Structures for Organizing Knowledge

Exploring Taxonomies, Ontologies, and Other Schemas

JUNE ABBAS

Neal-Schuman Publishers, Inc.
New York London

Published by Neal-Schuman Publishers, Inc.
100 William St., Suite 2004
New York, NY 10038

Printed and bound in the United States of America.

The paper used in this publication meets the minimum requirements of American National Standard for Information Sciences—Permanence of Paper for Printed Library Materials, ANSI Z39.48-1992.

Library of Congress Cataloging-in-Publication Data

Abbas, June, 1964-
Structures for organizing knowledge : exploring taxonomies, ontologies, and other schemas / June Abbas.
p. cm.
Includes bibliographical references and index.
ISBN 978-1-55570-699-9 (alk. paper)
1. Information organization. I. Title.

Z666.5.A23 2010
025—dc22

2010024861

To Charlie, Ben, and Clifford
My inspirations for organizing life

Contents

List of Figures and Tables

FIGURES

TABLES

Preface

Structures for organizing knowledge are an always present, but often unrecognized, part of our everyday personal and professional lives. They are the backbones behind the systems we use for work, for play, and for both physical and intellectual exploration. They not only help organize and retrieve "objects" in physical spaces like libraries, but they also give us the frameworks we use for making new connections, understanding disciplines, and making sense of professional and personal knowledge spaces.

Very young children begin organizing and grouping objects in their physical spaces. Pot lids and plastic containers strewn on the kitchen floor may look haphazard to the harried parent, but when one looks at the underlying structure, it is possible to see how children group everyday objects according to size, shape, color, texture, use, or even the sound they make. These groupings might be viewed as the beginnings of how children initially make sense of—and learn about—physical and mental spaces by developing and applying structures for organizing knowledge.

Library and information science professionals use structures for organizing knowledge when they catalog and classify objects in their collections, when they develop databases, or when they design customized taxonomies for application within a business context. Organizing structures are used when searching online to find articles in a database or travel information on the web, when browsing the shelves in a library or a favorite bookstore, or when downloading music and creating playlists. For example, a person planning a special event might create one playlist that holds music intended for use at the event, or a teen might create a playlist for music to listen to while studying for a test. At various points during every day, everyone organizes information and knowledge and interacts with structures for organizing knowledge.

Purpose and Scope

Structures for Organizing Knowledge: Exploring Taxonomies, Ontologies, and Other Schemas explores and explains how we organize knowledge by looking at three broad questions: (1) How do people organize objects in personal and professional contexts so that they make sense and are useful? (2) What roles do categories, classifications, taxonomies, and other structures play in the process of organizing? (3) What do information professionals need to know about human organizing behaviors in order to design useful structures for organizing knowledge?

Organization

To answer these questions, the book is organized using three major threads:

- *Traditional Structures for Organizing Knowledge*—Part I looks at structures used in libraries, such as MARC records, subject headings, and classification schemes, as well as traditional structures that may not be as familiar, such as those from natural science. The historical contributions to the organization of knowledge from fields such as library and information science, philosophy, natural science, and cognitive science are examined. Exemplars of how the structures have remained the same and/or have been adapted for use in the digital environment are also included in this section.
- *Personal Structures for Organizing Knowledge* are the focus of Part II. These are systems developed by individuals in both home- and work-related contexts. Several research streams from library and information science (knowledge organization and human information behavior) and human–computer interaction (personal information management) are introduced, and research in each area of personal knowledge structures is explored.
- *Socially-Constructed Structures for Organizing Knowledge*, or those that are beginning to emerge as the result of individual and collaborative uses of social bookmarking and social cataloging Web 2.0 sites, are examined in Part III. Research focused on these new environments is becoming more prevalent and providing information professionals with a glimpse into how people organize their own collections.

In Part I, which includes Chapters 1–4, the historical and multidisciplinary underpinnings of the development of traditional organizing structures such as categories, classification schemes, taxonomies, ontologies, controlled vocabularies, and others encountered along the way are reviewed. This study is not limited to those structures developed by library and information science, but, rather, a broad interdisciplinary net is cast in order to examine early structures that have informed current development of structures for organizing knowledge. Chapter 1 sets the stage for the explorations by introducing the reader to the concepts and theories that are central to understanding information, knowledge, and the representation and organization of information and knowledge. In Chapter 2 the contributions of multiple disciplines to the understanding of how and why people organize information and knowledge are examined. Conceptual frameworks and working examples of organizing structures of multiple disciplines such as philosophy, cognitive science, biology, and library and information science increase our understanding about human organizing behavior and application.

Organizing structures cannot be fully examined without also understanding the standards that are followed during development of the structures. Chapter 3 examines national and international standards related to the development and application of structures for organizing knowledge within several disciplines, such as those standards for thesaurus construction, controlled vocabulary development or subject headings list development, or specialized metadata schemes. Best practices for developing and applying organizing structures are also discussed.

Chapter 4 examines the principle functions of knowledge structures within disciplinary contexts through examination of different taxonomies in use and the standards developed to ensure the proper application of the knowledge structure. Chapter 4 presents an overview of the knowledge structures used within a sample of academic disciplines, including biology, zoology, social science, and library and information science. Examples of how the knowledge structures have translated into applications available in the digital environment, e.g., online databases for taxonomic identification, discipline-specific digital libraries of specimens or documents, and online archives, are reviewed as exemplars.

Part II addresses the questions of how people organize objects in personal and professional contexts. Chapter 5 outlines the research from fields, such as library and information science and computer science, related to how people organize information and knowledge in personal and professional contexts. Organizing structures such as categories, taxonomies, and ad hoc "artfully designed" organizing systems provide a means to organize the objects in professional and personal lives but also enable discovery and access of information and objects needed to satisfy information needs, to make purchases, to conduct work, or, quite simply, to live life. The development and use of organizing structures in everyday personal and professional knowledge spaces are explored through the lenses of personal information management (or PIM) and domain analysis.

Part III, composed of Chapters 6–8, introduces readers to socially-constructed knowledge organization. Chapter 6 discusses online social sharing sites, such as LibraryThing, Delicious, and Flickr. The Web 2.0 world has brought the professionally-constructed and personal organizing structures together in novel ways. Individuals now collect and organize personal information spaces online in social sharing sites for pictures, home collections of books, web bookmarks, and other multimedia such as videos, music files, podcasts, etc. Sites like Flickr allow for personal collections of pictures to be shared with friends, family, and online global contacts. LibraryThing provides an information space to organize and describe personal collections of books while also integrating professional organizing structures like the *Library of Congress Subject Headings* through what is called "tagmashing," or combining personal organizing structures with preestablished subject access schemes developed by library and information science professionals. This Web 2.0 context can be thought of as a Petri dish for researchers to learn more about how people organize personal information spaces, how they describe their collections and personal objects, and how they develop organizing structures individually and collaboratively. Chapter 6 also presents a framework for examining the research and perspectives focused on tagging, bookmarking, and social sharing behaviors, along with research related to social construction of structures for organizing knowledge.

Last, in Chapters 7 and 8, ways in which to connect the three threads of (1) traditional professionally-developed organizing structures, (2) personal structures for organizing knowledge spaces, and (3) socially-constructed organizing structures are investigated. In Chapter 7 the practical applications of shared folksonomies, both the impacts these potentially new structures will have on everyday professional and work-related lives and the implications for library and information science and related professions and disciplines, are explored. Practical applications, such as how to integrate socially-constructed technologies (in this instance, tags and their resulting folksonomies) into existing structures for organizing knowledge, such as library OPACs or existing controlled vocabularies (e.g., subject headings lists, thesauri), have the potential to change how knowledge is represented in libraries and other information organizations, but little is known at this point about the efficacy of doing so. Methods for refining or enhancing folksonomies, such as automatic and manual methods of "tag gardening" or reviewing and augmenting personal and/or community-based folksonomies, also are being explored by researchers in information science and computer science. Chapter 7 reviews the research into these issues and discusses the potential of integrating socially-constructed knowledge structures into traditional knowledge structures.

Chapter 8 weaves the three threads together through the use of two envisioning exercises designed to help the reader think through some of the issues and potentials of merging the three threads into new structures for organizing knowledge. First, readers are asked to construct their image of today's users, taking into account what they learned throughout the book and incorporating users' uses of technology into the picture. Second, readers will envision what a new structure for organizing knowledge might look like if the three threads of traditional (represented by the MARC record structure), PIM insights, and socially-constructed structures (represented by LibraryThing's Common Knowledge fields and others for readers to add) are woven together.

Each chapter follows the same structure: a box of bulleted "Focus Points" of issues and thoughts for the reader to consider, the main topics (as described earlier) along with helpful illustrations or "snapshots" of the different structures for organizing knowledge being discussed or used as examples, and a set of thought exercises designed to help the reader review and apply the topics being covered.

Audience

Structures for Organizing Knowledge is written for students of library and information science as well as for the practicing library and information science professional. The book is not meant to be a "how-to" guide for developing, applying, or implementing structures for organizing knowledge; rather, it is designed to present a conceptual discourse and to inspire thinking about taxonomic behavior, or how and why people organize knowledge, in various contexts. It also serves as a textbook on the historical development of structures for organizing knowledge and the current interdisciplinary theories and research related to the creation and application of structures for organizing knowledge. Furthermore, the book encourages readers to explore the new phenomenon of socially-constructed structures for organizing knowledge, such as those emerging in Web 2.0 social bookmarking and social cataloging sites, and to postulate how these socially-constructed structures for organizing knowledge may affect not only the existing structures already in use but also those developed in the future. Because library and information science professionals not only use structures for organizing knowledge but also develop and implement them, they must be thoroughly aware of how these structures function and how the structures are useful in differing contexts. To understand how to effectively develop and use structures for organizing knowledge, it is important that library and information science students and professionals understand the conceptual framework and rich history of structures for organizing knowledge, as well as the past and current understanding of organizing behaviors.

A secondary audience for the work is that of researchers in library and information science and related fields. Researchers will find the book's discussions of classical and newly developing folksonomies and metadata schemes and the reviews of the research literature useful to their work or to spark new ideas for research.

The three threads explored in the book present avenues for expanding our thinking on classification and classification schemes, taxonomy and ontology development, and structures for organizing knowledge. Learning more about how people naturally organize, categorize, name, and use organizing structures for making sense of their physical and mental spaces is important as the impacts of Web 2.0 and Library 2.0 developments and changes in user expectations are evaluated. This book will create new connections and ideas as historical perspectives are revisited, as more is understood about why and how people are taxonomists, and as the potentials of socially-constructed taxonomies are explored.

Acknowledgments

This work is the result of many conversations and projects I engaged in throughout the past 15 years. I can trace the first germinal thoughts of these ideas back to conversations with my friend and mentor Brian C. O'Connor while in one of my first courses as a master's student in the School of Library and Information Management at Emporia State University. Many of the ideas I struggled to effectively represent throughout this work stem from our conversations that took place on benches, in coffee shops and hotel lobbies, in hallways, and in academic offices. I hope I have done justice to your teachings, Brian. I also have drawn much inspiration from my students in the library and information studies programs in which I have had the pleasure to teach. Their ever curious inquiries have led me to explore new ways of thinking about, teaching, and expressing ideas about representation and organization of information. I have also been blessed by conversations with many knowledgeable colleagues, who challenged me, gave me the benefit of their insights, and helped me articulate many of the thoughts expressed in this work.

As for the actual writing of the book, my first thanks must go to my editor Sandy Wood at Neal-Schuman, whose patience and gentle guidance were essential for getting me out of ruts, seeing the work through others' eyes and perspectives, and pushing me at just the right moments. Many thanks to the anonymous reviewers who provided me with useful comments about gaps in the discourse and constructive feedback about the three threads that run throughout the book. A special thanks goes to my good friend Don Trainor from Shiny Object Media, who created the original graphics used throughout the book. Your work made it possible for me to visualize the thoughts I was attempting to convey through words.

Finally, I give heartfelt thanks to my husband Charles and my sons Clifford and Ben, who inspire me every day. Without their love and support this work would not have been possible.

Part I

Traditional Structures for Organizing Knowledge

1

Introduction to Structures for Organizing Knowledge

Focus Points

- What do we need to know about human information organizing behaviors in order to design useful structures for organizing knowledge?
- Why are organizing structures like categories, classifications, and taxonomies so important to everyday life?
- Think about the following sentence: "Everyone is a taxonomist at some point." What does this mean to you? How will this book help you explore this idea further?

Introduction

Someone gave me a picture once that has become one of the best examples for opening a conversation on organizing knowledge. The picture shows a collection at the Smithsonian Museum in Washington, DC. It is a picture of a person standing in a room that is filled with rows and rows of open drawers, each with objects of some sort in them. Only upon closer inspection can you see that it is a collection of small compartments, each containing a set of dead birds. Each bird has a tag attached to it (although the writing is too small to make out the representations) that serves as a structure for access into the collection. It is quite good fun to have this image up on the screen when students come back from a break and to see their initial horrified looks; then, as they realize *why* the picture is on the screen, their expressions turn to interest (see Figure 1.1).

Figure 1.1 illustrates many of the points that we will explore together in this book: (1) How *do* we organize objects in personal and professional contexts so that they make sense and are useful? (2) What roles do categories, classifications, taxonomies, and other structures play in the process of organizing? (3) What do we need to know about human information organizing behaviors

Figure 1.1. Ornithology Collection at the National Museum of Natural History

Ornithologist Roxie Laybourne amid the bird collection at the National Museum of Natural History (Smithsonian Institution), Photograph: Chip Clark.

Source: Andrew V. Suarez et al. "The Value of Museum Collections for Research and Society." *BioScience* 54, no. 1: 66–74.

in order to design useful structures for organizing knowledge? These three broad questions will be the basis for many of our explorations. We might also ask, "Why should we be interested in organizing behavior?" or "Why are organizing structures like categories, classifications, and taxonomies important to everyday life?" and "What are the implications for library and information science education, as well as practical application of organizing structures?"

It really goes without saying that the world is filled with information and what some will characterize as knowledge. Its forms and formats are numerous, and with each new technology that we use to generate even more information, new formats come also, presenting us with new dilemmas on how best to organize this information for access. For example, an involved discussion on how to catalog the new format of High Definition (HD) Blu-ray DVDs appeared on AUTOCAT, a listserv for catalogers, in March 2009. The participants were concerned with the practical application of how to best apply the AACR2 (*Anglo-American Cataloguing Rules*, 2nd edition revised) cataloging standard to this situation. This example illustrates how new formats of information present organizers of information and knowledge with new dilemmas as they develop standard practices for representation.

In library and information science we have developed many structures for organizing information, which is one of the primary reasons for writing this book. Together we will explore some of the structures developed to make access into collections possible—even though these systems are not always considered efficient or even effective by some.

To build these structures, it is prudent to know something about how people organize information for their own uses and how people organize their own personal and professional information spaces. To this end, the book is structured by using three threads: (1) traditional structures for organizing knowledge (those we have used in libraries, but also some we might not be familiar with, such as those in biology); (2) personal structures developed by individuals in both home and work-related contexts; and (3) socially-constructed structures that are beginning to emerge as the result of individual and collaborative uses of social networking, bookmarking, and cataloging Web 2.0 sites, such as Delicious, Flickr, and LibraryThing. Armed with the understandings we gain by examining these three threads, or at least a glimmer of understanding, we can build structures that enable useful access. During the course of this exploration, we will also review structures used in the fields of anthropology, biology, cognitive science, linguistics, and others as viewed relevant to our study of human organizing behaviors.

Framework for Exploring Organizing Behavior

Frames provide structures for holding something—like a picture frame holds a picture. They also serve as a means for allowing something to be used or useful. A framework then provides a structure for understanding that which is being presented or explored. Within the "frame" the boundaries are delineated and explained, and definitions are offered up as a means of further understanding of the author's intentions. The following framework will be used for exploring organizing behavior.

Scope

First, some limitations of this book are noted. While this book is an exploration of organizing structures, it is not intended to explicate the fine-grained detail of those structures, nor is it a textbook on how to construct and implement organizing structures within specific contexts, or how to create entries or representations within these systems. In other words, we will be looking at many examples of organizing structures, for example, bibliographic record systems used by libraries such as MARC record structures and related standards, classification schemes, taxonomies, ontologies, controlled vocabularies, and various metadata schemes, but our exploration will not include details at the level of defining database terminology, data modeling, metadata schema application, implementation, and evaluation languages, except as necessary for full understanding of the topic. Rather, the book will examine the underlying foundations, rationale, and uses of these organizing structures and will leave more in-depth technical discussions to other works on metadata, bibliographic control, information retrieval, and system design. The reader is referred to Zeng and Qin (2008) to read more about metadata and metadata schema development, implementation, and evaluation. Rowley and Hartley (2008) and Taylor and Joudrey (2009) present broad-based treatments of organizing knowledge that are instructive of many of the areas of organizing information and knowledge not covered in this work.

Interdisciplinary theories and perspectives will be introduced and integrated throughout as we look deeper into organizing structures and the human organizing behaviors that form the basis for these systems. The author does not purport to be an expert in each of these areas, but the combination of the ideas gleaned from them will serve as a backdrop for this exploration and will assist the reader in building new understandings on the subject of organizing structures for knowledge.

Definitions

Structure

The concept of *structure* is used throughout this work. It can be defined in many contexts. A structure can be a physical building or the foundation for an understanding. It can be a computerized structure, such as a metadata scheme or a database field design. Wendy Pullan (2000: ix) defines structure as

> a fundamental and sometimes intangible notion covering the recognition, observation, nature, and stability of patterns and relationships of entities. From a child's verbal description of a snowflake, to the detailed scientific analysis of the properties of magnetic fields, the concept of structure is an essential foundation of nearly every mode of inquiry and discovery in science, philosophy, and art.

Pullan's definition illustrates the flexibility a structure must possess in order to serve multiple purposes within varying personal and professional contexts, but it also points to the essential nature of structures as organizing and meaning-making.

Pullan's flexibility and meaning-making can be illustrated by further exploring how we might represent a collection of snowflakes. Wilson A. Bentley was the first person to capture a structure of a snowflake in a photographic image, thereby verifying that indeed each snowflake is unique. Bentley meticulously documented the specific weather conditions that were present at the time he photographed each snowflake. He kept this information in his journals, which were structured to help him make sense of each session. While working with the Buffalo Museum of Science to digitize and organize a collection of glass plate slide negatives of Bentley's snowflakes, students of the library and information science master's program were tasked with developing an appropriate metadata scheme that would be useful to many different user groups, such as children, researchers, or even meteorologists. The students decided that Bentley's journals really were the best way to describe each snowflake in the collection, so they used the structure he developed in his notebooks as the basis for the metadata scheme they used to describe the digital snowflakes in the collection (see Figure 1.2).

To view the digital collection, visit the Buffalo Museum of Science "Bentley Snow Crystal Collection" (bentley.sciencebuff.org). The specialized, though personalized, structure developed by Bentley himself afforded the flexibility needed to serve as an appropriate representation of the snowflakes for multiple user communities. The students also discovered the specialized classification scheme for snowflakes developed by Magono and Lee. This scheme is used as a navigation and browsing device in the snowflake digital collection.

Figure 1.2. Bentley's Snowflakes Metadata Scheme

http://www.bentley.sciencebuff.org/snowflake.asp?ID=103

• Classification:	P2d
• Snowflake:	0028
• Creator:	Wilson A. Bentley
• Date of Bentley Slide:	1/9/1896
• Crystal Description:	Dendritic crystal with sector like ends
• Weather Data:	Great storm all over the country. Taken all day. Best crystals in afternoon. Cloudy. Snowing hard.(forenoon) thinly (afternoon) wind W & W. Therm from 0 to +10F. No wind. Afternoon cloudy but quite light for cloudy day.
• Copyright:	© 2004 Buffalo Museum of Science

To see the organizing structure developed by Magono and Lee, visit the USDA website (emu.arsusda.gov/snowsite/Magono_and_Lee/Magono_and_Lee_Classification1.html).

For our purposes we might then define *structure* as "either a physical or a computerized foundation for representing an entity or collection of entities and the patterns and relationships among entities." This, however, seems too limiting for our purposes, as it does not get at the heart of structure as a means of representation beyond the physical thing. We could add Pullan's "fundamental and sometimes intangible notion covering the recognition, observation, nature and stability" (2000: ix) to this definition, but that construction seems artificial in this exploration. Perhaps the difficulty of defining *structure* comes because a structure is more than just a physical or computerized space to represent an entity and its relationships—but rather it somehow also encompasses the life experiences, understandings, and applications of the *organizer* (and even the culture of the organizer) in the structure itself, as well as the representations of the objects within the structure. An organizing structure is designed based on the organizer's knowledge base as well as on the purpose of the structure and, hopefully, a basic understanding of the user community. Figure 1.3 shows how each of these factors results in a structure for representing Bentley's snowflakes. The elements of Classification, Snowflake, Date of Slide, Crystal Description, and Weather Data were used by Bentley to both organize the collection and give further meaning to what he saw captured in each snowflake. Of significant importance to his exploration of snowflakes was the weather conditions during which each snowflake was captured. Additional elements to represent the snowflake collection include adding in copyright information to ensure the ownership of the image. Figure 1.3 also includes some additional elements we could consider including to represent this collection for other user groups, such as Size, Shape, and How Made for K–12 users and Formation, Typology, and Equipment Used for the meteorology community.

For our purposes, we *could* define structure as proposed above, but we will further define *organizing structures* as "either a physical or a computerized information space that represents an entity or collection of entities, and the patterns and relationships between entities, within the context of the life experiences, connections, understandings, and applications of the organizer."

Organizing structures are used not just in practical applications such as representations of information objects within libraries or within commercial contexts but we can also think of them as ways to *recognize*, *observe*, and *make sense* of the information being organized within the structure. Examples of organizing structures we will explore include categories, database and metadata schemes, classification schemes, taxonomies and ontologies, controlled vocabularies, and socially constructed taxonomies and folksonomies.

Information and Knowledge

When discussing organizing structures or structures for organizing, it important to also talk about *what* is being organized. As the title of this book indi-

Figure 1.3. Representing Bentley's Snowflakes for Multiple Users

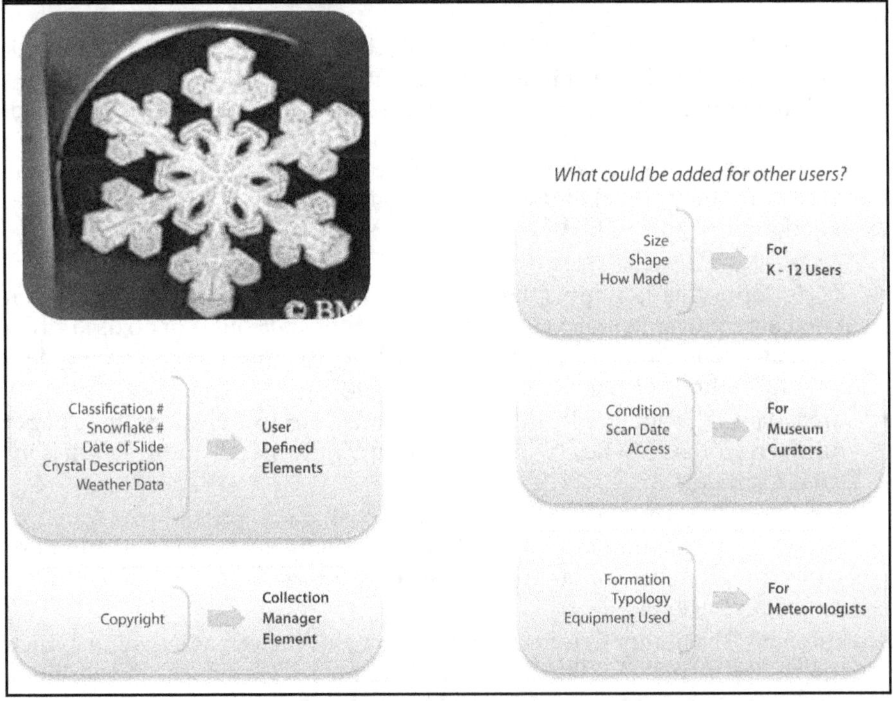

cates, its focus is on the organization of knowledge rather than information. Countless definitions and examples have been formulated in the fields of library and information science, cognitive science, computer science, and philosophy, to name but a few, in an attempt to understand the concepts of information and knowledge. The terms have been looked at from theoretical perspectives, evolutionary bases, cognitive functionality, as well as pragmatic applications within specific systems or disciplines. Bates (2005, 2006) presents perhaps the most comprehensive overview of the debate and varying perspectives presented by multiple disciplines in their attempts to define *information* and *knowledge*. The reader is referred to Bates (2005) for more readings on this debate from the field of information science and the emerging disciplines of evolutionary culture theory, evolutionary psychology, evolutionary neuroscience, and human behavioral ecology.

To further understand the author's choice of knowledge rather than information, let's explore a small set of the definitions and relationships that have been offered for each term. This set is by no means inclusive, nor does it attempt to be. The differing perspectives on the concepts of information and knowledge remain the most problematic and passionate discussions in the field of information science. The examples offered here are illustrative of those that have informed the author in her exploration of the concepts and in the selection of terms that will be useful in our investigation of organizing structures.

One of the most widely used methods of defining information and knowledge is to describe them as hierarchical in nature. Ackoff (1989) sees data, information, knowledge, and wisdom as structured into a hierarchical pyramid, referred to as the "DIKW hierarchy." As one moves up the hierarchy from data to wisdom, each entity becomes more defined, meaningful, and useful to the individual. Rowley (2007) and Rowley and Hartley (2008) offer the following explanation of Ackoff's DIKW hierarchy:

- *Data* is defined as "a symbol that represents a property of an object, an event or of their environment. It is the product of *observation* but is of no use until it is in a usable form." To Rowley and Hartley, "the difference between data and information is functional, not structural."
- *Information* is "contained in *descriptions*, answers to questions that begin with such words as 'who,' 'what,' 'when' and 'how many.' Information is inferred from data. . . ."
- *Knowledge* is seen as "know-how" and is "what makes possible the transformation of information into instruction. Knowledge can be obtained either by transmission from another who has it, by instruction, or by extracting it from experience."
- *Wisdom* is "the ability to increase effectiveness. Wisdom adds value, which requires the mental function that we call judgment. The ethical and aesthetic values that this implies are inherent to the actor and are unique and personal." (Rowley and Hartley, 2008: 5–6)

Rowley (2007: 170) describes *data* as being "discrete, objective facts or observations, which are unorganized and unprocessed and therefore have no meaning or value because of the lack of context and interpretation." Data then are derived from the act of observing but at this point have not been processed into meaning. According to Rowley (2007: 172), *information* is "organized or structured data, which has been processed in such a way that the information now has relevance (or meaning) for a specific purpose or context, and is therefore meaningful, valuable, useful, and relevant." Data becomes information to the individual when it has been processed or integrated with other data, information, or knowledge held by the individual and therefore becomes meaningful to the individual. O'Connor, Kearns, and Anderson (2008: 8) infer that *information* "has a connotation of evaluation, context, and consensus. Data have been reduced, modeled, and tested within some accepted framework." Furthermore, they suggest that "information is the reduction and synthesis of data for use in reasoning."

Knowledge, according to Rowley and Hartley (2008: 6), is consensually seen as "an elusive concept which is difficult to define." Much of the literature refers to knowledge as the product of the processing of information through synthesis, internalization, analysis, and reduction. Rowley and Hartley (2008: 6) point to the "added ingredients" many authors include as necessary in the processing of information into knowledge, including (1) contextual information, values, experiences and rules; (2) perception, skills, training, common sense, and experience; (3) information, expert opinion, skills, and experience; and (4) information combined with understanding and capability. O'Connor, Kearns, and Anderson (2008: 8) place their understanding of knowledge and wisdom in the field of evolutionary epistemology and state that "Each implies a greater degree of reduction, synthesis, and analysis of data, together with community agreement about the means of reduction and the value of the resulting outputs." They cite Plotkin's (1994) view that "knowledge is what gives our lives order and that 'knowing is living and surviving'" (O'Connor, Kearns, and Anderson, 2008: 8–9).

Furthermore, although seemingly unrelated, definitions of information and knowledge are proposed for use by the field of information science by Bates (2005). She suggests the use of Edwin Parker's (1974) definition of information "as a possible foundation for building a scientifically-based conception of information that also harmonizes with several of the more social-science–based theories of information in our field." Parker (1974: 10) defines information simply as "the pattern of organization of matter and energy."(This definition is labeled by Bates, 2005, as Information 1.) Bates (2005) further explains this definition in the context of defining "pattern" as "a combination of qualities, acts, tendencies, etc., forming a consistent or characteristic arrangement" (cited from Random House, 1993: 1423). A pattern in this context then can be understood to be

> a variety of features . . . knitted together in an overall system or integral design. A pattern of behavior implies repeated similar cycles of activity, that is, some coherence above and beyond the bunching and scattering of the frost on the window. . . . These patterns may be characterized as *emergent*, meaning that the sum of the elements constitutes something new, a whole with its own distinct qualities. (Bates, 2005)

Information then can be viewed as the organization of the repeated similar cycles of the qualities, actions, and behaviors of matter and energy that in themselves may become distinct qualities when they become meaningful to an individual. Bates (2005) expands on Parker's definition by defining what she calls Information 2 as "some pattern of organization of matter and energy given meaning by a living being." This expanded sense of *information* provides for the "foundational sense of information, in which information is understood to exist throughout the universe, whether or not humans or other living beings perceive or use it, *and* the social and communicatory sense in which living beings interpret and give meaning to information" (Bates, 2005). Following Bates' logic, knowledge then is defined by Bates (2005) as "information given meaning and integrated with other contexts of understanding."

Each of these definitions, although somewhat disparate at first glance, implies both sociobiological and sociocultural aspects to information and knowledge. As viewed in Figure 1.4, humans observe the environments in which we live via our senses, whether we characterize these environments on the macro level of a global world, the culture or ethnic group we may be a part of, or at a more micro level, of country, state, city, or family in which we reside. Our observations are data until we recognize in them the recurring patterns, reduce and/or synthesize these patterns to bits for consumption or use, and then integrate them into our life experiences and mental structures. In this manner the data become information and then knowledge when they become integrated into our overall understandings of our environments. These ideologies and subsequent definitions of *information* and *knowledge* will be further developed as we explore information-organizing behaviors. New dimensions of the sociocultural nature of both information and knowledge will become the focus of our later investigations in Part III of the book.

Organizing structures are designed with this view of knowledge in mind. The systems contain discrete pieces of data or information as representations of individual expressions, but what is being characterized, thereby organized, in these structures is the knowledge base of the *organizer(s)* and how they perceive and make meaningful their knowledge of their environments, as well as

Figure 1.4. From Data to Wisdom

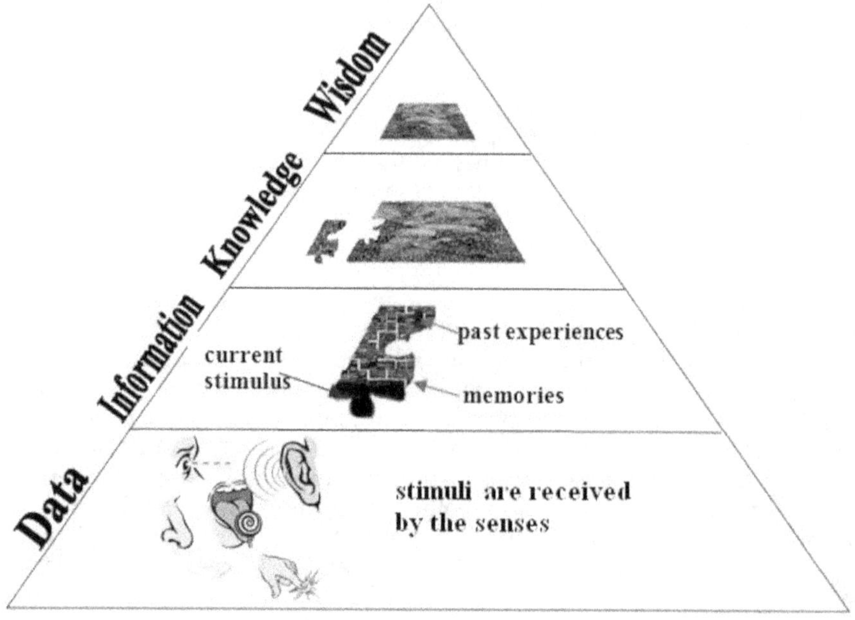

the documents or objects within the collection. Organizers also need to account for who will use the structures and build these understandings into the organizing structures. Rowley and Hartley (2008: 12) outline the following principles associated with the organization of knowledge:

1. knowledge needs to be organized for communities, which in turn means that all knowledge providers need to know their communities
2. in designing tools to support the organization of knowledge, community members' linguistic, semantic, and cognitive frameworks must be the central consideration
3. standards and standardization enhances interoperability between systems, which has benefits for both system designers and organizers and the communities they serve.

Abbas's (2001) model of age-appropriate indexing and sociocultural and sociobiological factors within organizing systems, as shown in Figure 1.5, can serve as an example of the interconnected variables within the structure of organizing systems. Her model, adapted from Cooper and O'Connor's Information Loss model (O'Connor, 1996: 6), includes the dimensions of the indexer's

Figure 1.5. Abbas's Model of Age-Appropriate Indexing

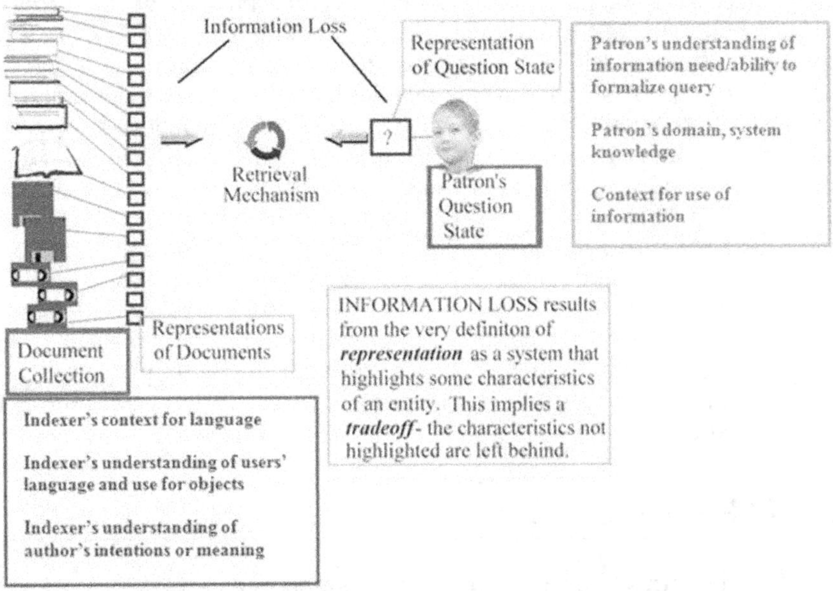

Source: Adapted from O'Connor, 1996: 6.

knowledge of the user community, the indexer's own experience, the domain knowledge of both the user and the indexer, as well as developmental, cognitive, and affective variables of each as central components of an age-appropriate organizing system for youth.

O'Connor, Kearns, and Anderson's notion of a "user template of meaning or understanding" can further illustrate the idea of the complexity of the structure of organizing systems as a product of the organizer(s)' knowledge base. They explain that each user's template is "constructed by a complex network of experiences, ideas, images, emotions, and knowledge" (O'Connor, Kearns, and Anderson, 2008: 18). While their idea of the user template is more specifically being applied to the meaning one may extract from the documents within an organizing system, the idea is useful here as illustrative of the complex factors that guide a designer of an organizing system.

Conclusion

Throughout this book we will examine the underlying knowledge base within the three threads outlined above: the traditional, the personal, and the socially-constructed structures for organizing knowledge, as well as the history and rationale for their design and development and the users and user communities that inform their construction. In Part I of the book, the traditional thread will be explored through the examination of exemplars of structures for organizing knowledge currently in use by library and information science, biology, and the social sciences. This section will also outline the role of standards and the process of standards development and take a closer look at emerging metadata schemes and other structures being developed to accommodate the digital initiatives present in each exemplar discipline. Part II will explore the second thread, the personal organizing behaviors, as readers are introduced to the research of personal information management (PIM), which aims to further our understanding of how individuals organize their personal home and work-related knowledge spaces. Part III will conclude this exploration by examining the third thread, the socially-constructed knowledge structures currently emerging within social networking, bookmarking, and cataloging Web 2.0 environments. This section concludes by proposing new ideas for rethinking structures for organizing knowledge that weave the three threads together.

Thought Exercises

1. Define the terms "information," "knowledge," and "structure." How do your definitions differ from those proposed in this chapter? How are they the same?

2. Develop a model of your understanding of the elements that are necessary to design a structure for organizing knowledge. Do you see the elements as all being of equal importance, or are there varying levels?
3. Compare and contrast what you know about the three threads presented in this chapter. Draw lines between the overlapping elements and dotted lines between those that are not related. Keep this sketch and revisit it after you finish reading Chapter 8.

References

Abbas, June. 2001. *Smoothing the Information Seeking Path: Removing Representational Obstacles in a Middle School Digital Library Environment*. Unpublished PhD dissertation. University of North Texas, Denton, Texas.

Ackoff, Russell L. 1989. "From Data to Wisdom." *Journal of Applied Systems Analysis* 16: 3–9.

Bates, Marcia J. 2005. "Information and Knowledge: An Evolutionary Framework for Information Science." Information Research 10, no. 4, paper 239. Available: InformationR.net/ir/10-4/paper239.html (accessed May 6, 2010).

———. 2006. "Fundamental Forms of Information." *Journal of the American Society for Information Science and Technology* 57, no. 8: 1033–1045.

O'Connor, Brian C. 1996. *Explorations in Indexing and Abstracting: Pointing, Virtue, and Power*. Englewood, CO: Libraries Unlimited.

O'Connor, Brian C., Jodi Kearns, and Richard Anderson. 2008. "Background Concepts and Models." In *Doing Things with Information* (pp. 1–20). Westport, CT: Libraries Unlimited.

Parker, Edwin B. 1974. "Information and Society." In *Library and Information Service Needs of the Nation: Proceedings of a Conference on the Needs of Occupational, Ethnic, and Other Groups in the United States* (pp. 9–50), edited by C.A. Cuadra and M. Bates. Washington, DC: U.S. Government Printing Office.

Plotkin, Henry C. 1994. *Darwin Machines and the Nature of Knowledge*. Cambridge, MA: Harvard University Press.

Pullan, Wendy. 2000. *Structure: In Science and Art*. Cambridge, England: Cambridge University Press.

Random House. 1993. "Information." In *Random House Unabridged Dictionary*, 2nd ed. (p. 1423). New York: Random House.

Rowley, Jennifer E. 2007. "The Wisdom Hierarchy: Representations of the DIKW Hierarchy." *Journal of Information Science* 33, no. 2: 163–180.

Rowley, Jennifer, and Richard Hartley. 2008. "Knowledge, Information and Their Organization." In *Organizing Knowledge: An Introduction to Managing Access to Information*, 4th ed. (pp. 1–19). Burlington, VT: Ashgate.

Taylor, Arlene G., and Daniel N. Joudrey. 2009. "The Organization of Recorded Information." In *The Organization of Information*, 3rd ed. (pp. 1–38). Westport, CT: Libraries Unlimited.

Zeng, Marcia L., and Jian Qin. 2008. *Metadata*. New York: Neal-Schuman.

Websites Noted in Text

Buffalo Museum of Science. "Bentley Snow Crystal Collection." Available: bentley.sciencebuff.org (accessed June 1, 2010).

U.S. Department of Agriculture. "Magono and Lee Classification Scheme for Snowflakes." Available: emu.arsusda.gov/snowsite/Magono_and_Lee/Magono_and_Lee_Classification1.html (accessed May 6, 2010).

2

Historical Perspectives and Development of Structures for Organizing Knowledge

Focus Points

- What can we learn from earlier conceptions of structures for organizing knowledge, e.g., classification schemes, encyclopedias, natural science collections, taxonomies, and cladistics?
- Did earlier classification schemes differ semantically from those currently in use?
- How do interdisciplinary needs and uses inform the design of structures for organizing knowledge?
- What have we/could we learn from studying "folk classifications"?

Introduction and Scope of the Chapter

Organizing objects in our environment is a fundamental activity of humans. We naturally categorize or group objects together to make sense of our environment, to determine practical issues like purchasing a breakfast cereal, or to be able to see connections or learn new insights while conducting scientific research. George A. Miller refers to humans as "informavores" (Miller, 1983: 111) and characterizes our propensity for gathering and organizing information as a hunger "for information in order to gather it and store it as a means for adapting to the world" (Pirolli, 2007: 13). Whether we are using an informal, ad hoc system of organizing or a formal one is probably directly related to the task at hand or to the context for the organizing activity.

Generally, structures for organizing knowledge are referred to at varying levels, or depending on context, as both *informal* and *formal* forms—*informal* meaning those developed for ad hoc or personal uses and *formal*, those developed for use in more standardized knowledge organizations such as scientific classification or information retrieval systems. Although informal and formal systems are used independently, they can also overlap or exist in conjunction with each other. For example, an information scientist may develop a scheme for conducting a content analysis. This scheme is based on the data gathered, the research goals of the study, and, most likely, the intellectual and conceptual frameworks of the researcher. The scheme's categories reflect the data gathered and are specific to the particular research project, but the guidelines for developing the scheme stem from a formal organizing structure for developing content analysis categories.

Informal Structures

Informal structures for organizing knowledge include those that are developed for personal use and those that serve a specific purpose at a specific time. For example, a system for organizing home collections, including the music, movies, books, and artifacts of an individual or family, represents the family's personal structure for organizing knowledge. On the web, using social sharing sites like LibraryThing or Delicious, users can organize their own collections of books or bookmarks for websites by creating their own subject terms, referred to as "tags" in these environments, or by using the preestablished schemes developed by the system's designers, which in the case of LibraryThing includes the users as well as the software developers of the site. A further example of an informal structure for organizing knowledge is a concept map that is developed by a student. Concept maps are a visual representation of a person's understanding and perspectives of a specific topic or issue. They also illustrate the relationships or connections to other concepts, topics, or issues. The relationships represented are developed by the individual and are specific to the task or context for the concept map. Concept maps are used to organize what is known about a particular topic or issue so that further learning can result by examining the relationships and making new connections. It should be noted that concept maps are also used within scientific disciplines to resolve problems or to visualize new understandings. In this context, categories and relationships may be predetermined or standardized by a discipline to ensure generalizability and usefulness of the data and conclusions of the research.

Formal Structures

Formal structures are those that have become standardized through development and use. These structures are not static structures that have a one-time, specific task-oriented use, but rather they are designed with a long-term, dynamic purpose in mind. Formal structures are used within library contexts or within varying disciplinary venues. For example, in library and information science, bibliographic control systems for organizing information objects in library collections have been developed. Print forms, and later database structures, were designed so that catalogers could create bibliographic records, or representative surrogates, of the objects in library collections. Beginning in the late 1960s, Henriette Avram at the Library of Congress developed the Machine Readable Cataloging (or MARC) organizing structure based on print-based structures for organizing knowledge, such as the book catalog or card catalog. Other examples of library and information science structures for organizing knowledge include, for example, classification schemes such as the Dewey Decimal Classification scheme (DDC), the Colon Classification scheme (CC), the Universal Decimal Classification scheme (UDC), as well as others. We can also extend this thinking to controlled vocabularies, defined simply as authorized lists of subject terms that represent the world of knowledge or the terminology within a specific discipline. Examples of controlled vocabularies include subject headings lists, such as the *Library of Congress Subject Headings* (LCSH) or *Sears List of Subject Headings* (Sears), which include as their scope the entire world of knowledge. Another form of controlled vocabulary that is more discipline specific is the thesaurus. Examples of thesauri include the *Medical Subject Headings* (McSH), which focuses only on concepts within medical disciplines, and the Educational Resources Information Center (ERIC) Thesaurus, which is designed for use with education-related materials.

Within the scientific disciplines, discipline-specific classification systems serve as knowledge-organizing structures for natural sciences such as biology, anthropology, evolutionary biology, and geology. Scientific naming and the concept of binomial nomenclature (explained later in this chapter) are used to classify objects from the natural world, such as plants or animals. The science of *systematics* focuses on developing classification schemes to organize the knowledge of the natural sciences. In the physical sciences, natural elements are structured into the Periodic Table of Elements, which shows in easily accessible visual form not only all of the known elements but also the properties of each element, their relationships to other elements, their scientific classification, and their abbreviated name form.

Informal and Formal Structures

As noted briefly, some organizing structures can include both informal and formal aspects or can be used in both informal and formal contexts. Taxonomy is an example of an organizing structure that can include both informal and formal aspects, as well as be used in varying personal or professional contexts. *Taxonomy*, which is a difficult concept to define, can be used as a noun, the product or result of taxonomic work (a taxonomy or a classification structure), or as a verb, the practice itself of categorization, classification, and taxonomy building (Grove, 2003). Taxonomy, according to Andrew Grove, was redefined in the 1990s to mean "any semantically significant, systematic organization of content" (Grove, 2003: 2770). A taxonomy, then, can be thought of as the conceptual, semantic structure underlying the organizing system. In an informal sense, a taxonomy may be developed without the use of more standardized categories, such as an ontology or database field structure within a specific context, for example, a corporate library or a craft supply store. The categories chosen and the resulting structure reflect the use for the system, the collection's objects and their general and unique attributes, or general characteristics, and the users of the system. In a corporate context, the taxonomy's categories and controlled vocabulary may be constructed using the language and terminology employed within the corporate culture, its correspondence, documents, and tacit knowledge stores. In a formal sense, the DDC and Library of Congress Classification schemes are examples of taxonomies. Both are formal, standardized organizing structures for assigning predetermined classes or categories and resulting notations to objects within a library's collection. Figure 2.1 shows examples of each form of structure for organizing knowledge.

This chapter takes a brief look at some of the significant early structures for organizing knowledge and the interdisciplinary influences that continue to inform the design of contemporary systems. The historical development of library and information science and natural science, as well as other scientific schemas, will serve as exemplars for this exploration. Interdisciplinary contributions from cognitive science will also be considered. In Chapter 4, we will take a closer look at discipline-specific examples of structures for organizing knowledge.

History of Structures for Organizing Knowledge

Structures for organizing knowledge throughout history have taken a variety of different forms and have resulted in many of the structures currently in use, although these organizing structures continue to evolve perhaps as frequently as the knowledge they represent. Depending on the perspective followed,

Figure 2.1. Examples of Different Forms of Knowledge-Organizing Structures

Informal Structure	Formal Structure	Combined Structure
Home collection system	Library online public access catalogs (OPACs) records	Small business ontology or database field structure
Social sharing site's categories	Classification schemes, e.g., Dewey Decimal or Library of Congress	Corporate taxonomy
Concept maps	Subject headings lists, e.g., Library of Congress Subject Headings	Display in a small business or specialty store
	Thesauri, e.g., ERIC Thesaurus	
	Periodic Table of Elements	

structures for organizing knowledge and their rich history include our earliest traces of human organizing behavior, such as clay tablets listing titles of early books; the first set of codified laws of a society set down on stone sculptures (the Hammurabi Codex); the Quipu or "talking strings" of ancient Incan messengers in Peru, which served as a repository of the laws or other information of this early society; and indexes that provided access into medieval collections in monasteries or private collections.

Beginning in the eighteenth century, the growth of natural science and other scientific disciplines can be linked to developing structures for organizing knowledge, such as natural history collections gathered for Renaissance and Victorian national collections and for wealthy collectors; early classification structures for organizing natural history, such as those constructed by Carl Linnaeus; encyclopedias chronicling the current world's knowledge; and bibliographic control systems in libraries. In contemporary times, we have witnessed the refinements of scientific classification schemes as the disciplines' members learned more about the objects in their purview and as technologies enabled further enhancements. We have augmented bibliographic control systems and, through the use of customized metadata schemes, taxonomies, and ontologies, are designing very user-centered and collection-specific structures and implementing them in digital libraries and in online and institutional repositories.

The aforementioned structures are products of the intellectual and social climate of the designer. Taking a closer look at the history of structures for organizing knowledge may reveal the rationale for their design, the conceptual framework of their designer(s), as well as insight into the purposes and uses of the structures.

Early Taxonomists and Their Contributions

Early Bibliographic Traces

Andrew Grove (2003: 2770) notes that "given the universal practice of organizing things, it is remarkable that only in the most recent 2500 years of human history has attention been paid to the principles and practices of categorization, classification, and taxonomy." Perhaps this lack of attention is due to the corresponding lack of evidentiary materials that can be used to document early structures for organizing knowledge. For example, some of the earliest known forms of structures for organizing knowledge include (1) early literature, such as biblical references in the book of Genesis to the naming of animals or to the categorizing of individuals by family names (Farber, 2000a); (2) artifactual evidences such as the oldest known list of books in the form of a Sumerian stone tablet found in Nippur dating from around 2000 BCE (Strout, 1956); and (3) the Hammurabi Codex stela that contain the first known set of codified laws of a human society. Arlene Taylor and Daniel Joudrey, crediting

Ruth Strout, outline some of the known archeological evidences of early bibliographic systems, including:

- the early use of colophons by the Hittites around 1500 BCE to provide details about the tablets in the collection, including its title, number in a series, and often the name of the scribe;
- one of the first known libraries in Nineveh around 650 BCE, which used a similar colophon system as the Hittites;
- the two great libraries of Greek civilization: Pergamum and Alexandria and the *Pinakes*, developed by Callimachus for Alexandria library, as thought to be possibly the first catalog, or a bibliography of Greek literature;
- early holdings lists of a medieval library dated in the eighth century, or inventories of libraries from the ninth through thirteenth centuries. (Taylor and Joudrey, 2009a: 67–70)

The early Renaissance, during the fourteenth through fifteenth centuries, saw some improvements in bibliographic control systems, such as the development of more lists, or what we might think of today as "shelflists," which included notations for physical shelf placement, content notes of each volume, and analytical entries related to author(s), title, or other works within the collection. Use of cross-references within the catalog also is evidenced during the fifteenth century. With the invention of the printing press, duplicates of original works could be obtained for private and university collections, which led to the new occupation of "bibliographer," or someone who constructed lists of works available. Toward the end of the fifteenth century, German bibliographer and librarian Johann Tritheim is credited with moving bibliographic control forward by developing the first alphabetical author index to accompany his bibliography of the collection (Taylor and Joudrey, 2009a: 70–71).

The sixteenth and seventeenth centuries are considered to be the golden age of libraries in Europe and the United States. With the rise of libraries and the growth of their collections came the need for, and development of, systems for cataloging or organizing the works held by libraries (Stockwell, 2001). During this time period, library inventories were beginning to be used as indexes or aids to accessing the works in a collection. The library catalog was further refined by Thomas Bodley, who included in the Oxford University catalog an alphabetical author index as well as analytical entries. Frederic Rostgaard proposed subdividing library catalogs by subject. He also proposed a printed catalog with a separate author and subject index (Strout, 1956; Taylor and Joudrey, 2009a).

Later Developments in Library and Information Science

The history of bibliographic control in libraries includes many examples of structures for organizing knowledge that were developed by the library and information science communities. Knowledge organizing structures include (1) *systems* that hold the representations of the knowledge objects, such as the library catalogs, bibliographies, and MARC metadata scheme (described earlier in this chapter and further in Chapter 4); (2) standardized structures for creating the *descriptive content* that is entered into systems for organizing knowledge, for example, cataloging codes for entering the descriptive content in library catalogs, such as the AACR2 (*Anglo-American Cataloguing Rules,* 2nd edition); and (3) structures for representing the *subject-related content* or "aboutness" of objects, including subject headings lists and classification schemes like the Library of Congress and DDC schemes. The next sections include an overview of the library community's efforts to standardize cataloging codes in Europe and the United States during the late nineteenth and early twentieth centuries. Development of classification schemes and subject headings lists will also be outlined.

Cataloging Codes

Toward the end of the eighteenth century, we see the first instance of development of a national cataloging code when in 1791 the new French government instructed its libraries to make catalogs of their collections (Strout, 1956). The nineteenth century, however, is often referred to as the period of codification, when some of the earliest efforts to codify or standardize bibliographic control systems took place. Major developments include the following:

- Anthony Panizzi, assistant librarian of the British Museum, published his cataloging code, the "91 Rules," in 1893.
- Charles C. Jewett published a code to be used in the catalog of the Smithsonian Institution in the United States in 1850. His code was based on the "91 Rules" of Panizzi. Both Panizzi and Jewett attempted to codify rules for creating bibliographic records in libraries and addressed many of the issues still in contention in today's bibliographic standards.
- Charles Cutter first published his *Rules for a Printed Dictionary Catalog* in 1876, which set out his principles for bibliographic records still followed today: (1) to enable a person to find a book on which either (a) author, (b) title, or (c) subject is known; (2) to show what a library has (a) by a given author, (b) on a given subject, (or) (c) in a given kind of literature; (and) (3) to assist in the choice of a book (a) as to its edition (bibliographically) and (b) as to its character (literary or topical) (Cutter, 1904, reprinted 1962: 12). Cutter's code was the first to include provisions for the creation and use of subject headings.

The first international cataloging code was created in 1908 through a collaborative effort between the British and Americans. The resulting code was designed to be used for the description of bibliographic elements in library records. In 1967, the Americans and British developed the first edition of the

Anglo-American Cataloguing Rules (AACR), which represented an international standard used in the United States, Great Britain, and other countries for descriptive cataloging and access points within bibliographic records. The AACR and its revised versions provide guidance to catalogers for the descriptive aspects of cataloging as well as developing access points or authorized headings for names and titles. Part I (Chapters 1–12) provides rules for description of specific formats of materials, with Chapter 1 focusing on general rules that could be applicable to any format. Part II provides guidance on choice of access points and rules for developing authorized headings for main and added entries in bibliographic records.

The second edition of the AACR, the AACR2, was published in 1978 to incorporate the new *International Standard Bibliographic Description* (ISBD) and to incorporate nonbook formats into the standard, to account for machine processing of bibliographic records, to reconcile differences between the American and British versions, and to align with the Paris Principles, developed by the international cataloging community in 1961. The AACR2 has continually been revised through the years (in 1988, 1998, 2002, 2003, 2004, and 2005). Significant revisions were made to the code in 2002 to integrate new digital formats into the standard. Updates to the AACR2 occurred in 2003–2005. No further updates are planned to the AACR2, as a new code, the *Resource Description and Access* (RDA), is being developed to replace AACR2 (Taylor and Joudrey, 2009a; Rowley and Hartley, 2008). The RDA will be explained further in Chapter 3. Refer to Chapter 3 also for additional content and technical standards developed to support the construction of bibliographic records.

Controlled Vocabularies

Controlled vocabularies, defined simply as authorized lists of subject terms that represent the world of knowledge or the terminology within a specific discipline, are structures for organizing knowledge developed by both the library and the information science communities and also in other disciplines, such as education, and for proprietary database systems that contain resources related to specific disciplines and designed for specific user groups, such as school-aged children. Examples of controlled vocabularies include subject headings lists, such as the *Library of Congress Subject Headings* (LCSH) and the *Sears List of Subject Headings* (Sears), which include as their scope the entire world of knowledge.

Another form of controlled vocabulary that is more discipline specific is a thesaurus. Examples of thesauri include the MeSH, which focuses only on concepts within medical disciplines, and the ERIC Thesaurus, which is designed for use with education-related materials.

Subject Headings Lists

Subject headings lists generally include as their scope the entire world of knowledge, organized in an alphabetical arrangement, with semantic relationships displayed to direct the user (both cataloger and library users) to terms that represent subject content within knowledge-organizing systems. Semantic relationships may include equivalence (synonymy), hierarchical (broader and narrower terms), and associative (part of, related to).

Subject headings lists began to be systematized in the late 1870s when Charles A. Cutter published his *Rules for a Dictionary Catalog* in 1876. The *American Library Association (ALA) List of Subject Headings*, published in 1885, draws from Cutter's work. In 1914, the first edition of the *Subject Headings Used in the Dictionary Catalogues of the Library of Congress* was published. It was later renamed the *Library of Congress Subject Headings* (LCSH) in 1975 and is today the preeminent authority list for subject headings throughout the English-speaking countries (Rowley and Hartley, 2008; Taylor and Joudrey, 2009a).

Subject headings lists are designed with a general homogeneous user in mind and may not always be useful for all knowledge-organizing systems. Discipline-specific structures have been developed in the form of thesauri, which will be detailed in the next section. There have also been efforts to develop or adapt an existing controlled vocabulary for a specific user group, namely, for children or younger users, including work by the Library of Congress to develop the Library of Congress's Annotated Card program. In 1966, the Library of Congress established the Annotated Card (AC) Program, which is currently administered by the Children's Literature Team of the Library of Congress History and Literature Cataloging Division. The program has adapted the Library of Congress's cataloging guidelines and practices and has modified the LCSH, as well as the guidelines for their application, to be more appropriate for the representation of resources for children up to the age of 15 years. The AC guidelines address issues of creating age-appropriate metadata in the description, name, subject, and classification elements in the MARC metadata scheme (Association for Library Collections and Technical Services, 1998; Abbas, 2005).

Another controlled vocabulary, predecessor to the AC list, is the *Sears List of Subject Headings* (Sears). It was designed for use by small libraries by Minnie Earl Sears in 1923. Sears differs from LCSH and AC in many ways that make it appropriate for representing children's resources or collections held within small or medium-sized libraries. For example, Sears contains fewer technical terms, prefers common names instead of scientific names, uses direct geographic subdivisions, and has converted inverted headings into direct forms (Miller, 1998; Abbas, 2005).

A further effort by members of OCLC's Knowledge Organization research team has produced *Subject Headings for Children*, a list of approximately 20,000 LCSH subject terms. The list was compiled by searching OCLC's WorldCat database of bibliographic records. The list includes LCSH terms and some specially devised terms. Name headings from LC's Name Authority File are also included. Reviews of the *Subject Headings for Children* indicate that the list is probably useful but still contains many inappropriate terms, such as "miscellanea," and doesn't incorporate terms in common use by children (Towsey, 1999; Abbas, 2005).

Thesauri

Thesauri, as mentioned earlier, are generally designed for use within a specific discipline, occupation, or proprietary database system. In contrast, subject headings lists represent the entire world of knowledge and are primarily used in libraries. During the mid-twentieth century numerous thesauri were developed for use within specific disciplines (such as education) or contexts (such as art museums). Thesauri do not include controlled terminology that represents the entire world of knowledge, but rather they capture the knowledge of the discipline, specific contextual environment, or profession that will be using the knowledge-organizing system. Thesauri generally include terminology that is derived from the discipline (or specialized setting, such as a corporation) and its publications. The terminology also tends to be more specific in nature than that found in subject headings lists. Thesauri contain structured semantic relationships similar to subject headings lists; however, the relationships that are included may be customized for the specific discipline. Examples of thesauri include the *Medical Subject Headings*, ERIC Thesaurus, and *Art & Architecture Thesaurus*. In Chapter 3, we will take a closer look at the structure and use of subject headings lists and thesauri.

Classification Schemes

Classification schemes such as the Dewey Decimal Classification scheme (DDC), the Library of Congress Classification scheme (LCC), the Colon Classification scheme (CC), the Universal Decimal Classification scheme (UDC), as well as others, are further examples of library and information science structures for organizing knowledge. Classification schemes divide the world of knowledge into manageable chunks of information that can then be processed by humans and by systems for organizing knowledge, such as integrated library systems (ILSs). Knowledge is divided into "classes" or groups of things or concepts that contain similar attributes.

The majority of library classification schemes in use currently are based on the "classical classification" theory developed by Aristotle for explaining the development of categories by humans. In "classical classification" there is a binary relationship within a class. A thing either belongs to a class of other things with the same attributes, or it does not. The classical classification theory has since been challenged by Eleanor Rosch and her colleagues in cognitive science. Researchers from linguistics, cognitive psychology, and other disciplines have developed alternative theories of categories and the process of categorization. The classical classification theory and the contributions to classification structures by philosophy, natural science, and cognitive science will be addressed later in this chapter.

Bibliographic Classification Schemes

As noted earlier, bibliographic classification schemes were developed before the ideologies of the classical classification theory were challenged. The most well-known bibliographic classification schemes are structured into hierarchical class structures that can be synthesized into notations that provide for the class inclusion of the object. In bibliographic classification, the main functions of classification are:

1. to serve a collocation function, or to gather together all items on the same or similar subject matter (library users can browse the library's collection and anticipate finding objects grouped together that contain the same or similar subject matter); and
2. as a locating device of the objects in the library's collection (classification notations assigned to objects provide a means for libraries to physically locate objects on library shelves).

There are two approaches to the division of classes: *enumerative* and *analytico-synthetic* (or faceted). In the enumerative approach, classes are predetermined within the structure of the scheme. Objects are then "fit into" the classes that they are most related to. Some early classification schemes, such as those developed within natural science by Linnaeus, would be considered an enumerative scheme. Both of the most widely used schemes today, the Dewey Decimal Classification and the Library of Congress Classification schemes, are enumerative, but each allows classifiers to build specific classification notations by use of the classes and subdivisions within the scheme or by using associated tables.

In the analytico-synthetic or faceted approach, facets, rather than classes, are predefined. *Facet* can be defined as a "basic component, attributes, characteristics or functions" (La Barre, 2010: 244) of objects. In the faceted approach to classification, facets are "clustered into categories to create a 'bottom-up' map of knowledge" (La Barre, 2010: 244). Objects are analyzed to identify the facets they contain. The classification notation then is constructed by following the guidelines for order of facets, as well as the codes to use to represent the facets. The Colon Classification and Bliss Bibliographic Classification schemes are examples of faceted or analytico-synthetic classification schemes. The *Art & Architecture Thesaurus*, while a specialized controlled vocabulary used to describe subjects of objects within museums, also provides codes that can be used as a faceted classification structure. Examples of these two approaches as well as advantages and disadvantages of both will be explored further in Chapter 4.

The development of bibliographic classification schemes is relatively recent in the history of knowledge organization. One of the earliest instances of bibliographic classification is Callimachus' *Pinakes*, which was noted earlier. The *Pinakes* contained ten broad categories or main classes. Arrangement, however, was based on author name rather than subject. In the late Middle Ages, university libraries based the division of the world of knowledge on the seven subjects taught in a medieval university, the Trivium (Grammar, Rhetoric, Logic) and the Quadrivium (Arithmetic, Music, Geometry, Astronomy). During the sixteenth and seventeenth centuries many different classification schemes were developed based on the division of knowledge of philosophers, including Francis Bacon. Bacon divided knowledge into three "faculties": history (natural, civil, literary, ecclesiastical); philosophy (including theology); and works of imagination (poetry, fables, etc.). When Thomas Jefferson developed his classification scheme for his collection, which he later donated to the Library of Congress, he based his scheme on Bacon's division of knowledge (Taylor and Joudrey, 2009b).

Development of classification schemes in the nineteenth and twentieth centuries included the major schemes that are still in use today. The first of these schemes was the Dewey Decimal Classification scheme (DDC), which was published in 1876 by Melvil Dewey. The DDC divided the world of knowledge into ten classes, with each of those further divided into ten divisions, and each of those further divided into ten sections, for a total of 1,000 potential categories into which books could be classified. The DDC also provided the first structures for "building numbers" or synthesizing more specific classification numbers by using the classes, divisions, and sections as facets that could be added to the base class number.

Shortly after the DDC was developed, Charles A. Cutter developed his own enumerative scheme, the Expansive Classification, which allowed classifiers to class objects using letters of the alphabet and then later expanded by numbers. Later when the Library of Congress developed its scheme, Library of Congress Classification, it was based largely on the structure designed by Cutter.

The Universal Decimal Classification (UDC) was developed in 1895 by Paul Otlet and Henri Fontaine. The UDC was based on the DDC but expanded the DDC with the addition of detailed subdivisions and the use of nondecimal symbols to represent complex subjects.

In the twentieth century, faceted classification schemes, or those based on the analytico-synthetic approach, were being developed as an alternative to enumerative schemes. One of the strengths of a faceted scheme is that it allows a classifier to express all aspects of a complex subject. S.R. Ranganathan was the first to use the term "facet" in the early 1930s in his Colon Classification (CC) scheme. The Colon Classification did not include predetermined classes into which objects were fit. It instead provided the individual facets or fundamental categories designated using the acronym of PMEST (Ranganathan, 1967):

- P (Personality)—the focal or most specific subject;
- M (Material or Matter)—a component;
- E (Energy)—an activity, operation, or process;
- S (Space)—a specific or generic place or location; and
- T (Time)—a chronological period, year, a season, etc.

Classifiers would determine the main or specific subject (P). Additional facets then would be added as applicable. Ranganathan's scheme inspired a group of classificationists in Great Britain known as the Classification Research

Group (or CRG). The CRG's work later resulted into the revision of the Bliss Classification and the creation of the PRECIS or Preserved-Context Indexing System (Taylor and Joudrey, 2009b). The Colon Classification scheme and the faceted approach have been used as the basis for classification schemes developed by e-commerce and in particular industries. Current efforts by classificationists to refine and develop new classification schemes for use in the digital environment, and simply to organize the growing body of knowledge today, will be discussed further in Chapters 3 and 4.

As noted, many of the existing structures for organizing knowledge are based on ideologies and theories developed by other disciplines than library and information science. Contributions from philosophy, natural science, and cognitive science are presented in the next sections. The structures examined below provide insights into current scheme development, as well as point us in new directions to explore.

Contributions from Philosophy

Philosophers such as Aristotle and Francis Bacon have played a central role in the development of organizing structures. Aristotle is often credited with setting out the basic principles of biological taxonomy and with being the father of what is referred to in cognitive and library and information science as "classical classification." Aristotle's methods are grounded in the philosophy of logic, more specifically, in that of deduction. Through observation one can define the inherent properties of a plant or animal such as form, habits, and habitat. Using deduction, one could posit that if animals share the same properties, or characteristics, they are similar to each other and can be grouped into categories. His work, the *Historia Animalium*, introduced the importance of using detailed observation, as well as the principle of grouping or categorizing nature based on inherent properties, which defined both similar and dissimilar characteristics. Aristotle's methodology of detailed observation influenced the work of seventeenth-century naturalists such as Georges-Louis Leclerc, Comte de Buffon, whose *Histoire naturelle* stressed the necessity of applying a rigorous standard of detailed, firsthand observation to the study of nature.

Aristotle's "classical theory of classification" influenced library and information science classification schemes and is evident in the definitions from library and information science literature. Classification, as defined by Taylor and Joudrey (2009b: 383), is "a structured system of categories used to collocate similar ideas or objects." For Elaine Svenonius (2000: 10), classification "brings like things together. . . . [L]ike things are brought together with respect to one or more specified attributes." Beginning in the sixteenth century, and also parallel to the growth of libraries, many different bibliographic classification schemes (those used for retrieval in bibliographic systems) were developed based on the classical theory of classification. Those of significance were based on either the philosopher Francis Bacon's division of knowledge into three basic "faculties": history (natural, civil, literary, ecclesiastical); philosophy (including theology); and works of imagination (poetry, fables, etc.) or the classification work of Thomas Jefferson. Other bibliographic classification schemes based on Aristotle's classical theory include those still in use today, the Dewey Decimal Classification scheme and the Library of Congress Classification scheme, as well as others mentioned earlier.

Aristotle's classical theory of classification and categories remained unchallenged until the mid-twentieth century when linguist Ludwig Wittgenstein showed that not all objects could be easily categorized based on similar properties. Using the concept of "games," Wittgenstein illustrated that not all "games" included common properties or general characteristics that would allow for the game to be categorized as a "game." Eleanor Rosch and other cognitive scientists continued to support and expand on Wittgenstein's challenge to classical classification. Cognitive science contributions to structures for organizing knowledge will be detailed later in this chapter.

Contributions from Natural History

A significant development in delineating structures for organizing knowledge can be attributed to the establishment of the discipline of natural history during the eighteenth century. Natural history systematically studies natural objects with the goal of naming, describing, classifying, and uncovering their natural order. This work is necessary so that further scientific analyses can be undertaken and knowledge of the natural world expanded (Farber, 2000a). The eighteenth-century naturalists Carl Linnaeus, a botanist from Sweden, and Georges-Louis Leclerc, Comte de Buffon, a French nobleman and student of nature, were central figures both in defining natural history as a discipline and for developing structures for organizing knowledge that prevail today in the natural sciences, such as biology, anthropology, and evolutionary biology. Linnaeus is credited with proposing a new system of classification for plants, animals, and minerals. In his *Systema Naturae*, Linnaeus laid the foundations for classifying plants based on sexual characteristics. Linnaeus designed a "brilliantly simple hierarchical system that arranged plants into twenty-four classes according to the number and relative position of their stamens (male parts)" (Farber, 2000a: 9). He further broke the classes into 65 orders, primarily based on the number and position of their pistils (female parts). Linnaeus later defined additional genera, or groups of species that possessed similar characteristics. Although his system of classification did not reflect any "real" natural order, Linnaeus's "artificial" system quickly gained wide acceptance throughout most of Europe. In addition to his classification system for plants, Linnaeus constructed a framework for grouping species into categories of species, genus, family, order, class, and phylum based on degrees of resemblance and dissimilarity (Squire et al., 2008: 1021). Stockwell (2001: 98) notes regarding Linnaeus's classification choices, "It is interesting to imagine how different our understanding of the world might be today had Linnaeus classified all of the animals by function, as some of the early scientists tried to do, rather than by bone structure. Bats, birds, and many insects might be in the same class, while men, ducks, and kangaroos would form another group."

Linnaeus also developed new rules for the naming of plants. Prior to Linnaeus no standardized system for naming plants was followed, which resulted in plants being given multiple names. His system of binomial (two-word) nomenclature first appeared in 1736 and proposed the use of two-part names: the first including a single name common to all the species in a genus, and the second, a specific name that distinguished the species from others in the genus. His *Species Plantarum*, released in 1753, recorded all known species of plants. This work, along with his binomial nomenclature standard for naming, is still in use (Farber, 2000a).

Linnaeus's structure for organizing knowledge represents a departure from the Aristotelian view of top-down classification. Linnaeus's "bottom-up" classification did not start with a set of classes based on similarities of characteristics to which objects were "fit," but rather he first examined the object and built the scheme based on what was observed in each individual species. Classes, or genera, were determined after examination of the specific characteristics of the object.

Linnaeus's classification system reflected his view of the world of knowledge and his own religious ideologies. According to Paul Farber, Linnaeus's drive to name and order the "products of Creation" was linked to his worship of God:

> Linnaeus's conception of order reflected his vision of Creation as a balanced and harmonious system. Classification, he thought, could reflect that harmony. . . . Every plant and animal fills a particular place in the network of life and helps maintain that network. . . . Such intricate relationships offered proof of a divinely sanctioned balance. (Farber, 2000a: 11)

The choice of terminology in his classification system, such as the names for his classes, reflected Linnaeus's cultural background. He used Greek names for "husband" (andria) and "wife" (gynia), which illustrated the predominate sociocultural view of the institution of marriage and relationships (Farber, 2000a: 9). Linnaeus's view of the world was characteristic of the time period, when religious, not secular, ideologies were representative of the accepted view of the world, and often these views were based on interpretations of nature.

Although Linnaeus's organizing systems were informed by his worldview, economic factors also played a role. He endeavored to catalog as much of the world of nature as possible. Building natural history collections became a source of income for young men who wished to study nature. Natural history, and identification of new sources of natural resources, was influenced by European imperialism. Natural history expeditions uncovered new resources and new markets and extended the arm of European imperialistic holdings further (Farber, 2000c: 24).

Linnaeus's main rival was Georges-Louis Leclerc, Comte de Buffon, a French nobleman and naturalist and Director of the French Royal Garden. Buffon's work represents a departure from the religious views that influenced Linnaeus and the Renaissance culture of the eighteenth century. As mentioned earlier in the chapter, Buffon was influenced by Aristotle's principle of direct, firsthand observation but also the necessity of detailed description. Aristotle's principles reinforced Buffon's conviction that in order for natural history to be a "science," more rigorous methods should be used. His "natural" system of describing and naming animals is based on observed relationships in nature rather than on the "artificial system" developed by Linnaeus. Buffon's *Histoire Naturelle* stressed the necessity of applying a rigorous standard of detailed, firsthand observation to the study of nature. This comprehensive work compiled an encyclopedic natural history of humans, minerals, quadrupeds, and birds as well as outlined a theory of the earth. Buffon's work also set out an additional knowledge structure to follow when studying nature, that of including knowledge on distribution, breeding habits, life stages, varieties, behavior, and environmental setting (Farber, 2000a: 14–16).

The contributions of both Linnaeus and Buffon laid the groundwork for the development of natural history as a discipline, but also for many of the structures for organizing knowledge used within the natural history and natural science disciplines. The collections amassed by each naturalist are also representative of structures for organizing knowledge. Naturalists, wealthy private collectors, and nations attempted to increase their knowledge of the world by creating large, global natural history collections. These collections included plants, animals, and minerals gathered from across the world.

The organizing systems of Linnaeus and Buffon were influenced by the worldview of each designer. Religious, cultural, and economic factors played a role in their convictions to design knowledge-organizing systems.

A further significant contributor to the development of natural science–related systems for organizing knowledge was Charles Darwin. In his work *Origin of Species*, published in 1859, Darwin proposed a new view on classification of species, that of tracing a species' evolutionary lineage. Linnaeus's classification was based on observable characteristics, or on what in modern terms is called a "phenetic" basis. Darwin's proposed idea transitioned biological taxonomy to a new way of thinking about structuring knowledge of natural science—classification based on the evolutionary lineage or history of genetically related groups or what is called the "phylogenetic" basis (Grove, 2003). Darwin recognized that "each living species represents the living tip of a largely dead branch of an extremely bushy tree of life. By examining other living tips of the tree, we can infer much about the organization of the brains (and other body parts) of ancestors that occupied the branching parts of the tree" (Squire et al., 2008: 1020). Darwin's classification "epitomized the new, secular, and specialized natural history characteristic of the early nineteenth century" (Farber, 2000b: 59). Darwin's proposed ideas of classification based on tracing evolutionary relationships was not widely accepted at first, and, since accepted by naturalists within a decade after it was proposed, it has been significantly modified by incorporating Darwin's ideas with those of other leading botanists, such as the religious views of Asa Gray in the United States, or the fossil evidence uncovered by paleontologists, who identified progressive trends in the fossil record.

What has resulted from a progression of the ideas of Linnaeus, Buffon, and Darwin is a science of classification within the natural sciences (including, for example, anthropology, biology, zoology, and neuroscience) known as "systematics." Systematics is based on the scientific understanding of phylogenetic (ancestor–descendant) relationships. As new discoveries are uncovered and understandings grow, this classification system is modified to reflect changes. Phylogenetic relationships are deduced from comparative evidence. Central to the construction of classification schemes is the concept of "clades" or the grouping of organisms that share a common ancestor. According to Squire and colleagues (2008: 1022), a clade is "simply a branch of the evolutionary tree, which is connected through a set of ancestors . . . to all the other branches in the tree."

Willi Hennig is credited with reinvigorating the field of systematics and for developing what is formally known as "cladistics" or a more rigorous comparative method of reconstructing clades (Squire et al., 2008; Trudge, 2000). Cladistics is defined as "a method of hypothesizing relationships among organisms—in other words, a method of reconstructing evolutionary trees" (University of California Museum of Paleontology, 2009). Taxonomists who practice cladistics are called "cladists." Hennig's method includes what he calls "character analysis" or the process of identifying "characters" or any observable feature or attribute of an organism. These characters can be anatomical and physiological characteristics, behaviors, or genetic sequences. His assertion is that closely related species will share more character states than distantly related species. Reconstructions of these evolutionary relationships, or clades, are then based on relationships among species that possess as many of these characters as possible. In fields such as neuroscience, clades guide the field's interpretation of the evolutionary history of brain organization (Squire et al., 2008: 1022). Clades (also referred to as "nodes") and the cladistic relationships (or "internodes") among them are depicted by branching diagrams that define the species groups (clades) as well as their taxonomic relationships. These trees of cladistic relationships are called "cladograms." An example of a cladogram is presented in Figure 2.2.

Cladistics merges tenets of classical classification (although the clades are based on more than similarities or dissimilarities), the detailed observation methodology of Buffon, and the comparative and phylogenetic or evolutionary lineage approach of Darwin. According to Arthur McCaffrey (1991: 86), "the new science of cladistics offered the promise of a 'value neutral' heuristic, which offered powerful and more empirical classification techniques without any of the theoretical hang-ups." We will look at current applications and ex-

Figure 2.2. Example of a Cladogram

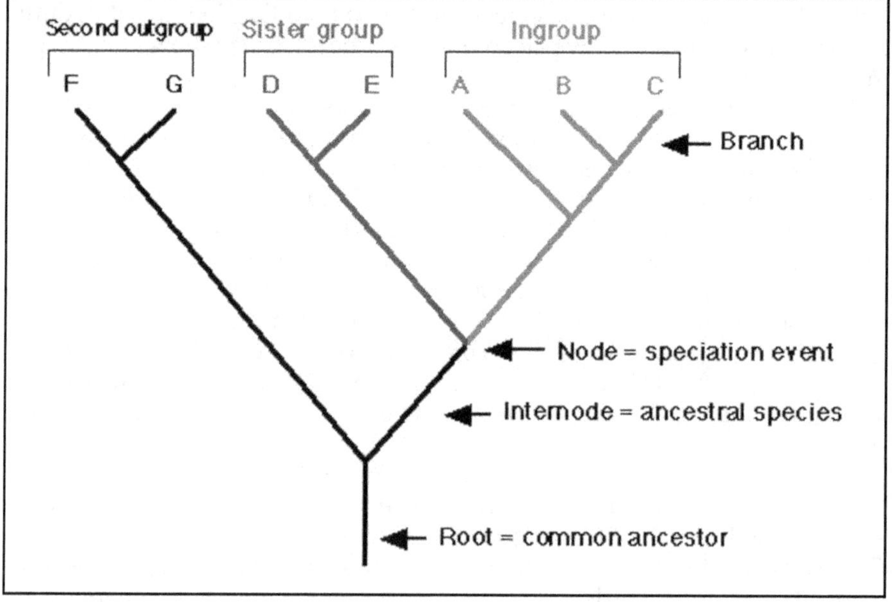

amples of systematics and cladistics in Chapter 4. For more on cladistics and Hennig, see the Hennig Society's website at www.cladistics.org/index.html.

Contributions from Cognitive Science

Cognitive science is a relatively new field that brings together many academic disciplines that focus on developing a greater understanding of the human mind and how it works. The disciplines include, for example, psychology, linguistics, anthropology, philosophy, and computer science. According to George Lakoff (1987b: xi), cognitive science seeks detailed answers to questions such as "What is reason?" "How do humans make sense of their experiences?" "What is a conceptual system and how is it organized?" "Do all people use the same conceptual system?" "Are there commonalities in the way that humans think?"

Many systems for organizing knowledge are based on the idea of categories or classing items together in either branched or hierarchical structures. The categories in structures for organizing knowledge, for example, thesauri or classification schemes, are based on understandings of the world's knowledge and how each class is related to the other classes contained in the whole structure. Categories and the formation of categories are central foci of what cognitive scientists study.

Classical View of Categories

Cognitive science views categories and categorization as the main way that we make sense of experiences. As is characteristic of all disciplines, there are opposing or changing views. In the traditional or classical view of cognitive science, now referred to as the "objectivist view" (in which reason is abstract and disembodied), categories are characterized solely by the properties that are shared with their members. Categories are characterized both as (1) being independent of the bodily nature of those doing the categorizing and (2) with no imaginative mechanisms (metaphor, imagery, metonymy) affecting the nature of the categories. In this cognitive science view, referred to as "experiential realism" or "experientialism," our bodily experiences and our use of imaginative mechanisms are central to how we construct categories to make sense of life's experiences (Lakoff, 1987b).

The classical view of categories is that concepts or things are grouped together into a category based on some similarities or common properties. As we move through our lives, we automatically categorize people, animals, and things into categories. According to George Lakoff, there is nothing more basic to our thought, perception, action, and speech than categorization. Whenever we reason about a kind of thing, such as a chair or an emotion, or whenever we intentionally perform any kind of action, for example, sorting laundry, we are employing categories that we have previously developed based on past experiences and motor actions. Categorization is "central to any understanding of how we think and how we function, and therefore central to an understanding of what makes us human" (Lakoff, 1987b: 6).

Prototype Theory

As noted earlier in this chapter, the classical view of categories, or classical classification, remained the predominant view in organizing knowledge until 1953 when Ludwig Wittgenstein pointed out that some categories did not fit the classical mold. He used the category of *game* as an example of how the *boundaries* (the properties the things in the category must have in common in order to belong to the category) that define *gameness* are not the same for all games. Some games are competitive, such as football or board games, and other games require skill or strategy, for example, chess; yet still others are purely for amusement, such as ring-around-the rosy. Wittgenstein proposed, instead, the idea of "family resemblances" in which members of a category resemble each other in various ways but may not share a common set of properties.

Although Wittgenstein's "family resemblances" was one of the first challenges to the classical view of categories, Eleanor Rosch has been credited with developing the theory of prototypes and basic-level categories or "prototype theory." Prototype theory proposes that human categorization is based on both human experience (of perception, motor activity, and culture) and imagination (of metaphor, metonymy, and mental imagery). Prototype theory challenges the classical view of reason as disembodied symbol manipulation and the mind-as-computer (mind as symbol-manipulating machine) metaphors. The prototype theory also calls into question the idea of "What is a category?" As noted earlier, we develop categories for *things*, and it is through these categories that we make sense of the world around us. What happens to these understandings of the world if we change our definition for what constitutes a category (Lakoff, 1987b)? These questions continue to be explored by researchers who support prototype theory and, later, the concept of cognitive models.

Some of the major contributors to prototype theory and the themes related to knowledge organization are described briefly in the next section. This section is by no means meant to be comprehensive and is presented here as a starting point for thinking through the contributions that cognitive science has made to structures for organizing knowledge.

Themes of Prototype Theory

George Lakoff sets out several of the central themes related to prototype theory that might be important to relate to structures for organizing knowledge:

1. *family resemblances*, or the idea that members of a category can be related to each other without possessing all of the same properties that define the category
2. *centrality*, or the idea that some members of a category may be "better examples" or exemplars of the category than others
3. *gradience*, or that some categories have degrees of membership or no clear boundaries for membership, and
4. *basic-level categorization*, the idea that categories are hierarchically organized from the general to the specific, but also, categories that are cognitively "basic" appear in the middle of the hierarchy. (Lakoff, 1987b)

As noted earlier, Eleanor Rosch, a cognitive psychologist, has been credited with developing the theory of prototypes and basic-level categories or "prototype theory." Rosch and her associates (e.g., Rosch, 1973; Rosch and Mervis, 1975; Rosch, Simpson, and Miller, 1976) are recognized by cognitive psychologists as having revolutionized the study of categorization within experimental psychology (Lakoff, 1987b: 39; Neisser, 1987). Ulrich Neisser describes Rosch and her colleagues' work as an "ecological view" that examines and describes the categories that humans use in everyday experience. Rosch and her associates' work "established basic facts about the structure of cultural and linguistic categories" and led to interdisciplinary collaborations among scholars in psychology, linguistics, anthropology, and philosophy interested in categories and category formation (Neisser, 1987: 3).

Rosch's research focuses on two areas—prototype effects and basic-level categories—but she was also instrumental in establishing research paradigms in cognitive psychology for demonstrating centrality, family resemblances, basic-level categorization, basic-level primacy, and reference-point reasoning. She is perhaps most well known for developing experimental protocols for exploring centrality within categories, or the idea that some members of a category are better examples of membership of the category.

Family Resemblances, Centrality, and Gradience

Ludwig Wittgenstein, as mentioned in the previous section, is credited with putting the first "crack" in the classical view of categories with his observation about the family resemblances present in some categories, such as games and numbers. He is also credited with the themes of centrality and gradience. In the classical view, no member of a category should be central; all members hold equal status. Wittgenstein observed that in the category of games, some games may actually be "better examples" of what we think of as a game.

J.L. Austin extended Wittgenstein's idea of centrality to words when he questioned why we call different kinds of things by the same word. His work examines whether or not people naturally use the same words for different senses or meanings and if this "use" is psychologically "real" or arbitrary. Austin's work helped to establish contemporary work on cognitive semantics, or applying prototype theory to the study of word meaning.

Lotfi Zadeh explored the theme of gradience—that not all categories include gradations of membership. In classical theory, there is a binary relationship in that an entity either belongs to a category or it does not. Take, for example, the category of "professor." A person either is or is not a professor. Other categories, however, include gradations of membership, such as categories related to economic status or physical characteristics. Zadeh devised a form of set theory now known as "fuzzy set theory," which supports the idea of gradience within some categories. In a fuzzy set, additional values or levels of membership are allowed within a category (Lakoff, 1987b; Neisser, 1987).

Basic-Level Categorization

Roger Brown is credited with the development of what is now referred to as "basic-level" categories or categorization. Through his observations of children he determined that there is a "first level" at which children name objects and learn categories. This level is neither general nor specific but rather in the "middle" of the hierarchy related to the object or the category of objects. Brown also observed that objects have many names. For example, a penny is also called money, a metal object, a thing, or, if one is fortunate enough to possess one, an Indian Head penny. The basic-level name, in this case the penny, is what we think of as the "real name." These real names tend to be shorter and to be used more frequently (Brown, 1958, 1965; Lakoff, 1987b).

Brent Berlin and his associates further supported the idea of basic-level categorization in their work on folk classification or folk taxonomy development. Berlin's research is often viewed as a response to the classical view that "the categories of the mind fit the categories of the world" or to the linguistic doctrine of Natural Kind Terms, which states that "the world consists very largely of natural kinds of things" and that natural languages contain names that fit these natural kinds (Lakoff, 1987b: 30; Berlin, 1992; Berlin, Breedlove, and Raven, 1974). Berlin and his associates studied the folk classification of the

Tzeltan-speaking people who live in Tenejapa in the Chiapas region of Mexico. What they discovered is that a single level of classification, the genus level, was the psychologically basic level at which the Tzeltan-speaking people named the plants and animals of their region. This level, called the "folk-generic level" by Berlin, was in the "middle" of the folk classification hierarchy, shown in Figure 2.3.

A further interesting finding of Berlin's research is that folk categories at the genus level match closely to scientific categories at the same level but do not match closely at other levels. This finding suggests the Doctrine of Natural Kind Terms may not be supported. If folk categories match only at the genus level, not at other levels, then the doctrine is not supported. Furthermore, Lakoff (1987b) points out that if you look closer at the examples used in the Doctrine (cow, dog, water), they are all from the basic level.

Berlin's research into the historical development of scientific classification shows that scientific classification grew out of folk classification. With this in mind, Linnaeus's development of the "genus," according to Berlin, may have been a result of his use of the psychological, general characteristics of a species. According to A.J. Cain (1958: 156), Linnaeus perceived genera as "practical units of classification" that biologists should all agree on and that would not "become confused and indistinct in the mind." In other words, the genus was set as the level "at which humans could most easily perceive, agree on, learn, remember, and name the discontinuities. The genus . . . was set up because it was the most psychologically basic level for the purposes of the study of taxonomic biology by human beings" (Lakoff, 1987b: 35).

Figure 2.3. Berlin's Folk Classification Hierarchy

UNIQUE BEGINNER (plant, animal)

LIFE FORM (tree, bush, bird, tree)

INTERMEDIATE (leaf-bearing tree, needle-bearing tree)

GENUS (oak, maple)

SPECIES (sugar maple, white oak maple)

VARIETY (cutleaf staghorn sumac)

Source: Berlin, Breedlove, and Raven, 1974: 240; Lakoff, 1987b: 33.

Mental Models

George Lakoff and his colleagues have explored the importance of theories in categorization or what is referred to as "idealized cognitive models" (ICMs). Their research illustrates that one or more ICMs is at the root of every cultural and linguistic model. Lakoff suggests that the graded structure seen in prototype theory is due to a lack of correspondence between our cognitive models and real-world experiences. To Lakoff (1987b: xv), "thought has an ecological structure. The efficiency of cognitive processing, as in learning and memory, depends on the overall structure of the conceptual system and on what the concepts mean." His theory of cognitive models incorporates views from traditional categorization, meaning and reason, prototype theory, and experiential realism. Lakoff's ICM theory suggests a different interpretation of Rosch's prototype effects research. In the prototype effects theory, there are two interpretations: (1) a person's representation of a concept is an abstraction or schema based on features or properties of a thing, or (2) a representation is based on a prototype, or an exemplar object, that best represents the thing. Lakoff argues that categories are formed by an individual's interaction with the world—by interactive functioning in our environment. Lakoff points to earlier research on mental models in cognitive science that support his theory. These include Rumelhart's "schemas," Minsky's "frames," and Schank and Abelson's "scripts," all of which explore our mental representation of knowledge (Lakoff, 1987a; Smith and Medin, 1981).

Philip Johnson-Laird is also well-known in cognitive psychology for his theoretical application of mental models to reasoning. He suggests that mental representations of concepts take the form of mental models. He views mental models as "knowledge structures that individuals construct in order to understand and explain their experiences." Furthermore, "the models are constrained by the individual's implicit theories about these experiences" (Sternberg, 1999: 236–237).

As noted earlier, cognitive science has contributed much to our understanding of humans' development of categories and their process of categorization. This section has presented a very cursory review of some of the major approaches and theories of category development and categorization. There are others that could be included that further explore each of the themes mentioned. Also, while contemporary theories of cognitive science continue to explore the themes of probabilistic, prototype, and experiential views of categorization, cognitive scientists are also applying these theories to learning and memory. Although these contemporary theories may be a bit of a departure from this exploration of structures for organizing knowledge, they may in fact provide us with ideas to incorporate into new structures for organizing knowledge.

Conclusion

This chapter presented a historical look at structures for organizing knowledge from the library and information science, philosophy, natural science, and cognitive science disciplines. The structures for organizing knowledge provide a means to "divide the world into manageable chunks" for further research and understanding. Library and information science has developed structures for organizing knowledge that not only "divide the knowledge into chunks" for learning or research purposes but also serve as devices for physical location and collocation and access. Tracing the development of natural science structures for organizing knowledge uncovered evidence of increasingly complex and interdisciplinary structures that synthesize the findings of current research with interdisciplinary approaches for representing understandings of a particular animal or plant. Cognitive scientists' theories inform development of structures for organizing knowledge. Systems that represent the knowledge of the world, or of a specific discipline (such as subject headings lists or thesauri), should take into account what cognitive science has discovered about human categories and the process of categorization.

Chapters 3 and 4 will take an ever closer look at the specific structures for organizing knowledge used within academic disciplines and specialized contexts and the standards that guide their development. The purpose of each structure within the discipline will be discussed, and its application to research, learning, and the development of new knowledge structures will also be explored.

Thought Exercises

1. Compare and contrast the major structures for organizing knowledge (Linnaean Hierarchy and clades/cladistics) developed by natural scientists. How are these structures related? What underlying principles led to their development and use?
2. Sketch a diagram(s) of your thinking about categories, classes, and facets. Do your diagrams look the same? If not, what are the differences you see among these three concepts?
3. If you were designing a structure to organize nature, whose scheme (Linnaeus, Darwin, Buffon, Hennig) do you think would be the most useful? How would your scheme differ from the one you chose?
4. Can Brown and Berlin's "folk classification" be used to understand the tagging and folksonomy development happening in social networking, bookmarking, and cataloging environments? If so, list how.

References

Abbas, June. 2005. "Creating Metadata for Children's Resources: Issues, Research, and Current Developments." *Library Trends* 54, no. 2 (Fall): 303–317.

Association for Library Collections and Technical Services (ALCTS). 1998. "Guidelines for Standardized Cataloging of Children's Materials." In *Cataloging Correctly for Kids: An Introduction to the Tools*, 3rd ed. (pp. 1–16), by S. Zuiderveld. Chicago: American Library Association.

Berlin, B. 1992. "Patterned Variation in Ethnobiological Knowledge." In *Ethnobiological Classification: Principles of Categorization of Plants and Animals in Traditional Societies* (pp. 199–131). Princeton, NJ: Princeton University Press.

Berlin, B., D.E. Breedlove, and P.H. Raven. 1974. "General Principles of Classification and Nomenclature in Folk Biology." *American Anthropology* 75: 214–242.

Brown, Roger. 1958. "How Shall a Thing Be Called?" *Psychological Review* 65: 14–21.

Brown, Roger. 1965. *Social Psychology*. New York: Free Press.

Cain, A.J. 1958. "Logic and Memory in Linnaeus's System of Taxonomy." *Proceedings of the Linnaean Society of London* 169: 144–163.

Cutter, C.A. 1904, reprinted 1962. *Rules for a Dictionary Catalog*, 4th ed. Washington, DC: Government Printing Office, 1904; reprint London: The Library Association, 1962.

Farber, P.L. 2000a. "Collecting, Classifying, and Interpreting Nature." In *Finding Order in Nature: The Naturalist Tradition from Linnaeus to E.O. Wilson* (pp. 6–21). Baltimore: Johns Hopkins University Press.

_____2000b. "Darwin's Synthesis: The Theory of Evolution." In *Finding Order in Nature: The Naturalist Tradition from Linnaeus to E.O. Wilson* (pp. 56–71). Baltimore: Johns Hopkins University Press.

———. 2000c. "New Specimens." In *Finding Order in Nature: The Naturalist Tradition from Linnaeus to E.O. Wilson* (pp. 22–36). Baltimore: Johns Hopkins University Press.

Grove, Andrew. 2003. "Taxonomy." In *Encyclopedia of Library and Information Science* (pp. 2770–2777). New York: Marcel Dekker, Inc.

La Barre, Kathryn. 2010. "Facet Analysis." In *Annual Review of Information Science and Technology* (pp. 243–284). Medford, NJ: Information Today.

Lakoff, G. 1987a. "Cognitive Models and Prototype Theory." In *Concepts and Conceptual Development: Ecological and Intellectual Factors in Categorization* (pp. 63–100), edited by Ulrich Neisser. Cambridge, England: Cambridge University Press.

———. 1987b. *Women, Fire, and Dangerous Things: What Categories Reveal about the Mind*. Chicago: University of Chicago Press.

McCaffrey, A. 1991. "Applied Cladistics: New Methodologies for Information Classification." In *Proceedings of the 2nd ASIS SIG/CR Classification Research Workshop* (pp. 85–100). Medford, NJ: Learned Information.

Miller, G.A. 1983. "Informavores." In *The Study of Information: Interdisciplinary Messages* (pp. 111–113), edited by Fritz Machlup and Una Mansfield. New York: John Wiley & Sons.

Miller, J. 1998. "Sears List of Subject Headings." In *Cataloging Correctly for Kids: An Introduction to the Tools*, 3rd ed. (pp. 67–70), edited by S. Zuiderveld. Chicago: American Library Association.

Neisser, Ulrich. 1987. *Concepts and Conceptual Development: Ecological and Intellectual Factors in Categorization*. Cambridge, England: Cambridge University Press.

Pirolli, P. 2007. "Information Foraging Theory: Framework and Method." In *Information Foraging Theory: Adaptive Interaction with Information* (pp. 3–29). New York: Oxford University Press.
Ranganathan, S.R. 1967. *Prolegomena to Library Classification*, 3rd ed. London: Asia Publishing House.
Rosch. E. 1973. "Natural Categories." *Cognitive Psychology* 7: 532–547.
Rosch, E., and Carolyn Mervis. 1975. "Family Resemblances: Studies in the Internal Structure of Categories." *Cognitive Psychology* 7: 573–605.
Rosch, E., C. Simpson, and R.S. Miller. 1976. "Structural Bases of Typicality Effects." *Journal of Experimental Psychology: Human Perception and Performance* 2: 491–502.
Rowley, Jennifer, and Richard Hartley. 2008. "Knowledge, Information and Their Organization." In *Organizing Knowledge: An Introduction to Managing Access to Information*, 4th ed. (pp. 1–19). Burlington, VT: Ashgate.
Smith, Edward E., and Douglas L. Medin. 1981. *Categories and Concepts*. Cambridge, MA: Harvard University Press.
Squire, Larry, Darwin Berg, Floyd Bloom, Sascha Du Lac, Anirvan Ghosh, and Nicholas Spitzer. 2008. "Human Brain Evolution." In *Fundamental Neuroscience* (pp. 1019–1038). Boston: Elsevier.
Sternberg, R.J. 1999. *Cognitive Psychology*, 2nd ed. New York: Harcourt Brace.
Stockwell, F. 2001. *A History of Information Storage and Retrieval*. Jefferson, NC: McFarland & Company.
Strout, Ruth French. 1956. "The Development of the Catalog and Cataloging Codes." *Library Quarterly* 26, no. 4 (October): 254–275.
Svenonius, E. 2000. "Information Organization." In *The Intellectual Foundation of Information Organization* (pp. 1–14). Cambridge, MA: The MIT Press.
Taylor, Arlene G., and Daniel N. Joudrey. 2009a. "Development of the Organization of Recorded Information in Western Civilization." In *The Organization of Information*, 3rd ed. (pp. 67–87). Westport, CT: Libraries Unlimited.
Taylor, Arlene G., and Daniel N. Joudrey. 2009b. "Systems for Categorization." In *The Organization of Information*, 3rd ed. (pp. 375–415). Westport, CT: Libraries Unlimited.
Towsey, M. 1999. "Subject Headings for Children." *Catalog & Index* 131 (Summer): 9–10.
Trudge, Colin. 2000. "The Natural Order: Darwin's Dream and Hennig's Solution." In *The Variety of Life: A Survey and a Celebration of all the Creatures That Have Ever Lived* (pp. 33–62). Oxford: Oxford University Press.

Websites Noted in Text

Hennig Society. Website for the Hennig Society. Available: www.cladistics.org/index.html (accessed May 10, 2010).
University of California Museum of Paleontology. 2009. Understanding Evolution Website. Available: evolution.berkeley.edu (accessed May 10, 2010).

3

Standards and Best Practices

Focus Points

- Are standards an important aspect to developing and maintaining knowledge structures? If so, why?
- Which national and international organizations are involved in standards development?
- What is the process for developing a standard?
- Who should be involved in standards development?
- What is meant by the phrase "best practice"?
- What role do best practices play in knowledge structures?
- What role do best practices play in standards development?

Standards and Standards Development

Structures for organizing knowledge are not developed in isolation, nor are they developed without a great deal of discussion and trial and error. Formalized structures for organizing knowledge, such as databases, bibliographic retrieval systems, or subject thesauri, for example, are developed according to national, regional, or international standards. A standard, according to the British Standards Institute (2009), is "an agreed, repeatable way of doing something. It is a published document that contains a technical specification or other precise criteria designed to be used consistently as a rule, guidance, or definition." Standards serve multiple functions and are developed by official standards organizations like NISO (National Information Standards Organization) and ISO (International Standards Organization), from industry consortia like the Unicode Consortium or W3C (Worldwide Web Consortium), from cooperative consortia of universities or other research organizations, and industrial organizations and business entities, like Microsoft and Adobe (Needleman, 2008). Standards can be voluntary or ad hoc and developed for specific purposes or products. Standards are developed and applied within a multitude of different contexts, from manufacturing, information management, and technology to agriculture and the sciences. Because standards are such a pervasive aspect of our lives, they play an essential role in society as they provide for the safety of products, ensure a healthy and clean environment, promote worldwide communication and collaborations for trade, and support innovation and economic development among countries (Hodge, 2008). The ISO (2009d) website outlines the following benefits of standards:

- make the development, manufacturing and supply of products and services **more efficient, safer and cleaner**
- **facilitate trade** between countries and make it **fairer**
- provide governments with a technical base for **health, safety and environmental legislation**, and conformity assessment
- **share** technological advances and good management practice
- disseminate **innovation**
- **safeguard consumers**, and users in general, of products and services
- make life simpler by providing **solutions** to common problems

This chapter examines national and international standards that are related to the development and application of knowledge structures, such as those standards for metadata schemas, thesaurus construction, controlled vocabulary development, or subject heading list development. The process for standards development, as well as the different organizations involved in the process, is outlined. Best practices and the role they play in standards development related to knowledge structures are also discussed. While there are standards for many aspects of daily life, the focus of this exploration will be on those developed specifically for information or knowledge systems. Examples of current standards related to systems for organizing knowledge, metadata schema development, metadata encoding, and controlled vocabularies like thesauri and subject headings lists will help us learn more about the complexity of standards and standards development, as well as the necessity of standards within structures for organizing knowledge.

Standards for Organizing Knowledge

The development of structures for organizing knowledge is a complex process that includes decisions about semantic, technical, and content creation that have to be determined before a system can be developed. Many of these aspects are informed by various national, regional, and international standards. Gail Hodge (2008) believes that "Today's information management requires attention to a vast array of standards, ranging from network protocols to format and content standards [and that] few information systems can be specified, procured, developed, or implemented without using multiple standards." Navigating through the various standards and standards organizations can be a daunting task, especially when dealing with information technology standards, which are often dependent on other existing standards or on those in development. No clear "map" of the standards terrain includes all aspects of standards, standards organizations, and standards development, and it is difficult to "draw" one as the landscape changes rapidly. It is also difficult to see how the various standards related to information technology fit together, as connected standards are often not identified. To gain a better understanding of standards and standards development related to structures for organizing knowledge, we will look at (1) the different organizations that develop standards, (2) the process for developing standards, and (3) the specific standards related to structures for organizing knowledge.

Standards Organizations: National Level

As noted earlier, standards are developed at national, regional, and international levels, as well as through cooperation among these different entities or their accrediting bodies. In the United States, the American National Standards Institute (ANSI) is an example of a standards-related entity that:

- "coordinates the U.S. voluntary consensus standards system";
- "accredits qualified organizations, whose standards development process meets all of ANSI's requirements, to develop American National Standards"; and
- "represents U.S. interests in regional and international standardization activities while overseeing conformity assessment activities that promote the global acceptance of U.S. products, services, systems and personnel." (ANSI, 2009)

ANSI itself does not develop standards but rather serves as coordinator of the U.S. private sector, voluntary standardization system. An organization that has been accredited by ANSI to develop American National Standards (ANS) related to the development of structures for organizing knowledge is NISO (the National Information Standards Organization). NISO (2009) is a nonprofit association accredited by ANSI that "identifies, develops, maintains, and publishes technical standards to manage information in our changing and ever-more digital environment. NISO standards apply both traditional and new technologies to the full range of information-related needs, including retrieval, re-purposing, storage, metadata, and preservation." NISO's Mission Statement emphasizes its commitment to standards development: "NISO fosters the development and maintenance of standards that facilitate the creation, persistent management, and effective interchange of information so that it can be trusted for use in research and learning" (NISO, 2009). NISO's voting members include industry leaders of over 70 organizations in the fields of publishing, libraries, information technology, and media, as well as experts and practitioners who serve on NISO working groups and committees and as officers of the association (NISO, 2009). NISO has been designated by ANSI to represent U.S. interests as the Technical Advisory Group (TAG) to the International Organization for Standardization's (ISO) Technical Committee 46 on

Information and Documentation, and NISO also serves as the Secretariat for Subcommittee 9 on Identification and Description.

Standards Organizations: Regional and International Levels

ISO is the world's largest developer and publisher of international standards. Since it was founded in 1947, ISO has published more than 18,000 International Standards on activities ranging from agriculture, construction, and mechanical engineering, to medical devices, to the newest information technology developments. The ISO (2009a) website characterizes the organization as a nongovernmental organization composed of a network of national standards institutes from 163 countries, as well as members from both private sector entities, such as national partnerships of industry associations, and member institutes that are part of the governmental structure of their countries, or are mandated by their government. ISO collaborates with international and regional partners in the development of standards. International partners include, for example, the International Electrotechnical Commission (IEC), the International Telecommunication Union (ITU), the World Trade Organization (WTO), and the United Nations (UN). ISO's technical committees have formal liaison relations with over 600 international and regional organizations. ISO's regional partners include, for example, the African Regional Organization for Standardization (ARSO), the European Committee for Standardization (CEN), and the Pan American Standards Commission (COPANT). The regional bodies commit themselves to adopt ISO standards as the national standards of their members. For a complete list of ISO's *international partners,* see www.iso.org/iso/about/discover-iso_isos-international-partners.htm; for *regional partners,* go to www.iso.org/iso/about/discover-iso_isos-regional-partners.htm.

ISO also collaborates with international organizations, such as the Association for Digital Documents Standards (ADDS), the International Art & Technology Cooperation Association (Artech), and the International Association for Information and Image Management (AIIM). For a complete list of international organizations that cooperate with ISO, see www.iso.org/iso/about/organizations_in_liaison.htm. International standards organizations like ISO serve to coordinate and collaborate with other international, regional, and national standards organizations. They develop standards in conjunction with or, in some instances, independent of, other standards organizations. Regional and national standards organizations also collaborate at the international, regional, and national levels to develop standards.

Standards Development Process

Standards Developers

Standards are developed by a community of experts from relevant industrial, technical, or business sectors. Representatives from government agencies, consumer associations, nongovernmental organizations, and academics can also be members of the technical committees that develop, review, and maintain standards. Standards are first proposed by leaders from these stakeholder groups when a need is found to create a new standard or to revise an existing one. Stakeholders propose their requirement to the national or international standards organization members, who in turn communicate this need to the appropriate technical committee working in the area of the needed standard. If the proposed standard does not match with existing technical committees, then a new committee can be formed.

Development Process

New, proposed standards, or standards being revised, go through a multistep process that differs slightly depending on which organization is developing the standard. For example, NISO follows the seven-phase process outlined briefly here:

Phase 1: Idea to Proposed Work Item (During this phase an item is proposed to the appropriate Topic Committee [TC] for consideration and Work Item is developed. This phase can take 18 months to complete.)
Phase 2: Approved Work Item (After Work Item is developed, then members have 30 days to vote on whether or not it should go forward for development. If vote is positive, then Working Group is recruited.)
Phase 3: Creating Work Plan (Working Group develops a Work Plan for the development of the standard.)
Phase 4: Work Plan to Draft Standard (During this phase, the Work Plan is followed to develop the standard. This phase may take up to 18 months to complete.)
Phase 5: Working Draft to DSFTU/Ballot (Working Draft of Standard is submitted to and voted upon by the Topic Committee.)
Phase 6: Approval (Once an affirmative vote is received from the Topic Committee, a multistep process ensues, which includes voting by NISO, a public commenting period, and then review of comments, etc., until a final draft is ready and voted on by TC and NISO membership.)
Phase 7: Maintenance (A Maintenance Agency or a Standing Committee is appointed to review the standard after a five-year period.)

For further explanation of NISO's development process and the particulars of each stage, refer to "NISO Operating Procedures" (NISO, 2008). ISO follows a similar six-stage process:

Stage 1: Proposal stage
Stage 2: Preparatory stage
Stage 3: Committee stage
Stage 4: Enquiry stage
Stage 5: Approval stage
Stage 6: Publication stage

The activities that take place during these stages are similar to those of NISO, so they are not explained in depth here. For further information on each stage, refer to "Stages of Standards Development" (ISO, 2009c). Figure 3.1 illustrates the ISO standards development process, as well as the deliverables from each stage.

Standards development is a very time-intensive process; it can take years to complete all of the stages required by the standards organization and its members. It is, however, important to note that the outcome of the process is not just to develop a new standard, or to revise an existing one, but to come to a consensus on the standard and how it will be applied. Consensus is essential to the process of standards development, as standards compliance is on a voluntary basis. ISO (2009b) defines consensus as "general agreement, characterized by the absence of sustained opposition to substantial issues by any important part of the concerned interests and by a process that involves seeking to take into account the views of all parties concerned and to reconcile any conflicting arguments." Both national and international standards organizations in these examples include a public review or commenting period, during which nonmembers of the standards organization can review and comment on the proposed new standard or revisions to existing ones. Any feedback that is submitted is then reviewed by the appropriate committee(s) and taken under consideration in revising the working draft for the standard. Through this part of the process, the public have the opportunity to make their opinions or suggestions known to the committee before the standard is approved and implemented.

Information Technology Standards

As noted by Hodge (2008) earlier in this chapter, standards related to structures for organizing knowledge can range from network protocols, to formatting, to content standards. William Moen (2000: 129) further supports Hodge:

> Technical standards affect the flow and processing of information. In the networked environment, robust interconnection and information exchange between systems require a broad range of standards: standards that specify data formats, network interfaces, operating systems, storage devices, computer-to-computer communications protocols, and other aspects of this complex information handling and processing environment.

Standards can be of a technical nature, dealing with encoding standards within specific technical standards (such as bibliographic databases like MARC), or they can be concerned with all aspects of record creation, including metadata schemas (field structures), technical infrastructure, and content entry rules, or the standard can be dependent on other related standards, such as technical standards for the encoding of data within XML or other data languages. This section will briefly outline some of the standards related to structures for organizing knowledge. The standards are, unfortunately, too numerous to account

Figure 3.1. ISO Standards Development Process

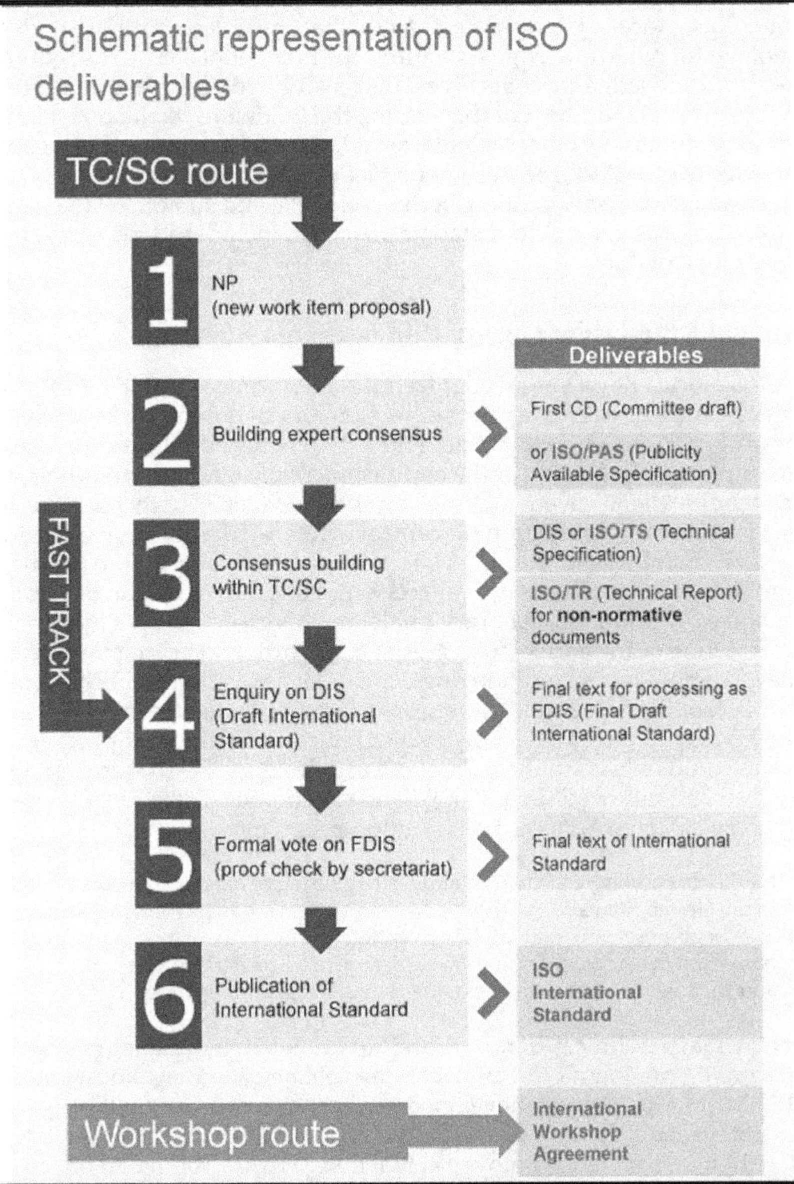

Note: TC in the ISO is a Technical Committee and SC is a subcommittee within the Technical Committee. Once the need for a new standard is determined, it is assigned to the appropriate TC or SC for development. If an appropriate TC or SC is not apparent, then a new SC will be developed within a related TC.

for them all here. One of the issues information professionals face is trying to keep up-to-date with relevant and related standards, and, as this section will illustrate, this concern is warranted. As we become even more dependent on technology for our knowledge structures, the number of standards required to make our knowledge systems work will also increase or become interconnected to other standards. For this reason, the following sections will be organized as such: (1) technical standards related to structures for organizing knowledge (e.g., MARC records or knowledge-organization systems); (2) standards related to content creation, both descriptive and subject-related content; and (3) standards related to metadata schemas, including structure, content, and exchange of data.

Technical Standards: Library Bibliographic Systems

Library agencies have long recognized the importance that standards or the standardization of rules play in the creation and maintenance in knowledge-organizing systems. Ronald Hagler (1989: 199) believed "the entire history of bibliographic control is that of the establishment of standards and their subsequent modification." Svenonius (2000) and Yee (2009) both note the many early visionaries in bibliographic control, such as Charles C. Jewett, Melvil Dewey, Herbert Putnam, and J.C.M. Hanson, whose visions for a national bibliographic catalog could not be realized without standardization of cataloging codes and cooperation from library cataloging divisions, such as the Library of Congress. One of the earlier successes at standardization came in the form of the new Anglo-American cataloging code, which was first published in 1908. Publication of the first Anglo-American cataloging code was preceded in 1901 by the Library of Congress's new cataloging card distribution program. This program could only continue to be successful if standards for cataloging were developed and followed (Yee, 2009). Elaine Svenonius (2000: 79–80) notes that the Library of Congress's card distribution program

> marks a technological advance and the beginning of union catalog building in the United States . . . [with] the drive toward standardization [as] strong. The beginning and end of the twentieth century were two such periods—first when card catalogs were introduced to replace book catalogs, and then again when online catalogs superseded card catalogs.

The primary technical standard used in knowledge-organizing systems in library online catalogs is the information exchange standard known today as MARC 21. MARC 21 was developed in 2000 as an agreement between the United States and Canada to merge the two MARC formats (USMARC and CAN/MARC) that were employed at that time. MARC 21 is based on the ANSI NISO Standard Z39.2, the American National Standard for Bibliographic Information Exchange (1971, revised 1985), and the ISO Standard 2709:1996, Information Documentation—Format for Information Exchange. Because MARC 21 is a cooperative merger between the United States and Canada, there are two offices or agencies that maintain the MARC 21 standard. The Network Development and MARC Standards Office plans and develops library and information network standards at the Library of Congress. It is the maintenance agency for several national standards, including the MARC 21 formats. The Standards Division at the Library and Archives Canada maintains and supports the MARC 21 formats and other library standards (Library of Congress, 2007b, 2008b).

The first MARC standard was developed in the United States and Great Britain concurrently during the late 1960s as a result of the MARC Pilot Program. Henriette Avram (2003: 1719) notes that factors including the availability of machine systems being used in libraries and the subsequent machine-readable form of cataloging data supplied by the Library of Congress; the possibility of sharing locally generated records; the potential for using computer programs across organizations to reduce the high costs of designing systems; and the need for hardware capable of handling large character sets were the impetus for the MARC Pilot Program. In 1969, the Project members submitted the new proposed ANSI standard, along with the equivalent proposed British standard, to the ISO. The MARC *format* structure, as a means of information interchange, was adopted by the major national U.S. libraries and others. In 1971 it became an ANSI standard, and it became an ISO standard in 1973 (ISO Standard 2709:1973 [E]) (Avram, 2003: 1720). There are more than 20 other national versions of MARC (e.g., UKMARC, RUSMARC, IBERMARC, etc.).

MARC 21 continues to be modified in order to remain viable with new metadata schemas being developed. The Library of Congress has launched a number of major initiatives relating to MARC 21, including MODs (Metadata Object Description Schema), an XML metadata scheme that uses selected data from MARC records and extends the records to include additional data elements; MADS (Metadata Authority Description Schema), an XML scheme for authorities data; XMLMARC, which translates the MARC record structure into an XML scheme; and the development of numerous metadata crosswalks between MARC and other metadata standards (Rowley and Hartley, 2008; McCallum, 2004; Guenther, 2004). Currently the MARC standard is undergoing revision by the Library of Congress RDA/MARC Working Group as a direct result of the new content standard being developed to replace the *Anglo-American Cataloguing Rules* (AACR2), the *Resource Description and Access* (RDA). The field structure for the MARC record is being adapted to more closely align with the new FRBR (*Functional Requirements for Bibliographic Records*) entity relationship requirements of the RDA within MARC records. To learn more about the current efforts to revise MARC, see the Library of Congress (2008a) "MARC Development" website.

A related MARC format for information exchange among national bibliographic agencies is UNIMARC. UNIMARC, like MARC 21, is intended to specify the content designators (tags, indicators, and subfield codes of a MARC record structure) to be assigned to bibliographic records in machine-readable form and to specify the logical and physical formats of the records. UNIMARC is a carrier format for exchange purposes. It does not stipulate the form, content, or record structure of the data within individual systems. UNIMARC does, however, provide recommendations on the form and content of data when it is to be exchanged. UNIMARC was developed in 1977 and has been revised as needed through the years. The most current version of UNIMARC includes updates through 2005. It is maintained by the International Federation of Library Associations (IFLA) Universal Bibliographic Control and International MARC Core Programme (UBCIM) (IFLA, 2008).

Data encoding standards are important to structures for organizing knowledge. As described earlier, the MARC 21 information exchange standard provides the backbone of the record structures held in current online catalog systems used in libraries in the United States, Great Britain, and Canada. Other countries worldwide use UNIMARC. Related data encoding standards that also serve the content format exchange function in structures for organizing knowledge include, for example:

- ISO Standard 1001:1996, Information Processing: File Structure and Labeling of Magnetic Tapes for Information Interchange
- SGML (Standard Generalized Markup Language), ISO Standard 8879:1986, Information Processing—Text and Office Systems, which defines the entities (objects) and attributes (general characteristics) of the data structure used to encode data about a collection's objects
- HTML (HyperText Markup Language), an SGML application designed for the creation of webpages
- XML (Extensible Markup Language), ISO Standard 8879, which implements SGML in the web environment
- Universal Coded Character Set (UCS or ISO/IEC 10646:1998) approved as a second encoding for MARC 21 records
- Unicode, ISO/IEC Standard 10646, Universal Multiple-Octet Coded Character Set, which defines a universal character set for encoding the characters in the scripts of the world's languages (Taylor and Joudrey, 2009a; Tull, 2002; Library of Congress, 2007a)

Technical Standards: Proprietary Databases

At present, standardization within knowledge-organizing systems other than library-oriented bibliographic systems is guided by the database vendors. As a result, each different database system is structured as appropriate for the specific knowledge being organized. According to Jennifer Rowley and Richard Hartley (2008: 69), "for large public databases, there has been little pressure to accept a standard format, and each database producer has in general chosen a record format to suit the particular database." There are efforts underway in the private and governmental sectors to develop standards for knowledge-organizing systems, but these efforts are mostly for content-related standards and not focused on technical or database structural standards. Developing knowledge-organizing systems standards will be discussed further later in this chapter.

Content Creation Standards

While technical standards provide the backbone and information exchange functions for structures that organize knowledge, content creation standards provide for the definition of elements to include in records, instructions for data entry, and controlled vocabularies that can be used to create content in records. The history of bibliographic control in libraries includes many examples of cataloging codes that were designed to help catalogers develop the content in bibliographic records. Chapter 2 included an overview of the library community's efforts to standardize cataloging codes in the United States during the late nineteenth and early twentieth centuries. In terms of standards for content creation, it was recognized by the library community that standardized principles and codes for creating bibliographic records were essential in order for libraries to share resources. Standardization also provides a degree of consistency within records, which in effect makes knowledge-organizing systems more efficient and useful.

Descriptive Cataloging: *Anglo-American Cataloguing Rules*

The first international content creation standard was created in 1908 through a collaboration between the British and Americans. The resulting code was designed to be used in the description of bibliographic elements in library records. In 1967, the Americans and British developed the first edition of the *Anglo-American Cataloguing Rules* (AACR), which represented an international standard used in the United States, Great Britain, and other countries for descriptive cataloging and access points within bibliographic records. The second edition of the AACR, the AACR2, was published in 1978 to incorporate a new international standard, the *International Standard Bibliographic Description* (ISBD), described in the next section, and to incorporate nonbook formats into the standard, to account for machine-processing of bibliographic records, to reconcile differences between the American and British versions, and to align with the Paris Principles, developed by the international cataloging community in 1961. The AACR2 has continually been revised through the years (in 1988, 1998, 2002, 2003, 2004, and 2005). Significant revisions were made to the code in 2002 to integrate new digital formats into the standard. Updates to the AACR2 occurred in 2003–2005. No further updates are planned for the AACR2 as a new code to replace AACR2 is being developed, the *Resource Description and Access* (RDA), which will be explained further later in this chapter (Taylor and Joudrey, 2009a; Rowley and Hartley, 2008). The AACR and its revised versions provide guidance to catalogers for the descriptive aspects of cataloging, as well as developing access points, or authorized headings for names and titles. Part I (Chapters 1–12) provides rules for description of specific formats of materials, with Chapter 1 focusing on general rules that could be applicable to any format. Part II provides guidance on choice of access points and rules for developing authorized headings for main and added entries in bibliographic records.

International Standard Bibliographic Description

The AACR and its revised editions provide guidance and rules for creating content within bibliographic records. A further important standard in content creation is the *International Standard Bibliographic Description* (ISBD), which serves as an international standard that defines a set of descriptive elements to include in bibliographic records. The ISBD resulted from an international meeting of cataloging experts convened by the IFLA in 1969. The ISBD (G), for General description, was issued by the IFLA in 1974. The objectives of the ISBD are to make records interchangeable among different sources, to facilitate their interpretation across different languages, and to facilitate the conversion of records to machine-readable form (Avram, 2003; Taylor and Joudrey, 2009a; IFLA, 2009a). There are ten specialized ISBDs related to (1) (A), older monographic publications, (2) (CF) computer files, (3) (CM) cartographic materials, (4) (CR) serials and continuing resources, (5) (ER) electronic resources, (6) (G) general, (7) (M) monographic, (8) (NBM) nonbook materials, (9) (PM) printed music, and (10) (S) serials. The IFLA worked on consolidating the ISBDs into one from 2003 to 2007 (IFLA, 2009c). In 2004, the IFLA ISBD Review Group began work on mapping the ISBD to the *Functional Requirements for Bibliographic Requirements* (FRBR) (Bianchini and Guerrini, 2009; Escolano and McGarry, 2009; IFLA, 2009a).

IFLA International Cataloguing Principles

In 2009, the IFLA's Cataloguing Section published the new "Statement of International Cataloguing Principles" (ICP). The ICP replaces the Paris Principles developed in 1961 as the standard international code for bibliographic description and access. The ICP was developed between 2003 and 2007. According to the IFLA (2009b) Cataloguing Section's website, The ICP

> replaces and broadens the scope of the Paris Principles from just textual works to all types of materials and from just the choice and form of entry to all aspects of bibliographic and authority data used in library catalogues. It includes not only principles and objectives (i.e., functions of the catalogue), but also guiding rules that should be included in cataloguing codes internationally, as well as guidance on search and retrieval capabilities.

The ICP "builds on the great cataloguing traditions of the world and also on the conceptual model in the IFLA *Functional Requirements for Bibliographic Records* (FRBR). It is hoped this statement will increase the international sharing of bibliographic and authority data and guide cataloguing rule makers in their efforts to develop an international cataloguing code" (IFLA, 2009b). The ICP has been translated into 20 languages for global use.

Resource Description and Access

As noted earlier, work on a content creation standard, the *Resource Description and Access* (RDA), to replace the AACR2 is in progress. The Joint Steering Committee for Development of RDA (JSC) began work in 2004. The online tool for accessing the RDA was released in June 2010. The RDA is based on the conceptual metadata models FRBR and FRAD (*Functional Requirements for Authority Data*), which were developed by the IFLA and the international cataloging community. It is also aligned with the principles of the ICP. The JSC provides a complete statement of the objectives on its website (JSC, 2009b). The development and release of RDA are also discussed on the JSC's website (JSC, 2009a).

Subject-Related Content Standards

The previous sections outlined the standards related to the descriptive aspects of content creation within bibliographic structures for organizing knowledge. The AACR2, ISBD, and ICP do not include provisions for subject description. The RDA has a placeholder for representing subject-related content, although it has not been developed as of 2010. Subject-related content standards include those that regulate the development of controlled vocabularies, such as thesauri and subject headings lists, and the standards related to the use and development of classification schemas, taxonomies, and ontologies. Subject-related content standards are developed by national and international standards organizations and within the library and World Wide Web communities.

Controlled Vocabulary Standards

At the national and international levels, standards for the development and use of thesauri include the following:

- ISO 2788:1986, Documentation–Guidelines for the establishment and development of monolingual thesauri. This standard was first published as an ISO standard in 1974. It was revised in 1986.
- ISO 5964:1985, Documentation–Guidelines for the establishment and development of multilingual thesauri. Work is currently underway to revise and combine ISO 2788 and ISO 5964 into an updated ISO 25964, Information and documentation—Thesauri and interoperability with other vocabularies. An international group of experts in indexing representing 11 countries is currently reviewing 2788 and 5964 and aligning them with the new BS 8723 (described later) (Clarke, 2008).
- ISO 5963:1985, Documentation–Methods for examining documents, determining their subjects, and selecting indexing terms. This standard describes

general techniques for document analysis that should apply in all indexing situations.

- ISO 214:1976, Documentation–Abstracts for publications and documentation. This standard provides guidelines for the preparation and presentation of abstracts of documents.
- BS 8723:2008, Structured Vocabularies for Information Retrieval. This standard, developed by the British Standards Institute, represents a combination and complete revision of BS 5723 and 6723. BS 8723 is being used as the basis for the development of ISO 25964.
- ANSI/NISO Z39.19:2005, Guidelines for the Construction, Format and Management of Monolingual Controlled Vocabularies. This standard presents guidelines and conventions for the contents, display, construction, testing, maintenance, and management of monolingual controlled vocabularies. It focuses on controlled vocabularies that are used for the representation of content objects in knowledge-organization systems, including lists, synonym rings, taxonomies, and thesauri.

These subject-related standards are used in the development of controlled vocabularies and classification schemes.

Subject-Related Standards Developed by the Library Community

As noted in Chapter 2, subject headings lists began to be systematized in the late 1870s when Charles A. Cutter published his *Rules for a Dictionary Catalog* in 1876 (Cutter, 1904). The *Library of Congress Subject Headings* (LCSH) draws from Cutter's work and is today the preeminent authority list for subject headings throughout the English-speaking countries (Rowley and Hartley, 2008). Because Chapter 2 outlines the developments of the major subject headings lists, controlled vocabularies, and classification schemes (the Dewey Decimal and Library of Congress schemes), these standards will not be discussed again in this section. While there are definitely other controlled vocabularies and classification schemes of note, the LCSH and DDC remain the most widely used currently.

Subject-Related Standards for the World Wide Web

Over the past 12 years web communities have focused on the development of standards for subject-related content creation and structures for organizing knowledge. The Semantic Web, a product of the W3C (World Wide Web Consortium) community, "provides a common framework that allows data to be shared and reused across application, enterprise, and community boundaries. It is a collaborative effort led by W3C with participation from a large number of researchers and industrial partners" (W3C, 2009b). The Semantic Web, the brainchild of Tim Berners-Lee, is intended to provide more structure to the web so that computers can deal with its content in more meaningful ways. The Semantic Web community has developed numerous metadata schemes and metadata specifications, such as the Resource Description Framework (RDF) and the SKOS (Simple Knowledge Organization) specification and associated standards. The RDF is "a language for representing information about resources in the World Wide Web. . . . RDF provides a common framework for expressing this information, so it can be exchanged between applications without loss of meaning" (W3C, 2009a). SKOS is an initiative underway in the Semantic Web community that is

> developing specifications and standards to support the use of knowledge organization systems (KOS) such as thesauri, classification schemes, subject heading systems and taxonomies within the framework of the Semantic Web. SKOS provides a standard way to represent knowledge organization systems using the Resource Description Framework (RDF). Encoding this information in RDF allows it to be passed between computer applications in an interoperable way. (W3C, 2008)

Metadata Schema Standards

More than any other area of standards development in structures for organizing knowledge, metadata schema development is a moving target. Numerous metadata schemes have been developed since the late 1990s. We have discussed a few of them previously in this chapter (MODS, METS), and some consider the MARC standard as a metadata scheme. One of the difficulties in discussing metadata standards is tied to the idea of "what is a standard." Many of the metadata schemes that have been or are currently being developed were designed for specific applications and not necessarily for large-scale use. As such, they may not be thought of as standards. However, a scheme may be considered as a standard by the community it serves once widely adopted and implemented. The following sections will present a representative sample of those standards that are used widely. It does not attempt to provide comprehensive coverage of all types of metadata standards/schemas, nor complete descriptions of each standard, as this is beyond the scope of the book. The reader is, however, referred to Zeng and Qin (2009) or Liu (2007) for more complete coverage of current and emerging metadata schemes.

This section will also address standards for metadata registries. Because metadata schemes are so numerous, efforts to organize them in meaningful ways have been developed within web communities. Metadata registries gather together related standards for a purpose, discipline, etc., and make them accessible through a web portal. The following section is organized based on a functional typology of metadata schemas: (1) general purpose, (2) cultural objects and visual resources, (3) educational purposes, (4) archival and preservation metadata, and (5) metadata registries.

General Purpose

Perhaps the most widely used metadata standard is the Dublin Core Element Set (DC). Development of the DC began in 1995 during a workshop in Dublin,

Ohio. A group of international experts from various fields (publishers, computer scientists, librarians, software developers, etc.) met with the goal of developing a general metadata standard that could be used by content creators of electronic documents. The core element set of the DC includes 15 general elements based on the principles of simplicity, compatibility, extensibility, and interoperability, which makes the element set general enough so that it can be used within many different contexts and for a variety of different applications. The generic nature of the scheme allows conformity with existing and emerging metadata schemas at an international level, as well as being interoperable with diverse collections and knowledge systems. The DC serves as the base for many metadata schemas that have been developed, for example, the GEM metadata scheme. GEM (Gateway to Educational Materials), a metadata scheme used to describe education-related resources, uses the DC core 15 elements, along with other discipline-specific and functional elements, for a total of 47 elements (GEM, 2009). The DC was approved as ANSI/NISO standard Z39.85 in 2007 and ISO 15836:2007. The Dublin Core Metadata Initiative (DCMI) oversees the development and implementation of the standard. "Dublin Core Metadata Element Set" (Dublin Core Metadata Initiative, 2009) provides more information on the DCMI.

Cultural Objects and Visual Resources

Cultural heritage organizations (e.g., museums, libraries, archives, historical societies), as well as local/state governments and private organizations, have increasingly been digitizing collections of culturally significant objects. These digitization projects have led to the need for standards that can be applied to the unique aspects of cultural and image collections, as well as provide administrative data describing the digitization, copyright, and use provisions of the objects. Two metadata schemas stand out as standards within the cultural heritage community: (1) the data structures and semantics standard CDWA (Categories for the Description of Works of Art) and its companion data content standard the CCO (Cataloging of Cultural Objects) and (2) the VRA Core (Visual Resources Association Core Categories). The CDWA was developed in the 1990s by members of the Art Information Task Force (AITF), funded by the Getty Information Institute and the National Endowment for the Humanities (NEH). The AITF included members of the cultural heritage community who provide access to art resources (e.g., museum curators and registrars, art librarians, visual resource managers, and technical specialists) (Baca and Harpring, n.d.). The CDWA provides "guidelines for the description of art objects and images, including a discussion of issues involved in building art information systems" (Baca and Harpring, n.d.). The CDWA was developed for the needs of those in the cultural heritage community who record, maintain, and retrieve information about art information, including academic researchers and scholars. The CDWA includes 532 categories and subcategories. A small subset of categories are considered *core* in that they represent the minimum information necessary to identify and describe a work. The categories and subcategories that are indicated as *core* are those that the task force agreed represent the minimum information necessary to uniquely and unambiguously identify and describe a particular work of art or architecture (Baca and Harpring, n.d.). According to Marcia Zeng and Jian Qin (2009), the purpose of the CDWA is to provide a framework for mapping existing art information systems and for developing new ones. It also guides users to additional resources for vocabulary control and provides guidelines for describing art resources. The CDWA has been mapped to other metadata standards, including, for example, the Dublin Core, MARC, VRA 4.0 XML, and MODS (Harpring, 2009).

The CCO, the companion content creation standard of the CDWA, is comprised of 116 elements and subelements derived from the CDWA. The CCO also identifies a *core* set of elements that should be used for the minimal description of art resources; however, the standard recommends the use of the full 116. The CCO also provides guidelines for selecting, ordering, and formatting data within the records.

The VRA Core was developed by the Visual Resources Association, Data Standards Committee, which is an international organization of visual media professionals. According to the VRA (2009) website, the

> VRA Core 4.0 is a data standard for the cultural heritage community. . . . It consists of a metadata element set (units of information such as title, location, date, etc.), as well as an initial blueprint for how those elements can be hierarchically structured. The element set provides a categorical organization for the description of works of visual culture as well as the images that document them.

VRA Core 4.0 was released in 2007 and includes 17 elements that can be used to describe resources at three levels: work, image, or collection level. VRA Core 3.0 also provided the groundwork from which the CCO content standards were developed. For further information on the VRA Core, refer to VRA (2009).

It should also be noted that other associated content creation standards developed by the Getty Information Institute are used in conjunction with the CDWA, CCO, and VRA Core. These include art-related controlled vocabularies used by cultural heritage organizations worldwide: the *Art & Architecture Thesaurus* (AAT), the *Getty Thesaurus of Geographic Names* (TGN), and the Union List of Artist Names (ULAN). Each can be accessed at the Getty Research Institute website (www.getty.edu/research/conducting_research/vocabularies/introvocabs/gettyvocabs.html#getty).

Educational Purposes

As mentioned earlier, the GEM metadata schema (Gateway to Educational Materials) is used to describe education-related resources. It uses the DC core base 15 elements, along with other discipline-specific and functional elements, for a total of 47 elements (GEM, 2009). Founded in 1996 as a project of the U.S. Department of Education and the Information Institute of Syracuse at Syracuse University, GEM is a consortium of more than 750 organizations and individuals. GEM has established and developed the architecture, software, and training materials necessary to build and maintain the Gateway to Educational Materials, which was introduced in 1997. GEM provides a mechanism for educators to share pedagogical resources used in K–12.The GEM metadata standards, GEM data files, and applications for creating GEM metadata records are used today by collection holders around the world (GEM, 2009; Liu, 2007).

The IEE Learning Technology Standards Committee (LTSC) began work on the LOM (Learning Object Metadata) standard in 1997. Development of the LOM is an international effort by LOM Working Group members from more than 15 countries. The LOM standard provides a minimal set of elements needed for the management, location, and evaluation of learning objects. The elements include areas for learning technology, digital rights, meta-metadata (data describing the data of the objects), and definitions related to areas of instruction of the object. LOM is a complex metadata standard that integrates descriptive, administrative, and technical metadata within its element set. According to the LTSC Purpose Statement, LOM is designed:

1. "to enable learners or instructors to search, evaluate, acquire, and utilize Learning Objects";
2. "to enable the sharing and exchange of learning objects";
3. to enable the development of learning objects by repurposing of existing objects in new ways;
4. to enable computer agents to automatically repurpose objects into new objects;
5. to complement the work on learning objects standards;
6. "to provide researchers with standards that support the collection and sharing of comparable data concerning the applicability and effectiveness of Learning Objects";
7. to define a simple yet extensible standard for multiple domains and jurisdictions to ensure that it is broadly adopted and applied; and
8. "to support necessary security and authentication for the distribution and use of Learning Objects." (LTSC, 2005)

The IEEE has been working with the DCMI to develop the educational categories and has collaborated with the Centre for Educational Technology Interoperability Standards (CETIS) to develop the Metadata for Learning Resources standards, ISO/IEC 24751-1:2008, Information technology—Individualized adaptability and accessibility in e-learning, education and training—Part 1: Framework and reference model; ISO/IEC 24751-2:2008, Information technology—Individualized adaptability and accessibility in e-learning, education and training—Part 2: "Access for all" personal needs and preferences for digital delivery; ISO/IEC 24751-3:2008, Information technology—Individualized adaptability and accessibility in e-learning, education and training—Part 3: "Access for all" digital resource description; and ISO/IEC 19796-1:2005, Information technology—Learning, education and training—Quality management, assurance and metrics—Part 1: General approach.

Archival and Preservation Metadata

In the archival community, the knowledge structure used for describing collections held by archives is the *finding aid*. Beginning in the mid-1990s a research project at the University of California Berkeley (conducted by the EAD Working Group) developed the metadata schema for encoding finding aids into digital form. The EAD (*Encoded Archival Description*) is a data structure that defines the elements to include in the finding aid. It is not a data content structure, but rather relies on other archival content creation standards such as the ISAD (G) (*General International Standard Archival Description*), which is similar in scope to the ISBD described earlier in this chapter. ISAD is designed to be used to create content in archival records or finding aids and to serve as the basis for the development of archival standards (International Council on Archives, 2000). DACS (*Describing Archives: A Content Standard*) is the content creation archival standard accepted by most of the U.S. archival community. DACS is based on the ISAD (G) and can be used for creating any level of content records in archives, including finding aids and catalog records (Society of American Archivists, 2004; Taylor and Joudrey, 2009b). The EAD Version 2002 is maintained by the Network Development and MARC Standards Office of the Library of Congress (Library of Congress, 2004).

Metadata Registries

In response to the numerous metadata schemes that have been or are currently being developed by different communities, metadata registries are being compiled that provide access to the variety of metadata schemes. According to Zeng and Qin (2009: 213), metadata registries "provide information for all metadata elements, schemas, and application profiles relevant to the application domain or domains; mappings of elements across standards and schemas; and a search and browse interface for discovering and locating metadata elements, value spaces, and schemas." According to Polydoratou and Nicholas (2001: 312), metadata registries' roles are:

1. To support data standardisation and documentation.
2. To support the management of basic semantics.
3. To function as an authoritative source of reference information about data.
4. To act as a medium for recording and disseminating data standards.
5. To function as a "mediator" to the source of information.

Metadata registries serve the function of "registration authority" for a specific domain, project community, or other standards creators. The ISO/IEC 11179, Information Technology—Specification and Standardization of Data Elements, is the international standard that establishes a data element registry and gives guidance on how to classify, describe, name, identify, and maintain both the data element descriptions and the metadata created using the schema (Polydoratou and Nicholas, 2001). What follows is a list of some metadata registries from different metadata communities:

- UKOLN's (U.K. Office for Library Networking) CORES Registry, available at cores.dsd.sztaki.hu (accessed June 3, 2010)
- Dublin Core Metadata Initiative Registry, available at dublincore.org/dcregistry (accessed June 3, 2010)
- SchemaWeb (which includes a directory of RDF schemas being used on the web as well as gathers information about non-RDF schemas used on the web), available at schemaweb.info (accessed June 3, 2010)
- The Agricultural Information Management Standards (AIMS) of the Food and Agricultural Organization of the United Nations Metadata Registry of Knowledge Organizing Systems (KOS) (which gathers into one interface agricultural-related thesauri, ontologies, classification schemes, etc.), available at aims.fao.org/en/website/Knowledge-Organization-Systems-%28KOS%29/sub (accessed June 3, 2010)
- National Center for Biomedical Ontology's BioPortal Ontology Registry (a web-based application for accessing and sharing biomedical ontologies), available at bioportal.bioontology.org/home/release (accessed June 3, 2010)

Gail Hodge reports on the 11th Open Forum on Metadata Registries meeting held in May 2008. Presenters described additional metadata registries and related projects of interest, including caBig (Cancer Bioinformatics Grid) and the DOE Science Grid, which are large data repositories for science-related data. The eXtended Metadata Registries Project is a pilot project implementing the conceptual model of ISO 11179 Edition 3 to test the ability of the registry to share semantic data and meaning using the concept scheme developed by the project (Hodge, 2008).

Issues Related to Standardization

In light of the previous sections, we might now ask, are standards really necessary? What value do they serve? Are there any reasons why standards would not be the best or most warranted course of action? Elaine Svenonius (2000: 80–81) outlines the dangers of excessive standardization within bibliographic control:

1. A standard may be in conflict with the principle of user convenience established by Cutter (1904). The standardized practice may be contrary to how

the user would represent and/or search for the information object being described in the knowledge system.
2. The reasons or principles underlying the standard and the community may become obscured. Is the rationale for the standard lost in the development process and the practice? Are all standards necessary or do they continue to be needed?
3. Overstandardization may inhibit change.

Standards should be dynamic and reviewed periodically to make sure they still work as projected or determine if revisions are needed. Clarke (2008) noted that the ISO indexing standards 2788:1986 and 5964:1985 were disgracefully outdated. They are currently being revised and will be combined into ISO 25964 if approved. Both the NISO and ISO include review provisions of five years so that standards can remain effective and up-to-date with the needs of the community. One issue, however, for an information professional, is the navigation and identification of the appropriate standard(s) in effect and their related standards. ISO provides links to other portions of the same standard, as well as potentially related standards of interest. However, there appears to be no mapping among NISO, ISO, and other national/international standards or even within the individual standards organization's standards themselves.

The real value of a standard is in its use by the community for which it is intended. Use by the community and cross-communities may serve as a legitimizing effect of the value and utility of the standard, but standards should continually be reviewed for currency, usability, and contextual usefulness.

Best Practices and Knowledge Organization Structures

According to Zeng and Qin (2009: 122), "Good design can easily be buried under the carelessness of incorrect execution." In other words, if clear instruction is not provided, then no matter how good a system or metadata scheme is, it will not be effective. Best practices and the guides that are developed to disseminate the best practices provide further information for how to implement a metadata scheme or for practical application of a cataloging code. A best practice is neither a standard nor a code, but makes standards and codes more useful by providing additional instruction to be used in implementation, such as content entry instructions, examples, or helpful advice on common errors to avoid. Best practices are developed by the standards developers and by the users in the community that use the standards. Best practices can be found in metadata schemes under comments or recommendation sections, where, for example, controlled vocabularies to use are listed. Often, best practices will include examples of application of a standard, such as those present in the AACR2, which give the content creator an example of how the data value will appear following the standard.

Best practices can also be "in house" or "local practice" within an information organization. Most cataloging departments have their own interpretation of standards that are conveyed either in print or verbally to employees. In this manner, content creation remains consistent with the "local practices" of the organization.

Best practices can evolve into standards or codes. If the best practice proves useful within the community or information agency, it may be suggested as an addition or provision of an existing standard or as the basis for a new standard. An example of this is the Library of Congress Rule Interpretations (LCRIs) that provide additional guidance for applying AACR2 within bibliographic records. LCRIs have been incorporated into revisions of the AACR2. As with standards, best practices must continually be reviewed for usefulness and appropriateness, updated and improved as needed, and disseminated within and among communities that use them.

Some additional examples of best practices and local practices in cataloging or metadata creation include the following:

- DLESE (Digital Library for Earth Science Education) Collection metadata framework version 1.0.0, which provides instructions, things to avoid, and examples (www.dlese.org/Metadata/collection/1.0.00/docs/framework-documentation.php)
- National Science Digital Library (NSDL) Metadata Guidelines, which provide guidance on metadata creation for the many participants of the NSDL collections (nsdl.org/collection/metadata-guide.php)
- The Claremont Colleges Digital Library Metadata Best Practices, which provide local practices to follow when creating Dublin Core records at Claremont College (ccdl.libraries.claremont.edu/inside/CCDLmetadata.pdf)
- Collaborative Digitization Project (CDP) Dublin Core Metadata Best Practices Version 2.1, which are guidelines for creating Dublin Core metadata records for digitized cultural heritage resources (www.bcr.org/dps/cdp/best/dublin-core-bp.pdf)
- The University of Akron Local Cataloging Practice, which establishes local practices to be used at the University of Akron's University Libraries (www3.uakron.edu/ul/depts/cataloging/local-practice.html)

Conclusion

In this chapter we reviewed what standards are, how standards are developed, and the necessary roles they play within structures for organizing knowledge. We also examined standards organizations and the various stakeholders in the standards development process and how each functions to develop standards. The next chapter will extend our exploration by looking at knowledge structures in use within a sample of academic disciplines, including biology, zoology, social science, and library and information science, and the principle functions knowledge structures play in each. Chapter 4 will also introduce initiatives in each of these disciplines to develop structures for organizing knowledge within the digital environment.

Thought Exercises

1. Now that we have reviewed the process of developing a standard at both the national and international levels, take a closer look at both processes. Where do they overlap? Are there any gaps that you see in the process(es)? Do the time periods for developing the standards seem reasonable/feasible? Other issues you found? Questions you asked?
2. Who are the major players in the development of standards? Does the process include all of the stakeholders you feel are *necessary*? If not, who *should* be involved in the standards development process? In your opinion, do you think that the users of the community are involved at the appropriate level or time in the development and approval process?
3. Do you think standards are necessary? Make a list of the pros and cons of using standards in structures for organizing knowledge. When would it be important *not* to use a standard?
4. What role do best practices play in structures for organizing knowledge? In application of standards and in standards development? Can you identify a best practice in your own organization and relate it to the organization of knowledge? Identify and list the strengths and weaknesses.

References

ANSI. 2009. "Frequently Asked Questions. ANSI Overview." ANSI. Available: www.ansi.org/about_ansi/faqs/faqs.aspx?menuid=1 (accessed May 12, 2010).

Avram, Henriette D. 2003. "Machine-Readable Cataloging (MARC) Program." *Encyclopedia of Library and Information Science* 1, no. 1: 1712–1730.

Baca, Murtha, and Patricia Harpring. n.d. "Introduction." Getty Information Institute. Available: www.getty.edu/research/conducting_research/standards/cdwa/introduction.html (accessed June 3, 2010).

Bianchini, Carlo, and Mauro Guerrini. 2009. "From Bibliographic Models to Cataloguing Rules: Remarks on FRBR, ICP, ISBD, and RDA and the Relationships between Them." *Cataloguing and Classification Quarterly* 47, no. 2: 105–124.

British Standards Institute. 2009. "What Is a Standard?" Available: www.bsigroup.com/en/Standards-and-Publications/About-standards/What-is-a-standard (accessed June 3, 2010).

Clarke, Sheila. 2008. "ISO 2788 + ISO 5964 + Much Energy = ISO 25964." *Bulletin of the American Society for Information Science and Technology* 35, no. 1 (October/November): 31–33.

Cutter, Charles A. 1904. *Rules for a Dictionary Catalog*, 4th ed. Washington, DC: Government Printing Office.

Dublin Core Metadata Initiative. 2009. "Dublin Core Metadata Element Set." DCMI. Available: dublincore.org (accessed June 3, 2010).

Escolano, Elena, and Dorothy McGarry. 2009. "International Standard Bibliographic Description: Updating the Consolidated ISBD." *International Cataloguing and Bibliographic Control* 38, no. 1 (January/March): 11–12.

GEM. 2009. "Gateway to 21st Century Skills: GEM in General." Available: www.thegateway.org/about/gemingeneral (accessed June 3, 2010).

Guenther, Rebecca S. 2004. "Using the Metadata Object Description Schema (MODS) for Resource Description: Guidelines and Applications." *Library High Tech* 22, no. 1: 89–98.

Hagler, Ronald. 1989. "The Consequences of Integration." In *The Conceptual Foundations of Descriptive Cataloging* (pp. 197–218). San Diego: Academic Press.

Harpring, Patricia. 2009. "Metadata Standards Crosswalk." J. Paul Getty Trust. Available: www.getty.edu/research/conducting_research/standards/intrometadata/crosswalks.html (accessed June 3, 2010).

Hodge, Gail. 2008. "Toward Interoperability: A Report from the 11th Open Forum on Metadata Registries and Related Standards." *Bulletin of the American Society for Information Science and Technology* 35, no. 1 (October/November): 25–30.

IFLA. 2008. "IFLA Universal Bibliographic Control and International MARC Core Programme (UBCIM). UNIMARC Manual. Bibliographic Format 1994." IFLA. Available: archive.ifla.org/VI/3/p1996-1/sectn1.htm (accessed June 3, 2010).

———. 2009a. "About the ISBD Review Group." IFLA. Available: www.ifla.org/en/about-the-isbd-review-group (accessed June 3, 2010).

———. 2009b. "Statement of International Cataloguing Principles." IFLA. Cataloguing Section. Available: www.ifla.org/files/cataloguing/icp/icp_2009-en.pdf (accessed June 3, 2010).

———. 2009c. "Superseded ISBDs." IFLA. Available: www.ifla.org/node/900 (accessed June 3, 2010).

International Council on Archives. 2000. *ISAD (G) General International Standard Archival Description.* Ottawa: International Council on Archives.

ISO. 2009a. "About ISO." ISO. Available: www.iso.org/iso/about.htm (accessed June 3, 2010).

———. 2009b. "How ISO Develops Standards." ISO. Available: www.iso.org/iso/about/how_iso_develops_standards.htm (accessed June 7, 2010).

———. 2009c. "Stages of Standards Development." ISO. Available: www.iso.org/iso/standards_development/processes_and_procedures/stages_description.htm (accessed June 3, 2010).

———. 2009d. "What Standards Do." ISO. Available: www.iso.org/iso/about/discover-iso_what-standards-do.htm (accessed June 3, 2010).

JSC. 2009a. "Joint Steering Committee for Development of RDA." JSC. Available: www.rda-jsc.org/index.html (accessed June 3, 2010).

———. 2009b. "RDA: Objectives and Principles." JSC. Available: www.rda-jsc.org/docs/5rda-objectivesrev3.pdf (accessed June 3, 2010).

Library of Congress. 2004. *EAD: Encoded Archival Description.* Version 2002 Official Site. Library of Congress. Available: www.loc.gov/ead (accessed June 3, 2010).

———. 2007a. "MARC 21 Specifications for Record Structure, Character Sets, and Exchange Media." Library of Congress. Available: www.loc.gov/marc/specifications/speccharucs.html (accessed June 3, 2010).

———. 2007b. "Network Development." Library of Congress. Available: www.loc.gov/marc/ndmso.html (accessed June 3, 2010).

———. 2008a. "MARC Development." Library of Congress. Available: www.loc.gov/marc/development.html (accessed June 3, 2010).

———. 2008b. "MARC Standards. FAQ." Library of Congress. Available: www.loc.gov/marc/faq.html#NDMSOdef (accessed June 3, 2010).

Liu, Jia. 2007. *Metadata and Its Applications in the Digital Library: Approaches and Practices.* Westport, CT: Libraries Unlimited.

LTSC. 2005. "IEEE WG12: Learning Object Metadata: Purpose of Proposed Project." LTSC. Available: ltsc.ieee.org/wg12/index.html (accessed June 3, 2010).

McCallum, Sally H. 2004. "An Introduction to the Metadata Object Description Schema (MODS)." *Library High Tech* 22, no. 1: 82–88.

Moen, William. 2000. "Interoperability for Information Access: Technical Standards and Policy Considerations." *Journal of Academic Librarianship* 26, no. 2: 129–132.

Needleman, Mark. 2008. "Introduction to Special Section on Information Standards." *Bulletin of the American Society for Information Science and Technology* 35, no. 1 (October/November): 12.

NISO. 2008. "NISO Operating Procedures." Available: www.niso.org/about/documents/NISOprocedures2008final.pdf (accessed June 3, 2010).

———. 2009. "About NISO." NISO. Available: www.niso.org/about (accessed June 3, 2010).

Polydoratou, Panayiota, and David Nicholas. 2001. "Familiarity with and Use of Metadata Formats and Metadata Registries amongst Those Working in Diverse Professional Communities within the Information Sector." *Aslib Proceedings* 53, no. 8 (September): 309–324.

Rowley, Jennifer, and Richard Hartley. 2008. "Describing Documents." In *Organizing Knowledge: An Introduction to Managing Access to Information*, 4th ed. (pp. 55–96). Burlington, VT: Ashgate.

Society of American Archivists. 2004. *Describing Archives: A Content Standard (DACS).* Chicago: Society of American Archivists.

Svenonius, Elaine. 2000. "Principles of Description." In *The Intellectual Foundation of Information Organization* (pp. 67–85). London, England: MIT Press.

Taylor, Arlene, and Joudrey, Daniel. 2009a. "Encoding Standards." In *The Organization of Information*, 3rd ed. (pp. 129–158). Westport, CT: Libraries Unlimited.

———. 2009b. "Metadata Description." In *The Organization of Information*, 3rd ed. (pp. 199–243). Westport, CT: Libraries Unlimited.

Tull, Laura. 2002. "Library Systems and Unicode: A Review of the Current State of Development." *Information Technology and Libraries* 21, no. 4 (December): 181–185.

VRA. 2009. "Welcome to the VRA Core 4.0." VRA. Available: www.vraweb.org/projects/vracore4/index.html (accessed June 3, 2010).

W3C. 2008. "SKOS." Available: www.w3.org/2004/02/skos/intro (accessed June 3, 2010).

———. 2009a. "RDA Primer." W3C. Available: www.w3.org/TR/rdf-primer (accessed June 3, 2010).

———. 2009b. "Semantic Web." W3C. Available: www.w3.org/2001/sw (accessed June 3, 2010).

Yee, Martha. 2009. "Wholly Visionary: The American Library Association, the Library of Congress, and the Card Distribution Program." *LRTS* 53, no. 2: 68–76.

Zeng, Marcia L., and Qin, Jian. 2009. "Current Standards." In *Metadata* (pp. 15–84). New York: Neal-Schuman.

Websites Noted in Text

CDP. 2009. Collaborative Digitization Project Dublin Core Metadata Best Practices Version 2.1. Available: www.bcr.org/dps/cdp/best/dublin-core-bp.pdf (accessed June 3, 2010).

Claremont College. 2009. Claremont College's Digital Library Metadata Best Practices. Available: ccdl.libraries.claremont.edu/inside/CCDLmetadata.pdf (accessed June 3, 2010).

Digital Library for Earth Science Education. 2009. DLESE Metadata Framework Version 1.0.0. Available: www.dlese.org/Metadata/collection/1.0.00/docs/framework-documentation.php (accessed June 3, 2010).

Dublin Core Initiative. 2009. Dublin Core Metadata Initiative Registry. Available: dublincore.org/dcregistry (accessed June 3, 2010).

ISO. 2009. "Organizations in Cooperation with ISO." Available: www.iso.org/iso/about/organizations_in_liaison.htm (accessed June 3, 2010).

J. Paul Getty Trust. 2009. Getty Research Institute Website. Available: www.getty.edu/research/conducting_research/vocabularies/introvocabs/gettyvocabs.html#getty (accessed June 3, 2010).

Library of Congress. 2009. MARC Standards. Available: www.loc.gov/marc/development.html (accessed May 12, 2010).

National Center for Biomedical Ontology. 2009. BioPortal Ontology Registry. Available: bioportal.bioontology.org/home/release (accessed June 3, 2010).

National Science Digital Library. 2009. NSDL Metadata Guidelines. Available: nsdl.org/collection/metadata-guide.php (accessed June 3, 2010).

SchemaWeb. 2009. Available: schemaweb.info (accessed June 3, 2010).

U.K. Office for Library Networking. 2009. UKOLN CORES Registry. Available: cores.dsd.sztaki.hu (accessed June 3, 2010).

United Nations. 2009. The Agricultural Information Management Standards (AIMS) of the Food and Agricultural Organization. Available: aims.fao.org/en/website/Knowledge-Organization-Systems-%28KOS%29/sub (accessed June 3, 2010).

University of Akron University Libraries. University of Akron Local Cataloging Practice. Available: www3.uakron.edu/ul/depts/cataloging/local-practice.html (accessed June 3, 2010).

4

Disciplinary Uses and Applications of Knowledge Structures

Focus Points

- What are the principle functions for knowledge structures within academic disciplines?
- Do these functions serve a different role within specific disciplines?
- Have knowledge structures adapted to disciplinary uses?
- How do knowledge structures translate into the digital environment?

Introduction and Scope of the Chapter

As noted in the exemplars discussed in Chapter 2, academic disciplines use knowledge structures to represent their understandings of the world. The conceptual bases for the knowledge structures developed within specific academic contexts vary significantly in order to meet the needs of the discipline in organizing the knowledge of the world, as seen through the lens of the discipline. We also saw evidence in Chapter 2 that development of knowledge structures was influenced by the current thinking of the discipline, as well as by other social and economic factors. With these ideas in mind one might then ask the following:

- What functions or roles do knowledge structures play beyond the representation of the knowledge of the discipline?
- Are knowledge structures used for comparative and explanatory purposes?
- Do they serve as a framework for learning?
- Do they serve as a framework for research and discovery?

This chapter will examine the principle functions of knowledge structures in general, but also within disciplinary contexts, through examination of different taxonomies in use and the standards developed to ensure the proper application of the knowledge structure. As a knowledge structure is not effective if it does not adapt and change with the disciplinary needs of its users, it is also informative to review how knowledge structures are translating into uses within the digital environment.

To explore the questions posed, this chapter will present an overview of the knowledge structures in use within a sample of academic disciplines, including biology, zoology, social science, and library and information science. Each section will include specific examples of knowledge structures, as well as their principle functions and the roles the structures play within the discipline. Examples of how the knowledge structures have translated into applications available in the digital environment will also be presented. These applications are in the form of online databases for taxonomic identification, discipline-specific digital libraries of specimens or documents, and online archives. Other developments within specific disciplines not only to make their resources available online but also to codify standards for taxonomic identification and metadata schema development are becoming more prevalent as the disciplines make use of the digital environment to disseminate ideas and make collections more accessible, thereby ensuring more collaboration within and across disciplines.

The chapter will not, however, outline in depth the development of the standards and codes used by each discipline. The reader is referred to Chapter 3, which provides the historical and current developments of standards and codes within library and information science, cultural heritage institutions, education, and interdisciplinary metadata schemes and registries.

Knowledge Structures within Biology

The Linnaean Hierarchy, as developed by Carl Linnaeus in 1735, established the rule-bound hierarchical structure that is still in use today by scientists worldwide. Refer to Chapter 2 for more information on Linnaeus and his contributions to the development of knowledge structures within the natural sciences. The Linnaean Hierarchy, a structure for organizing the knowledge of the living world, begins with the largest category an animal or plant can belong to, the Kingdom, followed by the Phyla (or Phylum in singular form), within which there are Classes, within which are Orders, etc. The Linnaean Hierarchy includes seven groupings that are used by scientists (biologists, zoologists, etc.) to classify natural living things. Figure 4.1 includes an example of the Linnaean Hierarchy and its application to *Homo sapiens* (or humans).

The Linnaean Hierarchy is used by taxonomists in the natural science disciplines of biology, botany, zoology, etc., to identify and classify new species. A

Figure 4.1. Linnaean Hierarchy for *Homo sapiens*

Kingdom	Animalia	(Animals)
Phylum	Chordata	(Vertebrates and kin)
Class	Mammalia	(Mammals)
Order	Primates	(Primates)
Family	Hominidae	(Hominids)
Genus	*Homo*	(Homo)
Species	*sapiens*	(humans)

simple workflow followed by taxonomists describing new taxa is provided by Larry Speers and James L. Edwards (2008: 88):

1. Reviewing all relevant species descriptions in the available taxonomic literature.
2. Compare these literature-based species descriptions with characters and character states of as large a series of closely related specimens as possible. Usually the specimens that are examined have been obtained by:
   a. selecting appropriate specimens from the collection at the researcher's home institution;
   b. obtaining similar specimens through new collecting efforts;
   c. visiting other institutions to examine their holdings for similar material; or
   d. requesting the loan of relevant material from the collections visited or other institutions.
3. Validating, where possible, the literature descriptions by examining all relevant type material, either through loans or by visiting the institutions holding this material.
4. Researcher can formally name this material as a new taxon . . . and submitting this new taxonomic description to the scientific community through the peer-reviewed publication process.

The Linnaean Hierarchy taxonomy serves as a framework for classification of a new specimen. However, also useful to this process is the existing literature published about the specimen or other related specimens. The taxonomist's knowledge structure includes not just the Linnaean Hierarchy but also the body of scientific literature (where the knowledge of the discipline is disseminated). Both are necessary in order to complete the work of a taxonomist.

Principle Functions

Throughout the years the principle structure for organizing knowledge within the biological sciences, the Linnaean Hierarchy, has continued to be used for its primary function, the classification and naming of living things. Using the Linnaean Hierarchy, taxonomists identify plants and animals within the established hierarchy and compare them to species that have already been classified and named. However, one of the most vexing issues facing early natural scientists, the naming of living things, continues to plague natural scientists. Establishing unambiguous names for living things is essential for effective scientific communication and development of new knowledge within scientific and scholarly communities. To accomplish this goal, John McNeill and Nicholas Turland (2006) believe that "names can only be unambiguous if there are internationally accepted rules governing their formation and use." Biologists have developed standard codes to ensure names will be unique, unambiguous, and published within the appropriate scientific literature, thereby establishing the name as valid. However, as can be the case with any standard or set of rules, not all individuals agree on what the rules should be, nor do they follow the rules as intended. According to Ernst Mayr and Peter Ashlock (1991: 383), "Underlying these very technical rules are certain basic principles or concepts that unfortunately are not understood by all taxonomists. Neglect of the conventional rules and ignorance of the underlying principles are the major reasons for the unsettled nomenclature of many groups of animals." Understanding the principles that underlie a standard, and the rationale for their development, can make it easier for an individual to apply the code. Mayr and Ashlock (1991: 384) outline a list of principles necessary for a system of nomenclature:

- **Uniqueness**: names must be unique as they are "the key to the entire literature related to that species or higher taxon. . . . there must be a clear-cut method of determining which [name is valid]."
- **Universality**: communication within the scientific community would be difficult without a singular language for the development of names. International agreements have been established that agree on a single language, a single set of names that are used worldwide.
- **Stability**: "[a}ny change of a well established name [will cause] confusion and [hinder] information retrieval [regarding the species]." Names of species should remain stable and unchanged unless determined by the community that the change is warranted.

To ensure that the international community of biologists understands and properly applies the Linnaean Hierarchy and rules for naming and placement of a species, codes of rules have been established. Because of the diversity of the field of biology, and by necessity born of the unique challenges of each biological discipline, multiple codes have been developed to address the specific issues encountered by scientists in applying the Linnaean Hierarchy, to establish rules for naming of new species, and to determine accurate naming of preestablished species. This section will present as examples three of the primary codes used by biologists and zoologists: *The International Code of Botanical Nomenclature*, *The International Code of Nomenclature of Bacteria*, and *The International Code of Zoological Nomenclature*. Other codes, including the *International Code of Nomenclature for Cultivated Plants* (International Society for Horticultural Science, 2009; information about this code is available at www.ishs.org/sci/icracpco.htm) will not be included in this discussion.

The *International Code of Botanical Nomenclature*

The *International Code of Botanical Nomenclature,* referred to as the *Vienna Code* due to the site of the Botanical Congress during which it was finalized, came into effect in 2006. It supersedes the Saint Louis Code published in 2000. The Vienna Code represents a 100-year history of international cooperation to develop a standard that governs the scientific naming in botany (including phycology and mycology), beginning with the first international code for botanists published in 1905, the *Regles Internationales de la Nomenclature botanique* or the *International Rules of Botanical Nomenclature* (referred to also as the *Vienna Rules*). The *International Code of Botanical Nomenclature* is published under the authority of the International Biological Congresses (ICBN) and has no legal status. It is dependent on the voluntary acceptance and use by the international community of botanists and others who use or establish plant names. The code itself is composed of Rules that are mandatory, Articles containing complementary information and advice on how to apply the code, Notes and Recommendations, nonmandatory provisions that are also recommended for use, and Examples of how the Rule is to be applied. A Glossary provides definitions and examples of proper use of terms within the code. Figure 4.2 shows an example of Article 1 and its associated Notes and Examples.

The Vienna Code is based on the underlying necessity for a precise and simple system of nomenclature that can be used by botanists worldwide. It contains provisions for denoting the ranks of taxonomic groups and for naming of botanical specimens. The Vienna Code "aims at the provision of a stable method of naming taxonomic groups, avoiding and rejecting the use of names that may cause error or ambiguity or throw science into confusion. Next in importance is the avoidance of the useless creation of names" (International Association for Plant Taxonomy, 2006a). The underlying principles outlined in the Vienna Code are the following (International Association for Plant Taxonomy, 2006b):

> Botanical nomenclature is independent of zoological and bacteriological nomenclature. . . .
>
> The application of names of taxonomic groups is determined by means of nomenclatural types.
>
> The nomenclature of a taxonomic group is based upon priority of publication.
>
> Each taxonomic group can bear only one correct name, the earliest that is in accord with the Rules, except in specified cases.
>
> Scientific names of taxonomic groups are treated as Latin regardless of their derivation.
>
> The Rules of nomenclature are retroactive unless expressly limited.

Figure 4.2. Article 1 of the Botanical Code

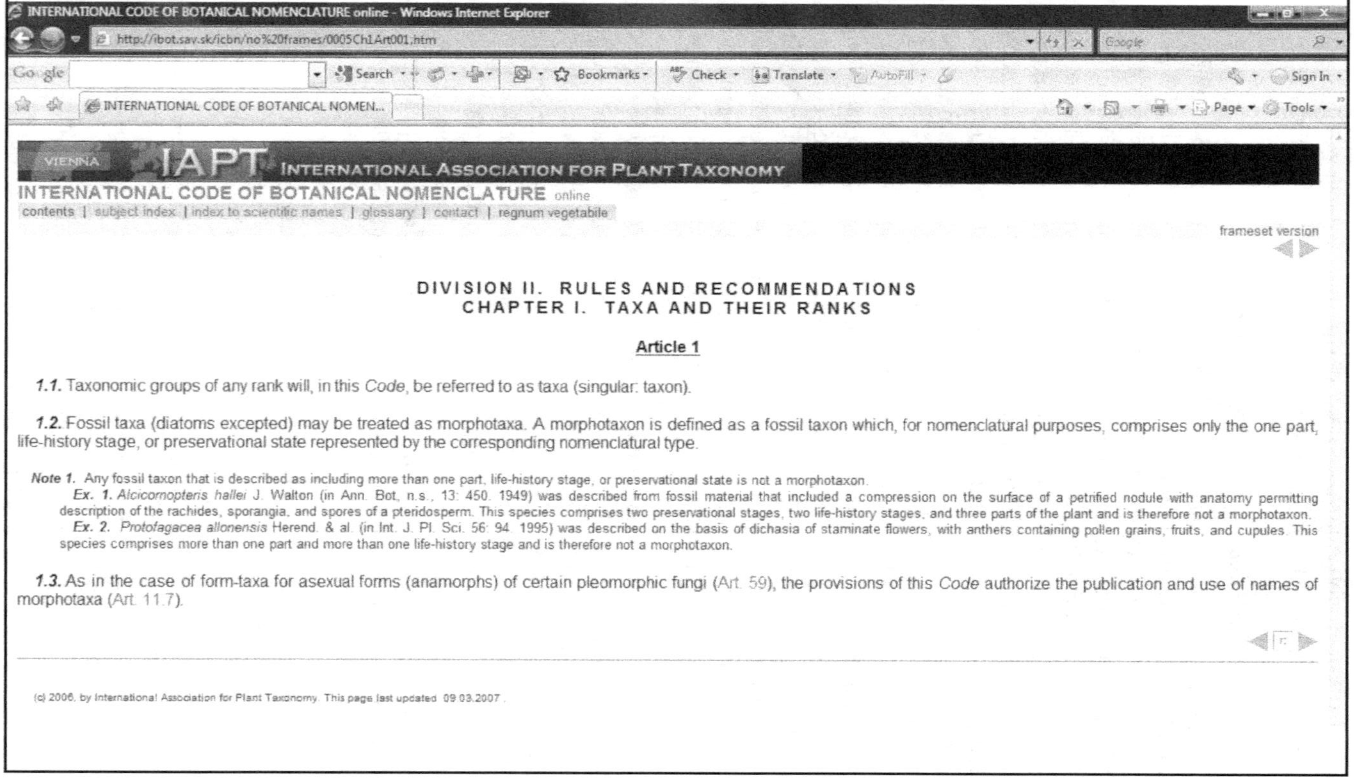
INTERNATIONAL CODE OF BOTANICAL NOMENCLATURE online - Windows Internet Explorer

http://ibot.sav.sk/icbn/no%20frames/0005Ch1Art001.htm

VIENNA IAPT INTERNATIONAL ASSOCIATION FOR PLANT TAXONOMY

INTERNATIONAL CODE OF BOTANICAL NOMENCLATURE online

contents | subject index | index to scientific names | glossary | contact | regnum vegetabile

frameset version

DIVISION II. RULES AND RECOMMENDATIONS
CHAPTER I. TAXA AND THEIR RANKS

Article 1

1.1. Taxonomic groups of any rank will, in this *Code*, be referred to as taxa (singular: taxon).

1.2. Fossil taxa (diatoms excepted) may be treated as morphotaxa. A morphotaxon is defined as a fossil taxon which, for nomenclatural purposes, comprises only the one part, life-history stage, or preservational state represented by the corresponding nomenclatural type.

Note 1. Any fossil taxon that is described as including more than one part, life-history stage, or preservational state is not a morphotaxon.

Ex. 1. *Alcicornopteris hallei* J. Walton (in Ann. Bot., n.s., 13: 450. 1949) was described from fossil material that included a compression on the surface of a petrified nodule with anatomy permitting description of the rachides, sporangia, and spores of a pteridosperm. This species comprises two preservational stages, two life-history stages, and three parts of the plant and is therefore not a morphotaxon.

Ex. 2. *Protofagacea allonensis* Herend. & al. (in Int. J. Pl. Sci. 56: 94. 1995) was described on the basis of dichasia of staminate flowers, with anthers containing pollen grains, fruits, and cupules. This species comprises more than one part and more than one life-history stage and is therefore not a morphotaxon.

1.3. As in the case of form-taxa for asexual forms (anamorphs) of certain pleomorphic fungi (Art. 59), the provisions of this *Code* authorize the publication and use of names of morphotaxa (Art. 11.7).

(c) 2006, by International Association for Plant Taxonomy. This page last updated 09.03.2007.

The full text of the Vienna Code is available online at ibot.sav.sk/icbn/no %20frames/Contents.htm.

The *International Code of Nomenclature of Bacteria*

The current edition of the *International Code of Nomenclature of Bacteria* (the Bacteria Code) was approved in 1990 by the International Committee on Systematics of Prokaryotes (ICSP) and published in 1992 by the American Society for Microbiology. The ICSP is responsible for the naming of prokaryotes, including both eubacteria and archaebacteria or archaea. The first Bacteria Code was developed in 1936 after the recognition by the international community of bacteriologists that the *Botanical Code of Nomenclature* would no longer work for the classification of bacteria. The Bacteria Code is comprised of Rules, which are mandatory, and Recommendations, which are guides for good practice. There are also sections with instructions on how to describe, name, and publish on a new bacterium and on how to request that the Judicial Commission review nomenclature issues encountered. The Bacteria Code also includes lists of names that are protected or conserved or those that must not be used. Figures 4.3 through 4.5 provide examples of Rules from the Bacteria Code.

According to Sneath (2003), the Bacteria Code is based on these underlying principles:

- **Stability**: Names should be stable. The first name published is retained, referred to as the *principle of priority*.
- **Unambiguity**: Names should be unambiguous. Unambiguity is ensured by establishing type cultures that function as indispensible points of reference.
- **Necessity**: Names should be necessary. Necessity is ensured by publication of descriptions of the bacterium and the rejection of names that are superfluous.

The nine principles published as part of the code agree with Sneath's summarization but also include provisions similar to those seen in the *Vienna Code*, including (International Union of Microbiological Societies, 1992):

1. Names are stable and necessary.
2. Nomenclature of bacteria is independent of botanical nomenclature.
3. Scientific names of all taxa are Latin or Latinized words treated as Latin regardless of their origin.
4. The primary purpose of a name is to serve as a point of reference, not to indicate history of the taxon.
5. Application of the names of taxa are determined by means of nomenclatural types, referred to as *types*.
6. The correct name of a taxon is based on valid publication, legitimacy, and priority of publication.

(continued p. 79)

Figure 4.3. Rules 5a and 5b from the Bacteria Code

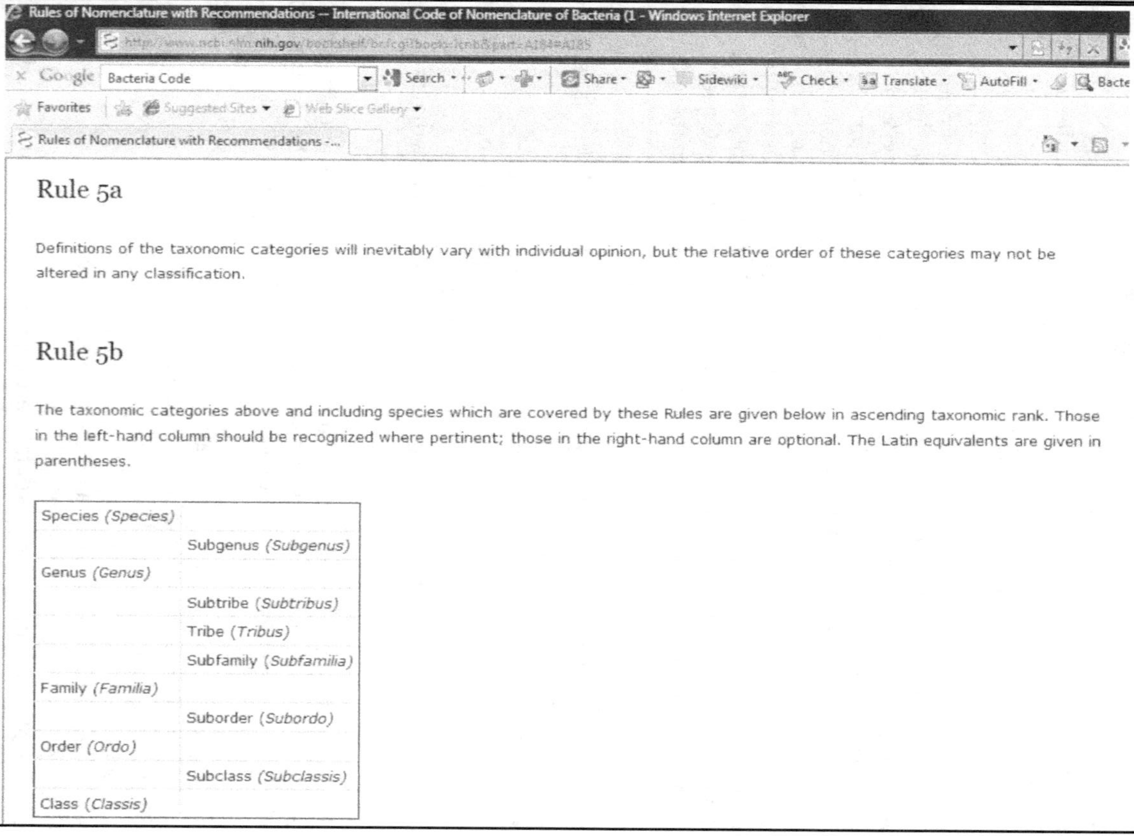

Rule 5a

Definitions of the taxonomic categories will inevitably vary with individual opinion, but the relative order of these categories may not be altered in any classification.

Rule 5b

The taxonomic categories above and including species which are covered by these Rules are given below in ascending taxonomic rank. Those in the left-hand column should be recognized where pertinent; those in the right-hand column are optional. The Latin equivalents are given in parentheses.

Species *(Species)*	
	Subgenus *(Subgenus)*
Genus *(Genus)*	
	Subtribe *(Subtribus)*
	Tribe *(Tribus)*
	Subfamily *(Subfamilia)*
Family *(Familia)*	
	Suborder *(Subordo)*
Order *(Ordo)*	
	Subclass *(Subclassis)*
Class *(Classis)*	

Figure 4.4. Rule 6 and Part of Rule 7 from the Bacteria Code

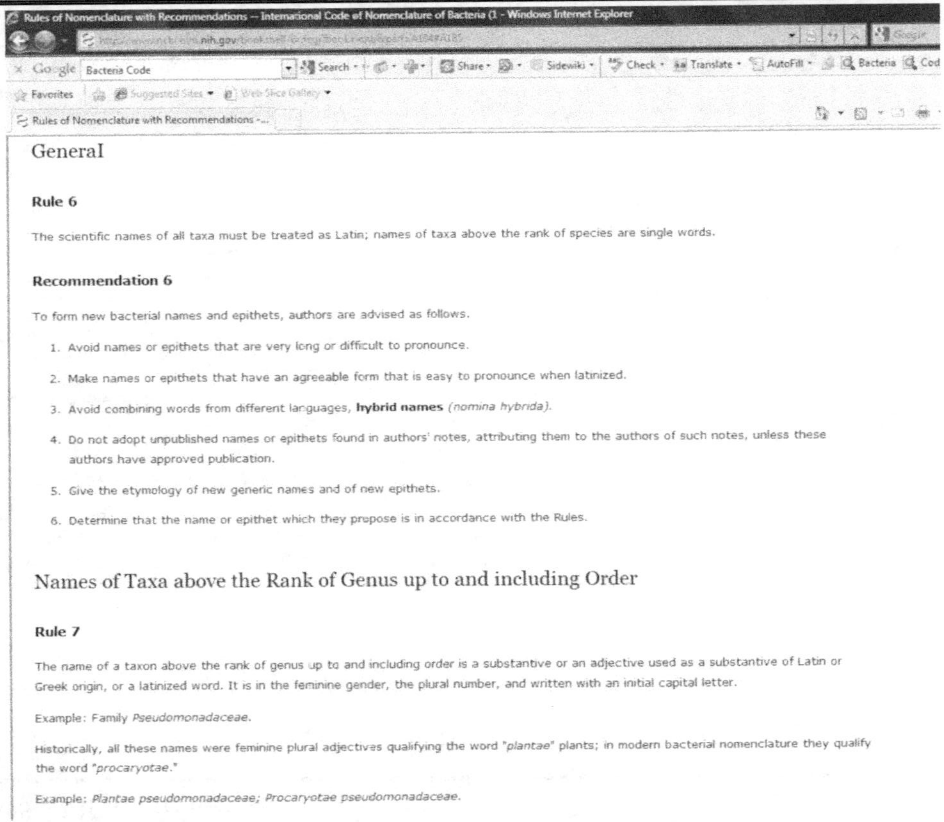

General

Rule 6

The scientific names of all taxa must be treated as Latin; names of taxa above the rank of species are single words.

Recommendation 6

To form new bacterial names and epithets, authors are advised as follows.

1. Avoid names or epithets that are very long or difficult to pronounce.
2. Make names or epithets that have an agreeable form that is easy to pronounce when latinized.
3. Avoid combining words from different languages, **hybrid names** *(nomina hybrida)*.
4. Do not adopt unpublished names or epithets found in authors' notes, attributing them to the authors of such notes, unless these authors have approved publication.
5. Give the etymology of new generic names and of new epithets.
6. Determine that the name or epithet which they propose is in accordance with the Rules.

Names of Taxa above the Rank of Genus up to and including Order

Rule 7

The name of a taxon above the rank of genus up to and including order is a substantive or an adjective used as a substantive of Latin or Greek origin, or a latinized word. It is in the feminine gender, the plural number, and written with an initial capital letter.

Example: Family *Pseudomonadaceae*.

Historically, all these names were feminine plural adjectives qualifying the word "*plantae*" plants; in modern bacterial nomenclature they qualify the word "*procaryotae*."

Example: *Plantae pseudomonadaceae; Procaryotae pseudomonadaceae.*

Figure 4.5. Rules 15 and 16 from the Bacteria Code

Rules of Nomenclature with Recommendations -...

General

Rule 15

A taxon consists of one or more elements. For each named taxon of the various taxonomic categories (listed below), there shall be designated a **nomenclatural type.** The nomenclatural type, referred to in this Code as **"type,"** is that element of the taxon with which the name is permanently associated. The nomenclatural type is not necessarily the most typical or representative element of the taxon. The types are dealt with in Rules 16–22.

Types of the various taxonomic categories can be summarized as follows:

Table 2

Taxonomic Categories

Taxonomic category	Type
Subspecies Species}	Designated strain; in special cases the place of the type strain may be taken by a description, preserved specimen, or an illustration
Subgenus Genus}	Designated species
Subtribe Tribe Subfamily Family Suborder Order}	Genus on whose name the name of the higher taxon is based
Subclass Class}	One of the contained orders

Rule 16

After the date of publication of this Code, the type of a taxon must be designated by the author at the time the name of the taxon is published in the IJSB (see Rule 27).

Note. Authors who intend to publish the name in the IJSB with reference to a previous effectively published description under Rule 27(2) are advised also to designate the type when publishing that description.

7. The name of a taxon has no status and no claim to recognition unless it is validly published.
8. Each taxon or order can bear only one name, the earliest.
9. The name of a taxon should not be changed without sufficient reason.

The full text of the Bacteria Code is available online at www.ncbi.nlm.nih.gov/bookshelf/br.fcgi?book=icnb.

The *International Code of Zoological Nomenclature*

The fourth edition of the *International Code of Zoological Nomenclature* (the Zoological Code) was published by the International Commission on Zoological Nomenclature in 1999 and provisions went into effect January 1, 2000, after undergoing eight long years of revision of the third edition. It has been adopted for use by the International Union of Biological Sciences (IUBS). The Zoological Code is the system of rules and recommendations for naming animals. According to the Preamble of the Zoological Code (International Commission on Zoological Nomenclature, 1999), the objectives of the code are to:

1. promote *stability* and *universality* in the scientific names of animals,
2. ensure that the name of each taxon is *unique* and *distinct*,
3. ensure that the *freedom of taxonomic thought* is not subservient or restricted by the provisions and recommendations of the code, and
4. recognize that *precision* and *consistency* in the use of terms are essential.

According to W.D.L. Ride (1999), the fundamental aim of the Zoological Code is to "provide the maximum universality and continuity in the scientific names of animals compatible with the freedom of scientists to classify animals according to taxonomic judgments."

The Zoological Code is composed of Articles that are mandatory and Recommendations, which include instructions for application. The Articles are "designed to enable zoologists to arrive at names for taxa that are correct under particular taxonomic circumstances" (Ride, 1999). Figures 4.6 through 4.8 provide the Table of Contents of the Zoological Code, so that the reader can see the range of topics covered, and examples of Articles from the Zoological Code relating to the source of the code and naming principles.

The underlying principles of the Zoological Code include:

1. Do not infringe on the taxonomic judgment of the taxonomists/biologists.
2. "Nomenclature does not determine the inclusiveness or exclusiveness of any taxon, nor the rank to be accorded to any assemblage of animals, but rather provides the name that is to be used for a taxon," within specific limits.
3. "The device of name-bearing types allows names to be applied to taxa without infringing upon taxonomic judgment." Names are permanently attached to a name-bearing type.

(continued p. 83)

Figure 4.6. Table of Contents of the Zoological Code

ICZN Code - contents

ICZN International Commission on Zoological Nomenclature
INTERNATIONAL CODE OF ZOOLOGICAL NOMENCLATURE *online*

iczn home | contents | search | glossary | help

Contents

Figure 4.7. Article 3 from the Zoological Code

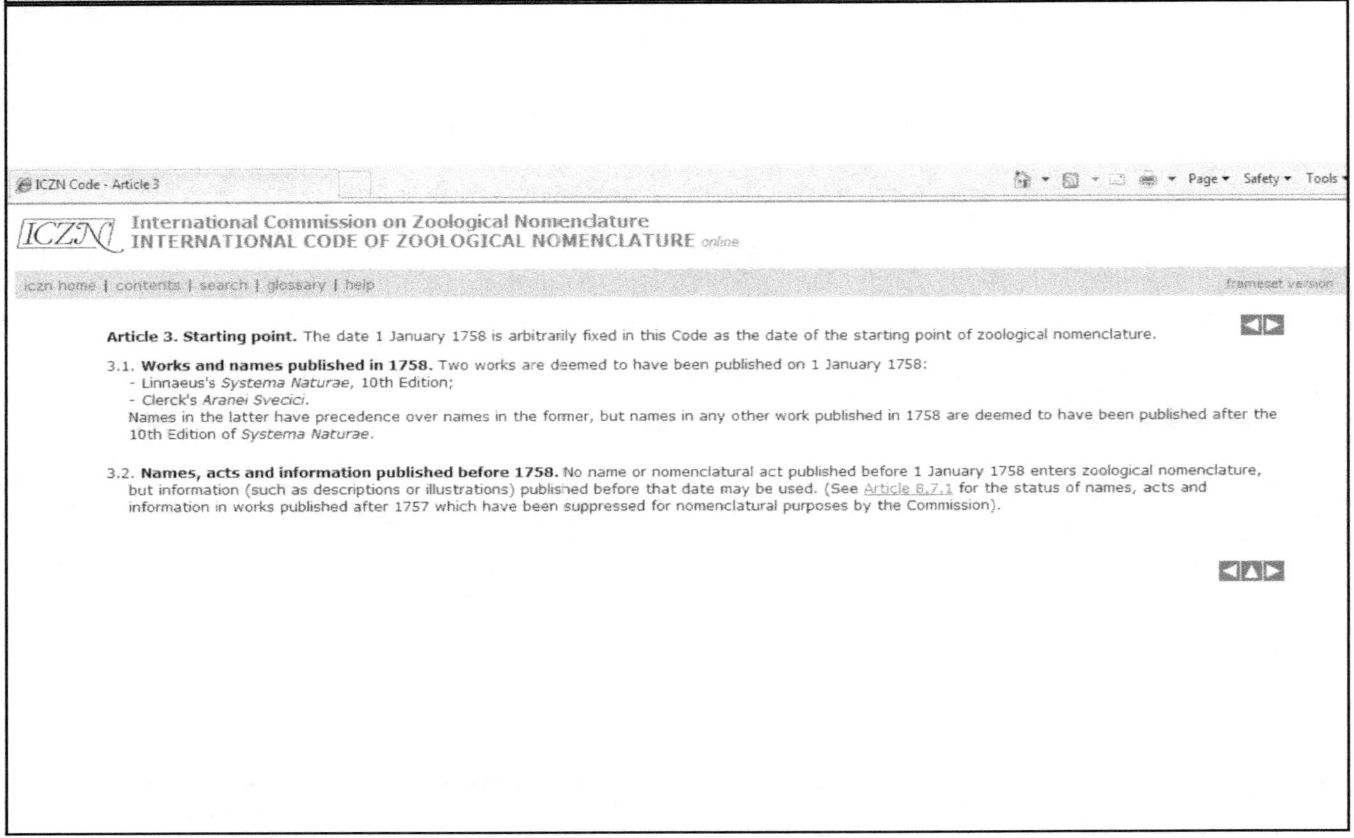

ICZN Code - Article 3

Page ▾ Safety ▾ Tools ▾

ICZN International Commission on Zoological Nomenclature
INTERNATIONAL CODE OF ZOOLOGICAL NOMENCLATURE *online*

iczn home | contents | search | glossary | help

frameset version

Article 3. Starting point. The date 1 January 1758 is arbitrarily fixed in this Code as the date of the starting point of zoological nomenclature.

3.1. **Works and names published in 1758.** Two works are deemed to have been published on 1 January 1758:
- Linnaeus's *Systema Naturae*, 10th Edition;
- Clerck's *Aranei Svecici*.

Names in the latter have precedence over names in the former, but names in any other work published in 1758 are deemed to have been published after the 10th Edition of *Systema Naturae*.

3.2. **Names, acts and information published before 1758.** No name or nomenclatural act published before 1 January 1758 enters zoological nomenclature, but information (such as descriptions or illustrations) published before that date may be used. (See Article 8.7.1 for the status of names, acts and information in works published after 1757 which have been suppressed for nomenclatural purposes by the Commission).

Figure 4.8. Article 5 from the Zoological Code

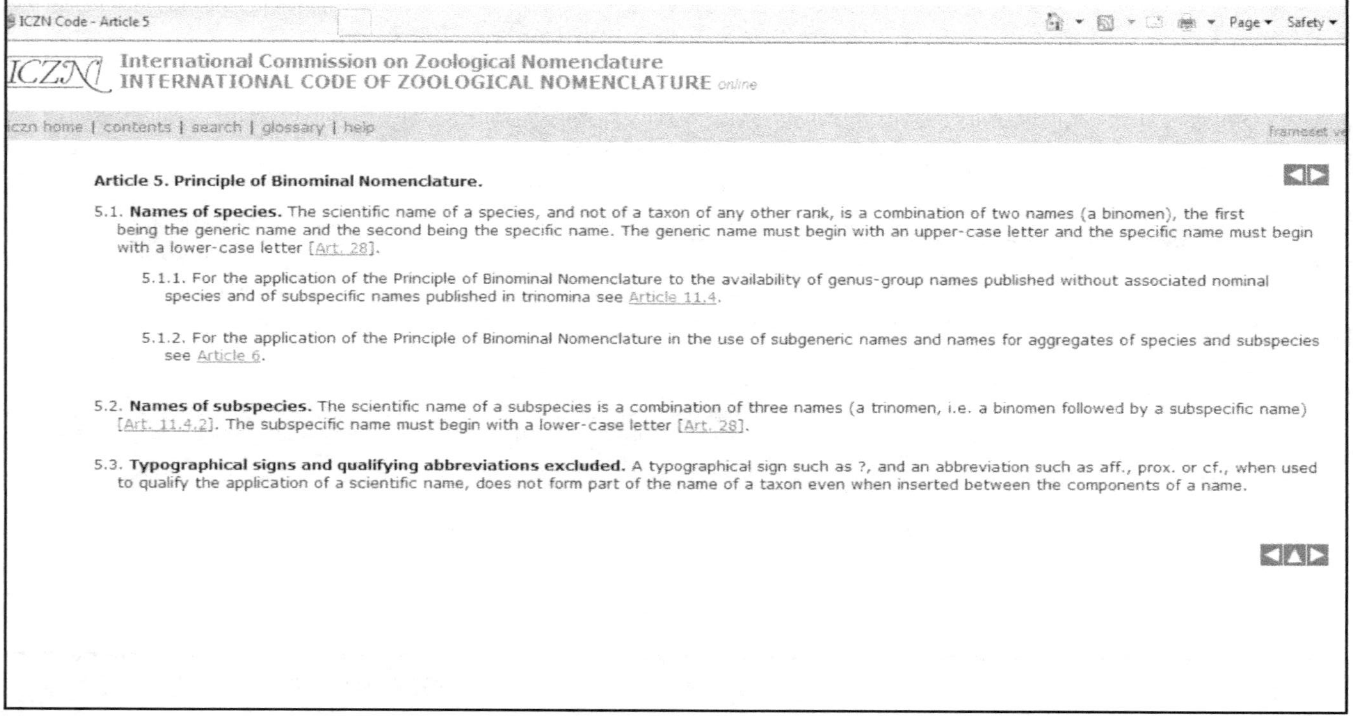

ICZN Code - Article 5

ICZN International Commission on Zoological Nomenclature
INTERNATIONAL CODE OF ZOOLOGICAL NOMENCLATURE online

iczn home | contents | search | glossary | help

Article 5. Principle of Binominal Nomenclature.

5.1. **Names of species.** The scientific name of a species, and not of a taxon of any other rank, is a combination of two names (a binomen), the first being the generic name and the second being the specific name. The generic name must begin with an upper-case letter and the specific name must begin with a lower-case letter [Art. 28].

5.1.1. For the application of the Principle of Binominal Nomenclature to the availability of genus-group names published without associated nominal species and of subspecific names published in trinomina see Article 11.4.

5.1.2. For the application of the Principle of Binominal Nomenclature in the use of subgeneric names and names for aggregates of species and subspecies see Article 6.

5.2. **Names of subspecies.** The scientific name of a subspecies is a combination of three names (a trinomen, i.e. a binomen followed by a subspecific name) [Art. 11.4.2]. The subspecific name must begin with a lower-case letter [Art. 28].

5.3. **Typographical signs and qualifying abbreviations excluded.** A typographical sign such as ?, and an abbreviation such as aff., prox. or cf., when used to qualify the application of a scientific name, does not form part of the name of a taxon even when inserted between the components of a name.

4. "Nomenclatural rules are tools that are designed to provide the maximum stability compatible with taxonomic freedom. . . . [t]he rules must recognize and allow for the Principle of Priority to be set aside on occasions when its application would be destructive of stability or universality, or would cause confusion."
5. "To avoid ambiguity, use of the same name for different taxa must not occur and is prohibited. This is the Principle of Homonymy."
6. Guidance to establish new names is provided, as well as the rules help to determine whether any name is available and with what priority and whether a name requires amendment.
7. Administration of the Code is provided for by the International Commission on Zoological Nomenclature.
8. Decisions on nomenclature issues are decided upon by the Commission and never by reference to precedent. (Ride, 1999)

As per the Zoological Code, Article 82, applications related to naming issues are first published in the *Bulletin of Zoological Nomenclature* and existing usage is to be maintained until the ruling of the Commission is published. Amendments to the 2000 Code have been proposed, but based on the information published about amendments on the ICZM website, change is very slow. For example, in 2002 a declaration to delete Article 74.7.3 was proposed. The declaration was approved and ratified five years later on May 13, 2007, by the International Union of Biological Sciences and the international community of biological scientists. For more information on the Zoological Code and the ICZM, refer to the Commission's website (www.iczn.org).

Additional knowledge structures ratified by the codes described in this section are *lists* of established names of plants, animals, and other organisms. These lists are essential to the effective naming of new species and for cases when names of species require changes. For example, "The Approved Lists of Bacterial Names" consist of two lists published in January 1980 in the *International Journal of Systematic Biology* (30: 225–420), including:

"Approved List 1. Names of taxa above the rank of genus," pp. 231–238, and
"Approved List 2. Names of genera, species, and subspecies," pp. 239–420.

Available as Appendix 4 to the Bacteria Code are five separate lists of conserved or rejected names for bacteria. These five lists are available online at www.ncbi.nlm.nih.gov/bookshelf/br.fcgi?book=icnb&part=A740. *The Official Lists and Indexes of Names in Zoology*, as updated July 2009, can be accessed at www.iczn.org/lists&indexes.pdf.

Role of Knowledge Structures in the Discipline

Ernst Mayr and Peter D. Ashlock (1991: 5) describe systematics and the role of taxonomy (the process, not the knowledge structure) in biology as

> not only the service functions of identifying and classifying but also the comparative study of all aspects of organisms as well as an interpretation of the role of lower and higher taxa in the economy of nature and in evolutionary history. It is a synthesis of many kinds of knowledge, theory, and method applied to all aspects of classification. The ultimate task of the systematist is not only to describe the diversity of the living world but to contribute to its understanding.

From this quote we can extract these roles of taxonomy:

1. To provide the *service functions* of identification and classification
2. To provide a framework for *comparative study* of organisms
3. To provide a framework for *interpretation* of the roles of higher and lower organisms within the structure of nature and evolutionary history
4. To *synthesize* biological knowledge
5. To *build new knowledge* based on existing knowledge of the organism

Mayr and Ashlock (1991: 6) summarize the roles of taxonomy (the process and the knowledge structure) to the discipline as:

> 1. "provides a vivid picture of the existing organic diversity of the Earth"
> 2. "provides most of the information needed for a reconstruction of the phylogeny of life"
> 3. "reveals numerous interesting evolutionary phenomena and thus makes them available for causal study by other branches of biology"
> 4. "supplies, almost exclusively, the information needed for entire branches of biology"
> 5. "supplies classifications which are of greatest heuristic and explanatory value in most branches of biology (e.g. evolutionary biochemistry, ecology, genetics, immunology)"
> 6. "makes important conceptual contributions . . . to experimental biologists. Thus it contributes significantly to a broadening of biology and to a better balance within biological science as a whole."

Taxonomy and, more specifically, the Linnaean Hierarchy provide the vital roles of not just service functions but also as comparative and interpretive tools for all branches of biology. Without the correct classification and naming of the organism, work within the biological sciences is severely hampered.

Digital Applications and Digital Knowledge Structures

Taxonomists and biologists have long struggled with access issues related to the resources needed to perform identification and classification. Resources are scattered, available only through print or subscription databases, or are accessible only by visiting the specific collection or obtaining loans from it. Beginning in 2000, the community of biologists began to envision digital solutions to the dispersed nature of biological specimens and resources through the use of the Internet. E.O. Wilson (2003) envisioned an electronic encyclopedia of all life. His essay was the impetus for digital projects like the Encyclopedia of Life (available at eol.org). This section will outline some of the significant digital projects and digital knowledge structures and provide examples of their goals, the roles they play in biology, and developments in standardizing knowledge structures that serve as their infrastructure.

According to the TDWG (the Biodiversity Information Standards, formerly the Taxonomic Database Working Group) website (available at www.tdwg.org), it has currently identified 658 digital biodiversity projects available online and 56 digital biodiversity networks. (To search their database of projects, go to www.tdwg.org/biodiv-projects/projects-database or to www.tdwg.org/biodiv-networks/networks-database to browse the biodiversity networks. Both databases illustrate the range of different biodiversity projects either developed or in development.) While there are significant efforts underway to construct the digital taxonomy network, it is estimated that only 10 percent of all biological resources are available online (LINNE, 2009). Digital initiatives include a vast array of resources:

1. the development of online collections, digital libraries, and repositories of biological resources, such as collections of current and historical images or organisms or historical and current biological literature (e.g., botanicus.org);
2. the development of the infrastructure for the digital projects, including technical and application standards and best practices, to ensure universal use by the biological community and interoperability between systems (e.g., TDWG or the GBIF—Global Biodiversity Information Facility); and
3. large-scale efforts that incorporate standards and/or develop new standards as needed to provide access to the entire world of biological knowledge (e.g., Encyclopedia of Life).

The listings from the TDWG databases illustrate the richness of the resources available within the community, but they also make very evident the need for some synthesis or collaboration among the different projects (if possible) to combine their efforts in order to provide the biological community with a concise set of resources with which to conduct their work. The next three sections take a brief look at each of the three forms of initiatives and provide examples of each. The reader is also directed to the TDWG Biodiversity Information Projects of the World database (www.tdwg.org/biodiv-projects/projects-database) to review other digital initiatives.

Development of Online Collections

There are numerous online collections devoted to biological resources being constructed. For example, **Botanicus** is a freely accessible portal to historic botanical literature from the Missouri Botanical Garden Library, funded by support from the Institute of Museum and Library Services, the W.M. Keck

Foundation, and the Andrew W. Mellon Foundation. Botanicus was created to improve access to scientific literature, a problem that plagues the biological community. The project began digitizing materials in 1995 and focuses primarily on beautifully illustrated volumes from their rare book collection. The project undertakes four aims:

1. Develop a model for digitized scientific literature: a universal data structure and metadata schema that will define how scientific disciplines, museums, or individual scientists use and configure available digitized literature on their subjects to initiate or support a research project;
2. Program and test an extensible reference system based on the scientific literature model and universally applicable to all areas of natural history;
3. Capture a robust, targeted subset of systematic botanical literature as images and associated defining metadata for those references, and employ automated OCR and XML markup protocols to convert the image to text and embed links to external data sets;
4. Provide a Web Portal to the scientific literature system that will facilitate research and intensify the vital work on science-based conservation of the world's biological diversity through an interactive, intelligent interface to systematic botanical literature. (Botanicus, 2009)

Figures 4.9 and 4.10 show the subject search interface on the Botanicus site and a sample page retrieved using the search terms "Systema Vegetabilium."

Development of Infrastructure and Standards

The **TDWG** is a not-for-profit scientific and educational association that is affiliated with the International Union of Biological Sciences. TDWG was formed to establish international collaboration among biological database projects. TDWG promotes the wider and more effective dissemination of information about the world's heritage of biological organisms for the benefit of the world at large. Biodiversity Information Standards (TDWG) focuses on the development of standards for the exchange of biological/biodiversity data. The mission of the TDWG is threefold:

- Develop, adopt and promote standards and guidelines for the recording and exchange of data about organisms
- Promote the use of standards through the most appropriate and effective means and
- Act as a forum for discussion through holding meetings and through publications. (TDWG, 2009b)

TDWG has been very active in establishing infrastructure (technical specifications) and application standards, as well as best practices to follow when applying standards. Currently TDWG has several standards approved and being

Figure 4.9. Subject Cloud Interface on the Botanicus Digital Library Homepage

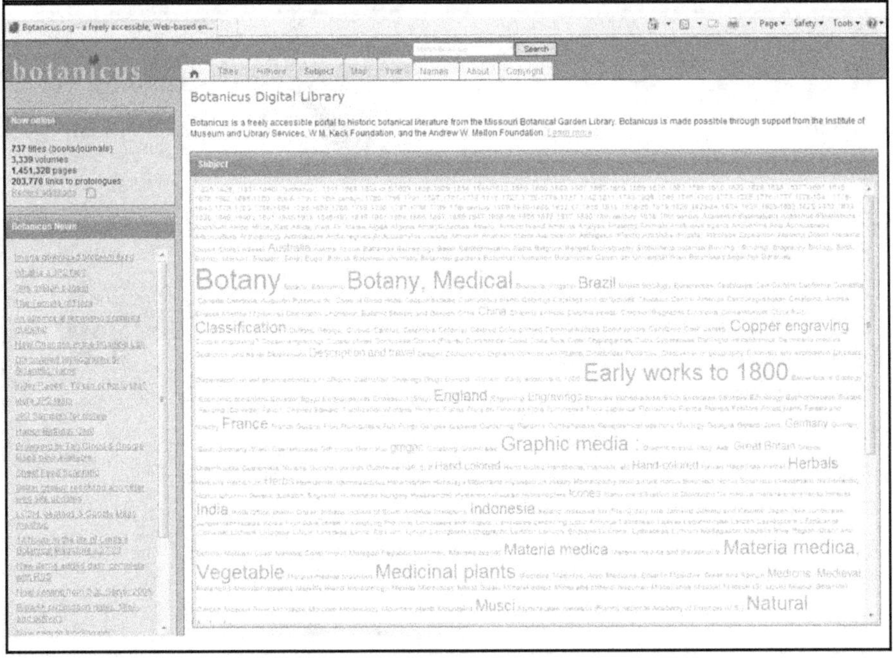

used in biodiversity projects and five standards in draft form. For example, the Darwin Core standard is a technical specification standard designed to

> facilitate the discovery, retrieval, and integration of information about organisms, their spatiotemporal occurrence, and the supporting evidence housed in collections (physical or digital). The primary goal of the Darwin Core is to provide a stable reference to standard terms about biodiversity, which can be used in a variety of contexts. The Darwin Core derives its vocabulary from community-based experience in data discovery, sharing, and integration, while its form is derived from the practices developed by the Dublin Core Metadata Initiative except where otherwise noted. (TDWG, 2009a)

The Darwin Core technical standard consists of (1) a vocabulary of terms (properties, elements, fields, concepts), (2) the policy governing the maintenance of these terms, (3) decisions resulting in changes to the terms, (4) the history of the terms including detailed attributes, (5) a generic application schema for use in the construction of new application schemas based on Darwin Core, and (6) a metafile schema to allow for the description of Darwin Core fielded text files. Figure 4.11 provides the XML structure of elements included in the Darwin Core.

Figure 4.10. Sample Page from Botanicus Showing Results of Search for "Systema Vegetabilium"

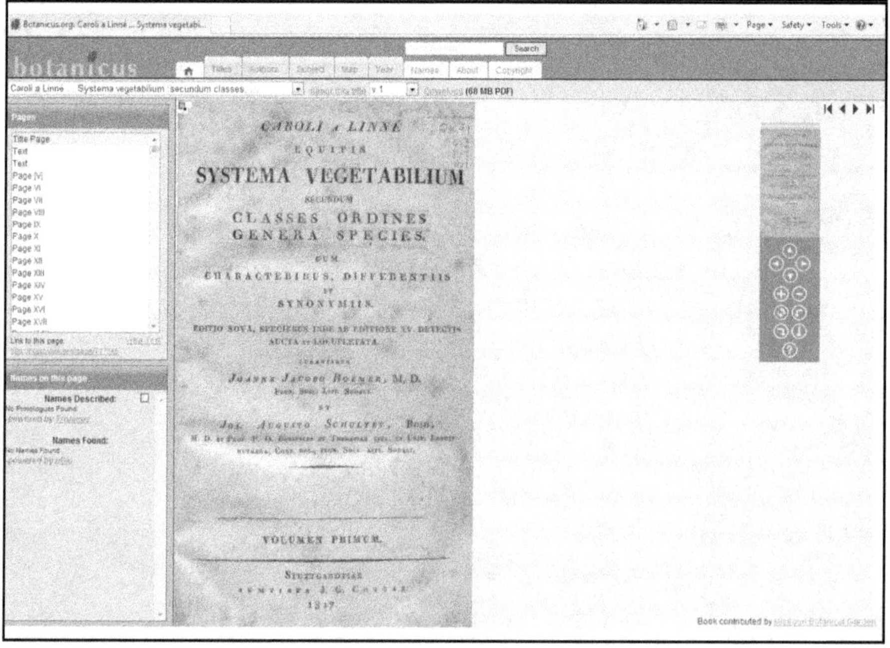

The Natural Collections Descriptions (NCD) is a data standard for exchanging data describing natural history collections at the collection level. The NCD standard covers all types of natural history collections, such as specimens, original artwork, archives, observations, library materials, data sets, and photographs or mixed collections such as those that result from expeditions and voyages of discovery. NCD lies between general resource discovery standards for analog and print resources such as Dublin Core (DC) and rich collection description standards such as the *Encoded Archival Description* (EAD) used by archives and museums (NCD, 2009).

The **uBio Project** is an initiative within the science librarians' community to join international efforts to create and utilize a comprehensive and collaborative catalog of known names of all living (and once-living) organisms. The Taxonomic Name Server (TNS) catalogs names and classifications to provide tools to help users find information on living things using any of the names that may be related to an organism. Two of the uBio projects include:

- **NameBank**—a repository of millions of recorded biological names and facts that link those names together. NameBank promotes the emergence of a layered biological informatics infrastructure that allows different expert sys-

Figure 4.11. Excerpt from Darwin Core XML Schema

Darwin Core XML Schema http://www.tdwg.org/standards/450/

- __MACOSX
  - DwC25May09
    - .DS_Store
    - ._DS_Store
    - archive
    - DarwinCore_files
      - blank.gif
      - default.css
      - default.js
      - general.js
      - javascript_757c080409.js
      - main.css
      - moore_logo.jpg
      - print.css
      - RTEmagicC_rss-feed-icon_02.gif.gif
      - stylesheet_564c72b602.css
      - TDWGlogo_Twiki.gif
      - valid-xhtml10.gif
      - vcss.gif
    - examples
      - rdfa_content
        - rdfa2rdf.py
        - sciname_1.html
        - sciname_2.html
        - sciname_location.html
    - text
      - example_star_archive.xml
      - example_text.xml
      - example_text2.xml
      - example_text_relationship.xml
      - example_text_simpledwc_complete.xml
      - simplemetafile.xml
      - images
        - dwc-a_logo.png
        - extension.png
        - related.png
        - single.png
        - star.png
        - unrelated.png
        - usage.png
      - diagrams.graffle

tems to share common information. This conserves scarce resources and enhances the means to support continued expert work (NameBank, 2009).

- **ClassificationBank**—a collection of multiple classifications and taxonomic concepts that are the result of expert opinions. It extends the functionality of NameBank (ClassificationBank, 2009).

Figures 4.12 and 4.13 show the homepages of the NameBank and ClassificationBank websites.

Another significant initiative to enable better, more accurate access to biological resources includes the **Life Science Identifiers** (**LSIDs**) project. LSIDs are "persistent, location-independent, resource identifiers for uniquely naming biologically significant resources including species names, concepts, occurrences, genes or proteins, or data objects that encode information about

Figure 4.12. uBio NameBank Homepage

Universal Biological Indexer and Organizer

Find name...

Introduction - NameBank separates facts from opinions

NameBank contains nomenclatural metadata that is not in dispute

NameBank is composed of factually-related data elements. These elements, once correctly recorded, are persistent and applicable to any subjective treatement.

Experts may disagree over how an organism should be classified and what specimens might actually refer to a taxon. This is a healthy aspect of systematics. Effectively modelling this within an information system is a matter of continued contention but this belies the fact that many data elements within taxonomy are not in contention. Nomenclatural (homotypic) relationships, recorded instances of names within publications, and recorded uses of vernacular names with scientific names are based on objective criteria. One may dispute their valid usage but not their objective basis.

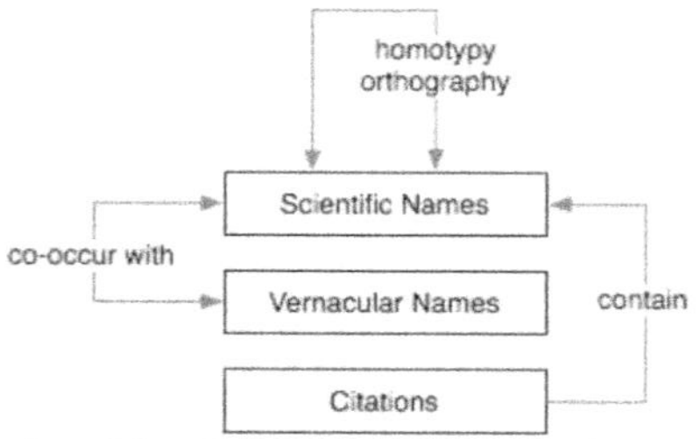

This separation of objective reference nomenclature from any particular subjective treatment allows any accrued factual knowledge within NameBank to be made available to any subsequent subjective use of the name. This also provides a foundation for collaboration with other names-gathering initiatives.

	Examples	Basis
Authority and Publication	*viridescens is* described by Rafinesque and placed in the genus, *Triturus* in Ann. Nat. Lexington, 1(22) resulting in the new name *Triturus viridescens*	Objective
Homotypic variation	*Notophthalmus viridescens* is a new combination of the same *viridescens*	Objective
Cited use	"*Notophthalmus viridescens*" appears in Smith, 1953, Herpetologica, 9:95-99	Objective
Use of vernacular forms	"Common Newt" co-occurs with *Notophthalmus viridescens* in Stejneger and Barbour, 1907 Checklist of N. Amer. Amphibians	Objective
Homotypic variation	*Notophthalmus viridescens viridescens* appears in Handbook of Salamanders (Bishop 1943) and is based on the same *viridescens*	Objective
Misspellings	*Notophthalma viridescens* is a misspelling of *Notophthalmus viridescens* appearing in Proc. Zool. Soc. London	Objective
Non-objective	*Salamandra dorsalis,* Harlan, 1829, is determined to be synonymous with *viridescens* by Baird, 1850.	Subjective

Mission statement | Advisory board | People | Contact us
uBio copyright © 2009 by The Marine Biological Laboratory

Figure 4.13. uBio ClassificationBank Homepage

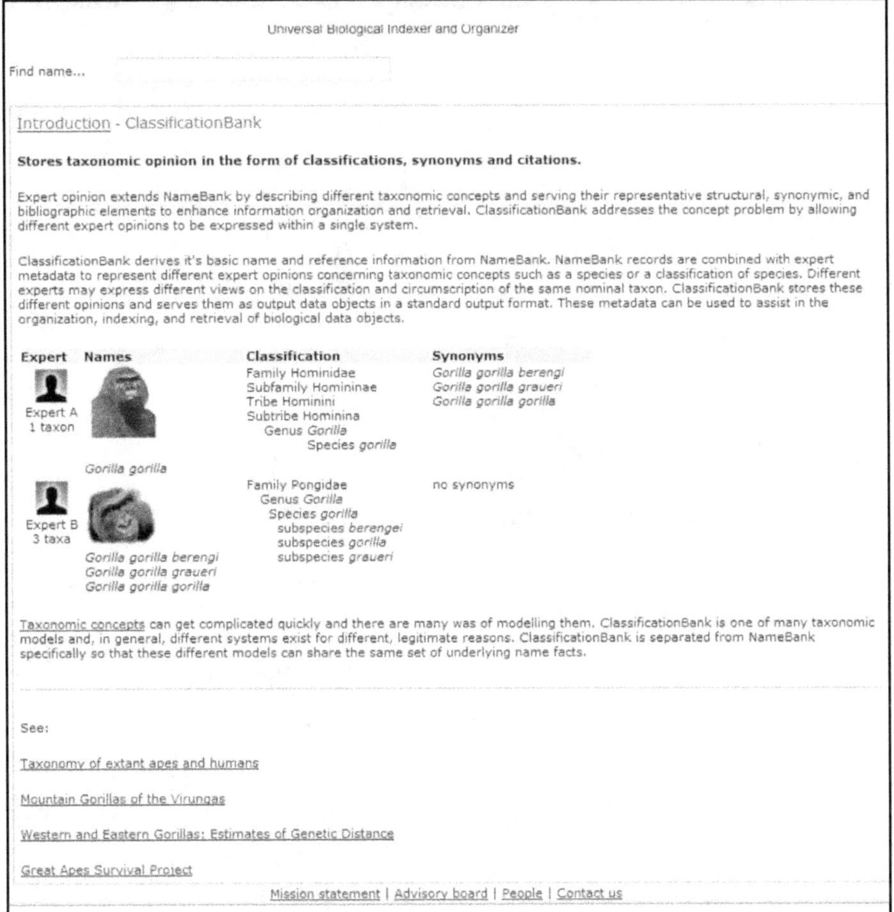

them. To put it simply, LSIDs are a way to identify and locate pieces of biological information on the web" (LSID, 2009).

The LSID concept introduces a straightforward approach to naming and identifying data resources stored in multiple, distributed data stores. By defining a simple, common way to identify and access biologically significant data, LSID provides a naming standard that enables global access and interoperability among digital biological systems. See Figure 4.14 for the LSID schema. See also the LSID website (lsids.sourceforge.net) for more information on this initiative. LSIDs are used in the GBIF Data Portal and Encyclopedia of Life projects described in the next section.

Figure 4.14. LSID Homepage

Welcome to the Life Sciences Identifiers (LSID)

Life Science Identifiers (LSIDs) are persistent, location-independent, resource identifiers for uniquely naming biologically significant resources including species names, concepts, occurrences, genes or proteins, or data objects that encode information about them. To put it simply, LSIDs are a way to identify and locate pieces of biological information on the web.

The LSID concept introduces a straightforward approach to naming and identifying data resources stored in multiple, distributed data stores in a manner that overcomes the limitations of naming schemes in use today. Almost every public, internal, or department-level data store today has its own way of naming individual data resources, making integration between different data sources a tedious, never-ending chore for informatics developers and researchers.

By defining a simple, common way to identify and access biologically significant data, whether that data is stored in files, relational databases, in applications, or in internal or public data sources, LSID provides a naming standard underpinning for wide-area science and interoperability.

The Life Sciences Identifier is an Object Management Group (OMG) Final Adopted Specification developed by the Life Sciences Research (LSR).

What does an LSID look like?

LSIDs are Universal Resource Names (URN) that conform to the following syntax:

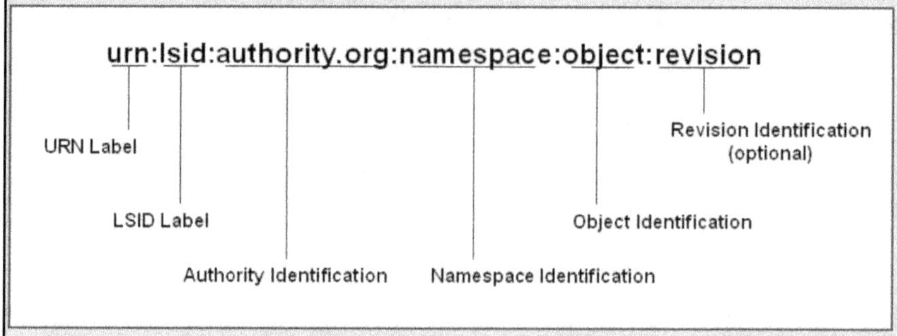

Every LSID consists of up to five parts, each separated by a colon:

1. the **Network Identifier** (NID), i.e., the "**urn:lsid:**" label;
2. the **Authority Identification**, usually the root DNS name of the issuing authority;
3. the **Namespace Identification** chosen by the issuing authority;
4. the **Object Identification** unique in that namespace; and
5. an optional **Revision Id** to represent versioning information.

Large-Scale Efforts

There are many large-scale efforts to develop collaborative, comprehensive resources for use by the biological community. A sample of large-scale projects is provided in this section but the reader is again referred to the TDWG Biodiversity Information Projects of the World database (www.tdwg.org/biodiv-projects/projects-database) to review other digital initiatives.

GBIF (the Global Biodiversity Information Facility; www.gbif.org) is an international government-initiated and -funded project focused on making biodiversity data available to anyone for scientific research, conservation and sustainable development. GBIF provides three core services and products:

1. **An information infrastructure**—an Internet-based index of a globally distributed network of interoperable databases that contain primary biodiversity data—information on museum specimens, field observations of plants and animals in nature, and results from experiments—so that data holders across the world can access and share them
2. **Community-developed tools, standards and protocols**—the tools data providers need to format and share their data
3. **Capacity-building**—the training, access to international experts and mentoring programs that national and regional institutions need to become part of a decentralised network of biodiversity information facilities. (GBIF, 2009a)

The GBIF mission is to collaboratively share in the development of standards, tools, and collections through its network of contributors. The GBIF network has also compiled an online collection of taxonomic and geospatial biodiversity resources. The GBIF Data Portal provides access to millions of data records provided by the GBIF's 316 data providers. When last accessed (July 1, 2010), there were a total of 10,957 data sets available through the data portal (GBIF, 2009b). Figures 4.15 and 4.16 show the search results and overview screens of a search for *Palliolisentis quinqueungulis* in the GBIF Data Portal.

The overview screen also provides a link to the ITIS Report (as shown in Figure 4.17) about the species with additional classification and origination information. The GBIF Data Portal uses the ITIS (Integrated Taxonomic Information System) as a taxonomic backbone or infrastructure for organizing the information present in the data sets. To learn more about ITIS, visit its website at www.itis.gov.

The **Encyclopedia of Life** (EOL; eol.org) is an online reference and database covering all 1.8 million species currently known to science. The mission of the EOL is to "help all of us better understand life on our planet" (EOL, 2009a). E.O. Wilson of Harvard University articulated the idea for an encyclopedia of all life and has been one of the leading supporters of the EOL. The project is funded by the John D. and Catherine T. MacArthur Foundation and the Alfred P. Sloan Foundation. What is interesting about the EOL is that it is a collaborative effort between scientists and the general public.

> The Encyclopedia of Life is an unprecedented global partnership between the scientific community and the general public. Our goal is to make freely available to anyone knowledge about all the world's organisms. Anybody can register as an EOL member and add text, images, videos, comments or tags to EOL pages. Expert curators ensure quality of the core collection by authenticating materials submitted by diverse projects and individual contributors. Together we can make EOL the best, most comprehensive source for biodiversity information. (EOL, 2009b)

The website and project also makes use of Web 2.0 technologies, such as allowing users to provide tags to pages, to add comments or submit pictures of

(continued p. 97)

Figure 4.15. GBIF Data Portal Search for *Palliolisentis quinqueungulis*

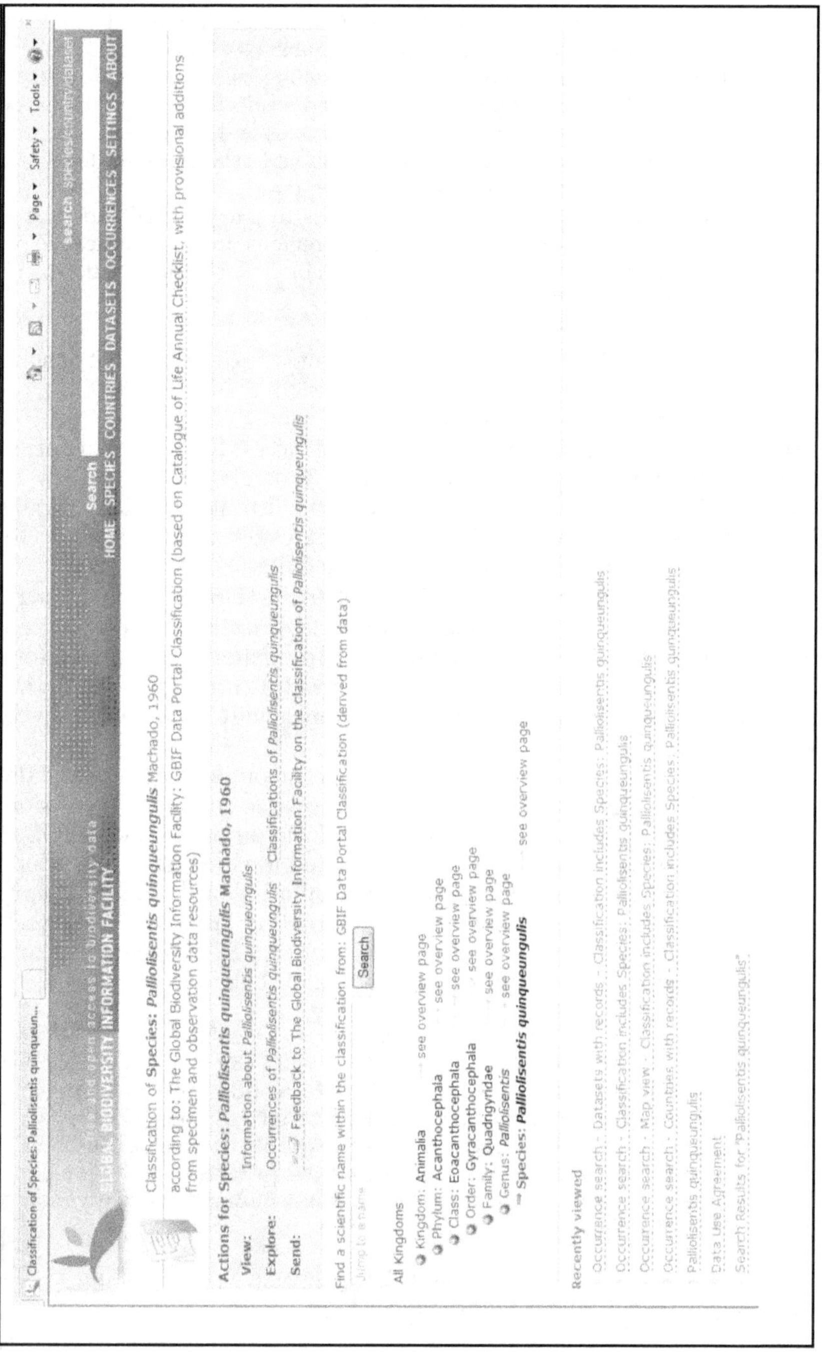

Figure 4.16. Overview Screen for *Palliolisentis quinqueungulis* in the GBIF Data Portal

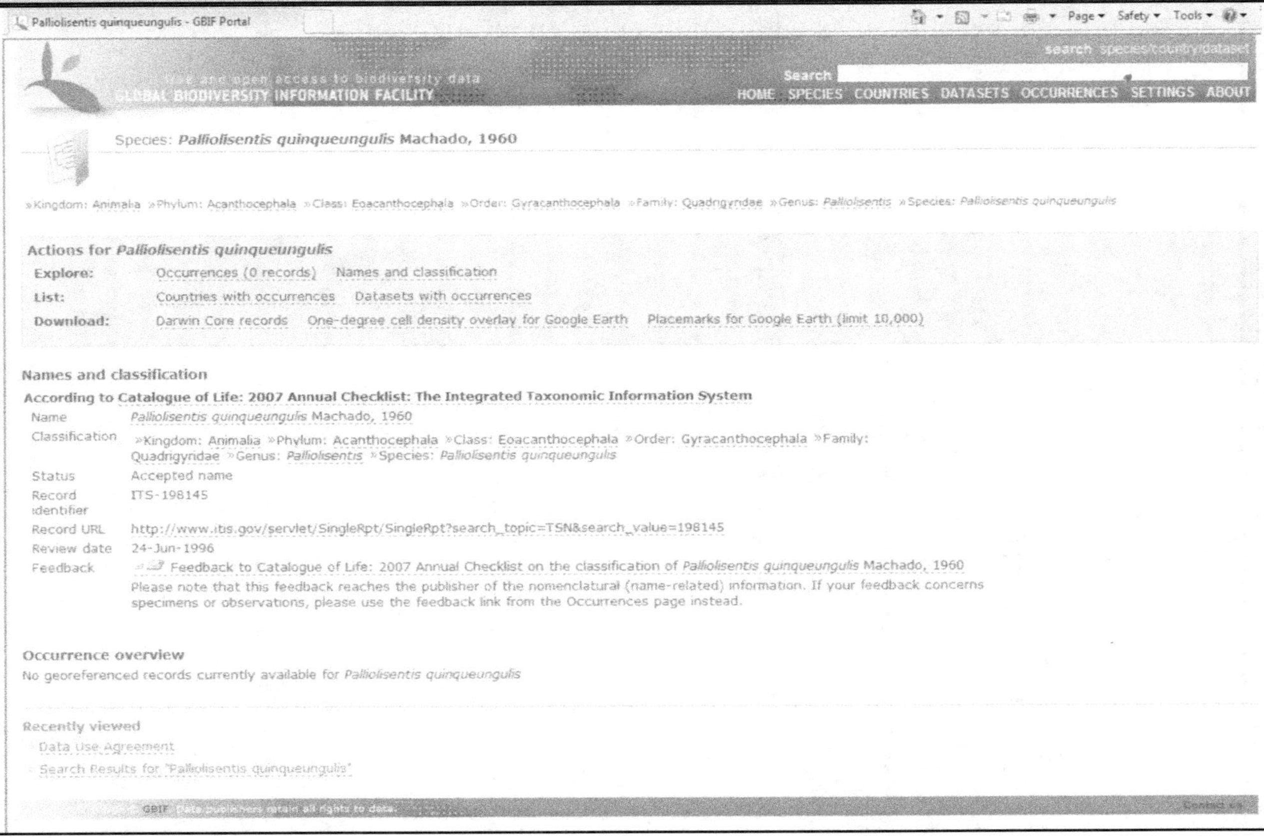

Figure 4.17. ITIS Report on *Palliolisentis quinqueungulis* Machado, 1960

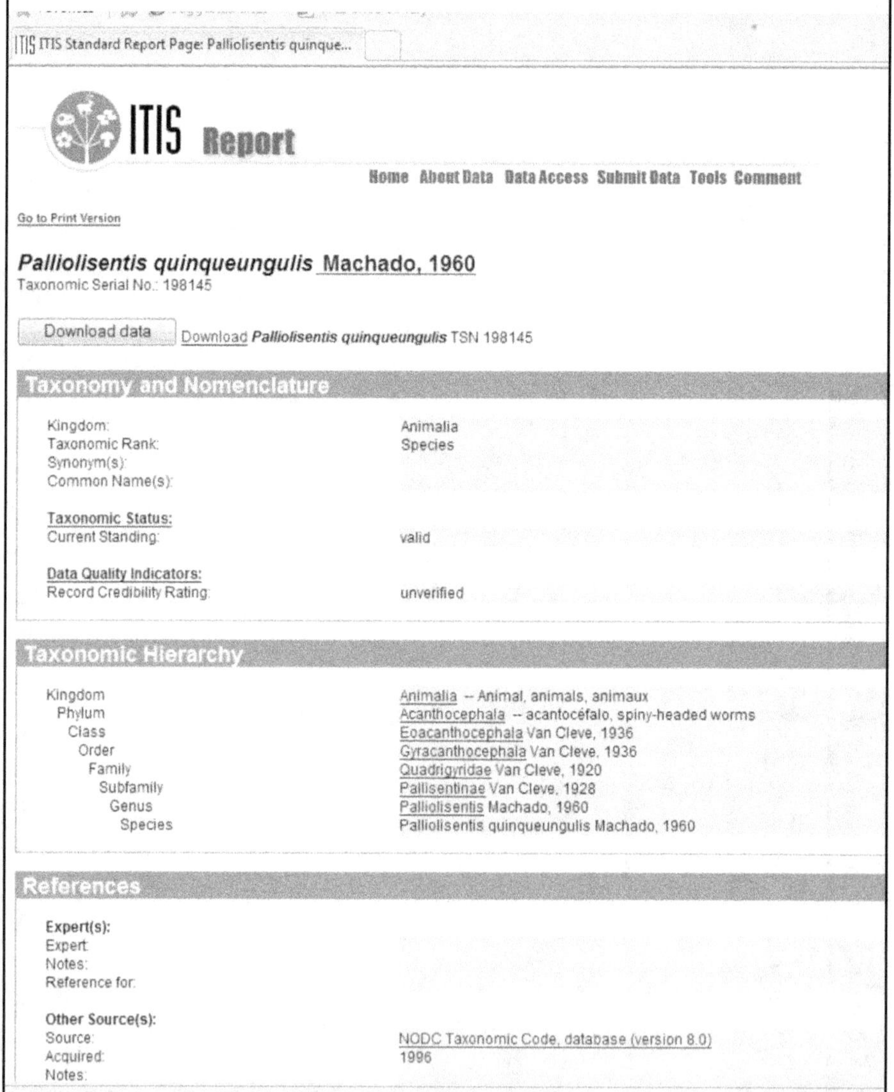

ITIS Standard Report Page: Palliolisentis quinque...

ITIS Report

Home About Data Data Access Submit Data Tools Comment

Go to Print Version

Palliolisentis quinqueungulis Machado, 1960

Taxonomic Serial No.: 198145

Download data Download *Palliolisentis quinqueungulis* TSN 198145

Taxonomy and Nomenclature

Kingdom:	Animalia
Taxonomic Rank:	Species
Synonym(s):	
Common Name(s):	
Taxonomic Status:	
Current Standing:	valid
Data Quality Indicators:	
Record Credibility Rating:	unverified

Taxonomic Hierarchy

Kingdom	Animalia -- Animal, animals, animaux
Phylum	Acanthocephala -- acantocéfalo, spiny-headed worms
Class	Eoacanthocephala Van Cleve, 1936
Order	Gyracanthocephala Van Cleve, 1936
Family	Quadrigyridae Van Cleve, 1920
Subfamily	Pallisentinae Van Cleve, 1928
Genus	Palliolisentis Machado, 1960
Species	Palliolisentis quinqueungulis Machado, 1960

References

Expert(s):	
Expert:	
Notes:	
Reference for:	
Other Source(s):	
Source:	NODC Taxonomic Code, database (version 8.0)
Acquired:	1996
Notes:	

species, to participate in the EOL Twitter community, and receive RSS feeds. The site's records include images of the species, a taxonomic breakdown, and links to significant articles about the species, including the source article that established the name of the taxon for the species. Figure 4.18 shows the EOL's homepage, and Figure 4.19 shows a sample EOL record.

ZooBank (www.zoobank.org/Default.aspx) is an online registry of zoological nomenclature. It is intended to be the official registry of zoological taxonomic registration, according to the International Commission on Zoological Nomenclature (ICZN). Richard L. Pyle and Ellinor Michel (2008: 40) note:

> Development of a registry for new animal names (prospective registration) and a complete listing of existing names (retrospective registration) has long been a goal for biologists. The stakeholders for a gold-standard registry of animal names are diverse and central to the functioning of many biological sciences and to policy concerned with the living world. They

Figure 4.18. Encyclopedia of Life Homepage

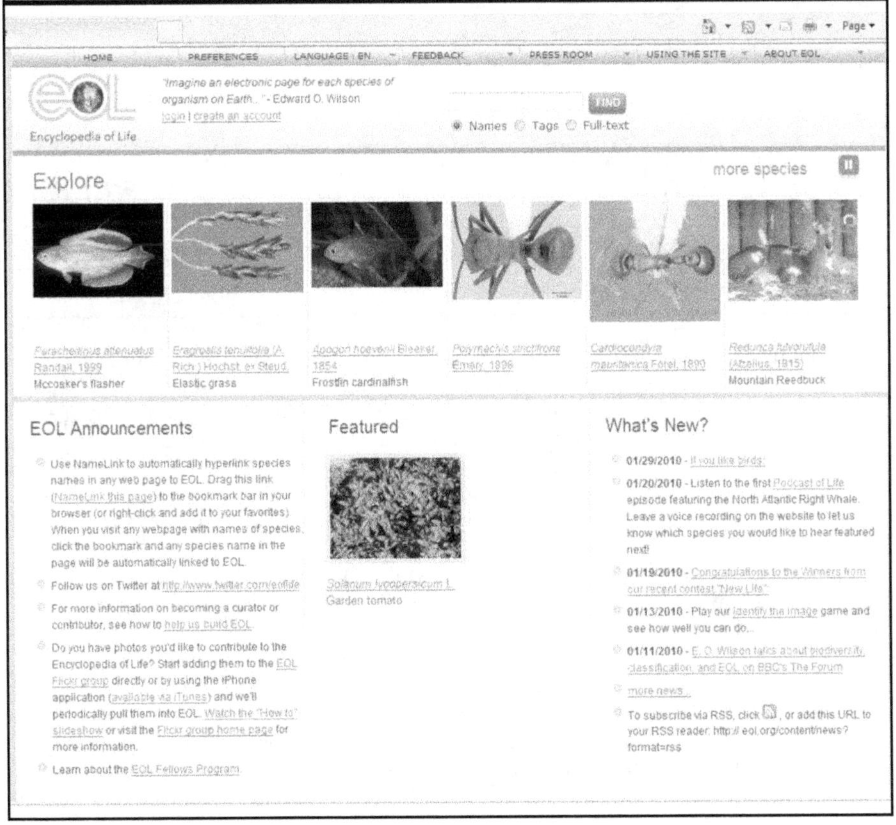

Figure 4.19. Record in the Encyclopedia of Life

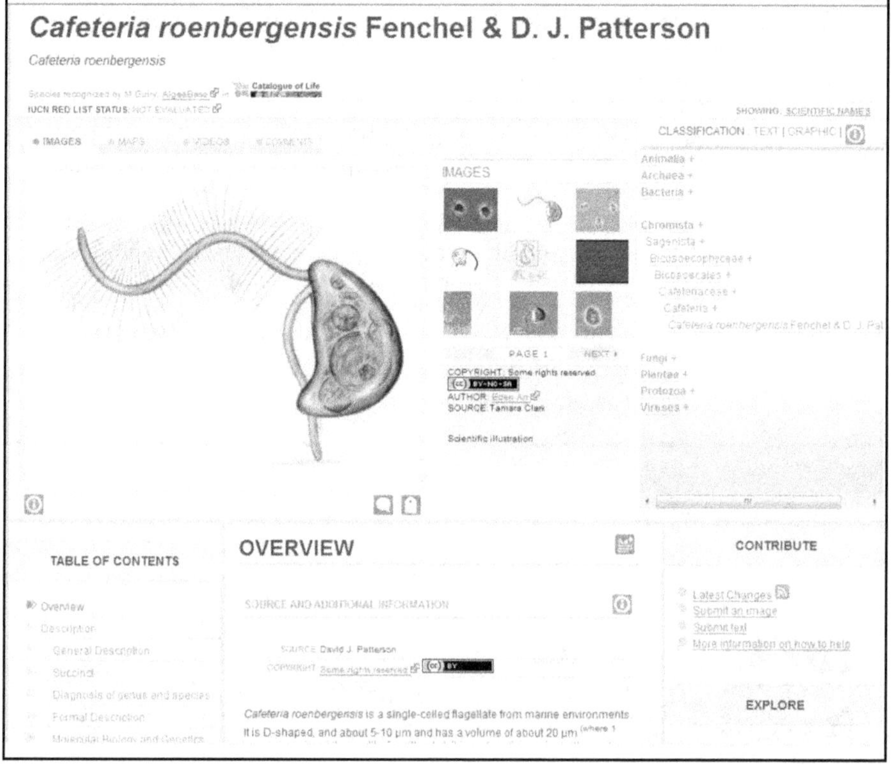

> include not only taxonomists, ecologists, and biodiversity informatics specialists but also conservationists, medical and veterinary workers, planners, policy makers, lawyers and even customs enforcers. Their requirements include ready access to a system of unambiguous answers to questions on the availability and validity of animal names that can be retrieved both by ordinary people and machines. The ICZN is meeting this need by developing ZooBank, a web-based registry of animal names.

ZooBank includes four "domains" of data: Authors, Publications, Nomenclatural Acts, and Type Specimens. One of the primary functions of ZooBank, according to the website,

> is to issue Globally Unique Identifiers (GUIDs) to each registered data object. GUIDs are necessary because taxonomic names, author names, publication citations, and references to type specimens are not unique (e.g. homonymy of names), are subject to inconsistent representations in textual

form (e.g. *Homo sapiens* vs. *H. sapiens*; Linnaeus vs. Linn vs. L.; etc.), and are generally fraught with ambiguity. (Pyle, 2009)

ZooBank uses LSIDs (described earlier in this chapter) to assign a unique number to each species record. Figure 4.20 shows an example of a ZooBank species record, and Figure 4.21 shows an example of a ZooBank Publication record.

Knowledge Structures within Library and Information Science

In contrast to knowledge structures developed and used within the natural science disciplines, knowledge structures developed within library and information science are used by information professionals to provide subject access to resources in collections, but the knowledge structures are also used by *anyone* who uses these information retrieval systems to access the information and knowledge resources of the entire world of knowledge. Knowledge structures developed by library and information science include (1) library bibliographic catalogs (online public access catalogs or OPACs) and the metadata structure for representing data about objects in collections; (2) controlled vocabularies, including, for example, subject headings lists, discipline- and subject-specific thesauri, ontologies, and taxonomies; and (3) classification schemes. Chapter 2 outlined the history of each of these knowledge structures, and Chapter 3 discussed the development of standards used within knowledge structures constructed by library and information science. The following sections will take a closer look at each of these three types of knowledge structures developed by library and information science and provide examples of each.

Metadata Structures and Content Creation Standards

The primary goal of knowledge structures within library and information science is to link users with the information and knowledge resources they need to satisfy an information need, whether the need is task related, for leisure purposes, or for any other goal-directed activity. Each structure provides users with a mechanism to access the information and knowledge resources of local and global collections in many contexts, for example, a public, academic or special library, a cultural heritage organization, a digital library or institutional repository, or a corporate intranet. Within a library context, access is provided through the use of bibliographic catalogs (either analog or digital) that contain descriptive and subject-related representations of the objects held within the collection locally, but also digital resources available from a variety of sources (subscription databases, webpages, digital libraries and online repositories, etc.). Each representation, or bibliographic record, is developed by using national and international standards that govern both the technical and encoding structures of the record as defined by the cataloging community and local

Figure 4.20. ZooBank Record for *Tectodamaeus longus* Registered 9-17-2009

Figure 4.21. Record Structure for a ZooBank Publication Record

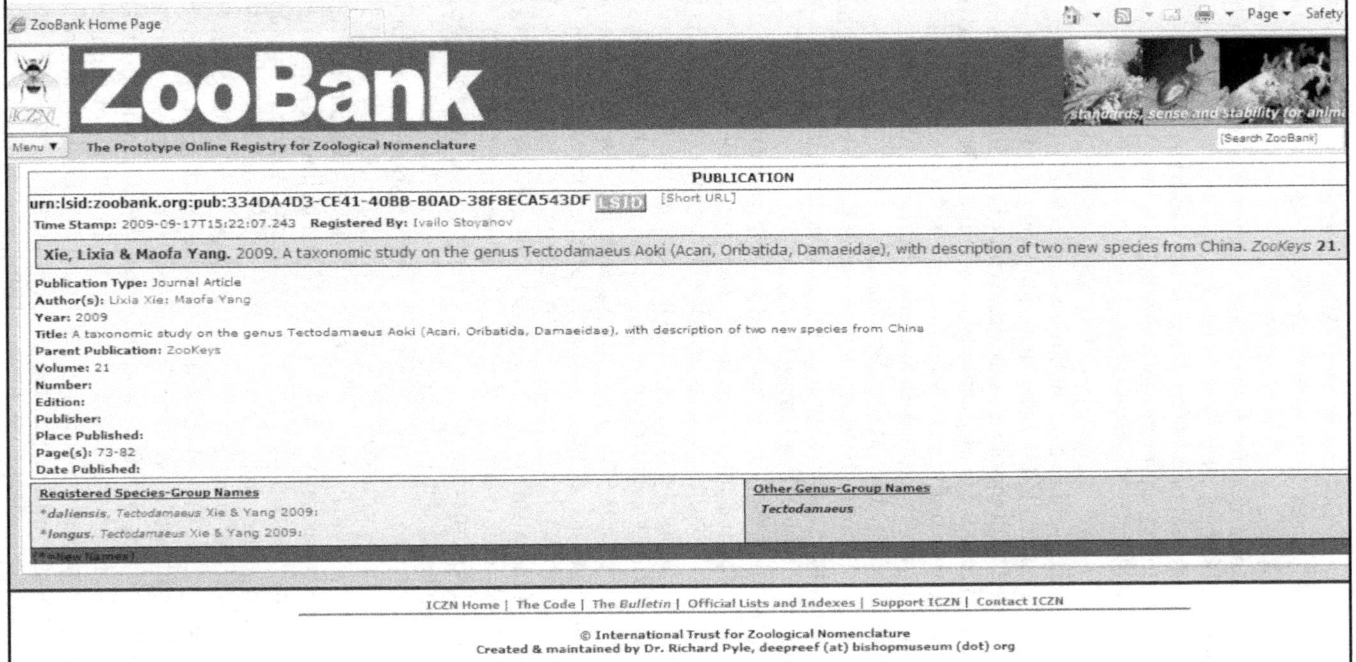

practices of the cataloging agency. A bibliographic record contains information about the *descriptive* aspects of the objects, for example:

1. who is responsible for its creation (author, translator, sculptor, musical group, publisher, etc.);
2. information that names the object (title, subtitle); and
3. information that describes the format, size, and other physical characteristics of the object.

Bibliographic records also include *subject-related* information, which can be terms from a controlled vocabulary that provide information about the subjects associated with the object and also a classification notation that provides a subject-based means for physical placement and subject-related collocation or grouping together of the objects on the same subject. Figure 4.22 shows how a representation is structured to include the descriptive and subject-related elements defined by the cataloging community.

The combination of these elements results in the bibliographic record that represents the object in the library's OPAC. Figure 4.23 provides an example of a bibliographic record in a library OPAC.

As we examine the structures used by libraries for representing objects in their collections, we might begin to question if the current representation scheme used in bibliographic records has incorporated elements that users actually find useful for describing items in their personal collections. Library bibliographic record structure continues to be based on Cutter's objects of a catalog that he proposed in 1876. The Objects include (1) to enable a person to find a book on which either (a) author, (b) title, or (c) subject is known; (2) to show what a library has (a) by a given author, (b) on a given subject, (c) in a given kind of literature; and (3) to assist in the choice of a book (a) as to its edition and (b) as to its character (Cutter, 1904, reprinted 1962: 12).

Patrick Wilson, among others, takes issue with Cutter's objects and principles for subject access in bibliographic catalogs in that they are too limiting and do not accurately convey the degree to which we should provide subject access to objects in library catalogs. Wilson asserts that not only should we be representing more than just at the whole "book" level (we can really use the term "book" to mean basically any format of object in libraries or other collections) but that "short descriptions [subject headings] of overall subject matter just don't reveal much explicitly about content" (Wilson, 1983: 14). Wilson further asserts that subject access in library catalogs is not based on how the user searches for a book. He believes that users are looking for "a *good* book, not just for a book or all books on a specific subject. Users instead want retrieval systems to filter out the *bad* books and only provide them with useful books" (Wilson, 1983: 14). In essence, Wilson is proposing some of the features we see developing in social networking sites such as LibraryThing or Flickr. These sites allow users to add subject terms that represent any level of the "book" being described (called *tagging*). LibraryThing also gives users options for writ-

Figure 4.22. Descriptive and Subject-Related Elements of a Bibliographic Record

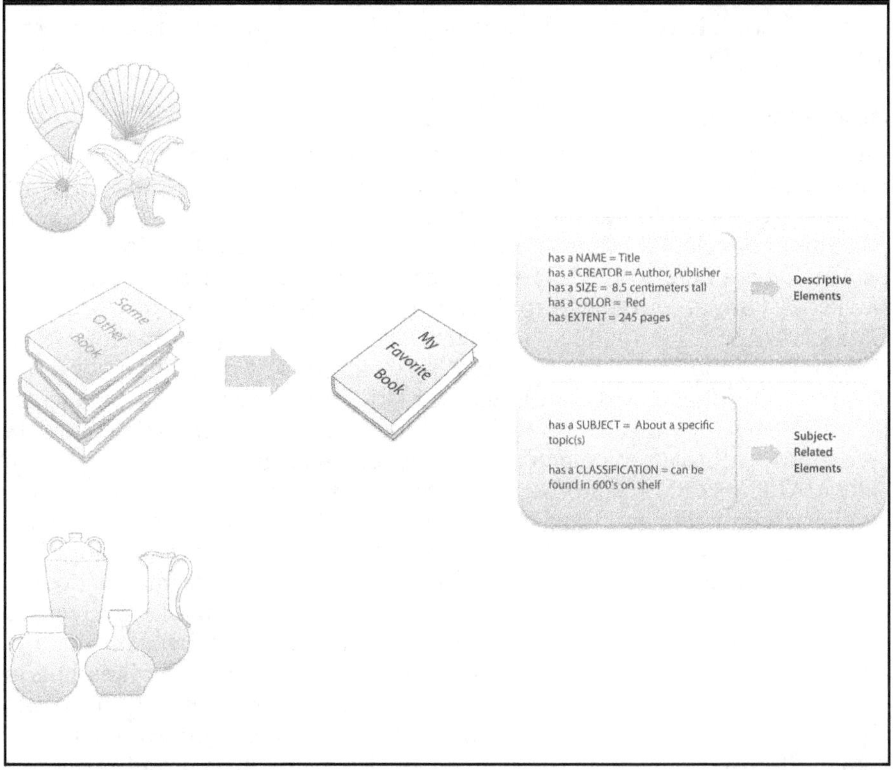

Figure 4.23. Example of a Bibliographic Record in a Library OPAC

Library of Congress subject headings : principles and application **Change Display**
Chan, Lois Mai.

Personal Author:	**Chan, Lois Mai.**
Title:	**Library of Congress subject headings : principles and application / by Lois Mai Chan.**
Edition:	4th ed.
Publication info:	Westport, Conn. : Libraries Unlimited, 2005.
Physical descrip:	xvi, 549 p. ; 25 cm.
Series Title:	**(Library and information science text series)**
Held by:	BIZZELL
Subject term:	**Subject headings, Library of Congress.**

Bizzell Library	Copies	Location
Z 695 .Z8 L5226 2005	1	Stacks

ing reviews or including comments about books, which can serve as a means for users to "filter" out the *bad* books. We will explore more about these emerging socially-constructed ways of providing subject access in Chapters 6–8.

Machine-Readable Cataloging

The structure that underlies the bibliographic record is referred to as the metadata scheme or database field structure. In library catalogs, the metadata scheme used is the MARC record structure (Machine Readable Cataloging), which was developed in the late 1960s. The MARC 21 standard (currently in use) includes a family of five MARC 21 communication formats, including (1) MARC 21 Format for Bibliographic Data, (2) MARC 21 Format for Authority Data, (3) MARC 21 Format for Holdings Data, (4) MARC 21 Format for Classification Data, and (5) MARC 21 Format for Community Information. Libraries and other information organizations use MARC standards for the representation and exchange of bibliographic, authority, holdings, classification, and community information data in machine-readable form.

A MARC record is composed of three elements: the record structure, the content designation, and the data content of the record. The *record structure* is an implementation of the international standard Format for Information Exchange (ISO 2709) and its American counterpart, Bibliographic Information Interchange (ANSI/NISO Z39.2). The elements included in the MARC record structure are derived from (1) the *International Standard Bibliographic Description* (ISBD), which is a technical bibliographic system standard (described in Chapter 3); and (2) subject-related elements. The *content designation*, the codes and conventions established to identify and further characterize the data elements within a MARC record (such as the field labels or "tags"), and to support the manipulation of that data, is defined by each of the MARC formats. The *data content*, the content that is entered into the record fields, is developed using the following content creation standards:

1. The *Anglo-American Cataloguing Rules* for bibliographic or descriptive content
2. Controlled vocabulary standards, such as those for subject headings lists (e.g., *Library of Congress Subject Headings*) or thesauri (e.g., *Medical Subject Headings*)
3. Classification schemes (e.g., Dewey Decimal Classification or the Library of Congress Classification)

The MARC record structure contains ten sets of fields, called "tags." The basic divisions include:

0XX Control information, numbers, and codes
1XX Main entries related to personal and corporate names

2XX	Titles, edition, imprint (including the title, statement of responsibility, edition statements, and publication information)
3XX	Physical description information
4XX	Series statements
5XX	Notes (including, for example, target audience, literary form, inclusion of supplementary materials, summary of content, restrictions, etc.)
6XX	Subject added entries
7XX	Added entries other than subjects or series (including, for example, personal or corporate name information, geographic names)
8XX	Series added entries
9XX	Locally defined uses, such as barcode number. The 9XX fields may also be used by the library or a vendor to include other types of information related to the record.

The 1XX, for example, indicates a range of tags or record fields within the 100 division. The 1XX fields (100, 110, 111, and 130) hold information about the main personal or corporate author or uniform title related to the information object being cataloged. To view the entire MARC record structure, see the *MARC 21 Format for Bibliographic Data,* available on the Library of Congress website (www.loc.gov/marc/bibliographic). A useful tutorial developed by the Library of Congress for understanding the structure of MARC 21 as used in bibliographic records is available at www.loc.gov/marc/umb, and a tutorial related to the structure of MARC 21 for authority records is available at www.loc.gov/marc/uma. Figure 4.24 illustrates what a library catalog record in the MARC format looks like.

Other metadata schemes are being developed to augment or adapt MARC for use in different system environments (e.g., MODS, METS, MARCXML) and also in response to the application of new content creation standards, such as the *Resource Description and Access* (RDA) cataloging standard, released in 2010. The MARC structure is undergoing revision to accommodate changes in descriptive cataloging included in the RDA. Discussion on both the history of the MARC record structure and the content creation standards of AACR and RDA are included in Chapters 2 and 3.

Other Metadata Schemas

Additional metadata schemas have also been developed over the past 10–15 years to provide non-MARC knowledge structures for representing information and knowledge resources, including the Dublin Core Metadata Element Set (DC), maintained by the Dublin Core Metadata Initiative group. As noted in Chapter 3, the development of the DC began in 1995 and continues currently. The core element set of the DC includes 15 general elements, as shown in Figure 4.25.

The DC is based on the principles of *simplicity, compatibility, extensibility,* and *interoperability,* which makes the element set general enough so that it can be

Figure 4.24. MARC Record for *Library of Congress Subject Headings* by Chan

Library of Congress subject headings : principles and application / Lois...

Relevance:

LC Control No.: 85024115

LCCN Permalink: http://lccn.loc.gov/85024115

000 00904cam a2200265 a 450
001 970857
005 19950113101707.6
008 851024s1986 coua b 001 0 eng
035 __ |9 (DLC) 85024115
906 __ |a 7 |b cbc |c orignew |d 1 |e ocip |f 19 |g y-gencatlg
010 __ |a 85024115
020 __ |a 0872875431 : |c $45.00
040 __ |a DLC |c DLC |d DLC
050 00 |a Z674 |b .R4 no. 19 |a Z695
082 00 |a 020 s |a 025.4/9 |2 19
100 1_ |a Chan, Lois Mai.
245 10 |a Library of Congress subject headings : |b principles and application / |c Lois Mai Chan.
250 __ |a 2nd ed.
260 __ |a Littleton, Colo. : |b Libraries Unlimited, |c 1986.
300 __ |a xvi, 511 p. : |b ill. ; |c 25 cm.
440 _0 |a Research studies in library science ; |v no. 19
504 __ |a Bibliography: p. 485-498.
500 __ |a Includes index.
650 _0 |a Subject headings, Library of Congress.
991 __ |b c-GenColl |h Z674 |i .R4 no. 19 |t Copy 1 |w BOOKS

CALL NUMBER: Z674 .R4 no. 19
Copy 1

used within many different contexts and for a variety of different digital and analog applications. The generic nature of the scheme allows conformity with existing and emerging metadata schemas at an international level, as well as being interoperable with diverse collections and knowledge systems. The DC serves as the base for many metadata schemes that have been developed (e.g., the GEM metadata scheme) and is the underlying infrastructure for many digital library projects (e.g., the National Science Digital Library). Visit the Dublin Core Metadata Initiative website (dublincore.org) for more information on the DC.

Metadata Structures in Cultural Heritage Organizations

In a cultural heritage organization, such as an archive or historical society or museum, the primary knowledge structure in use is the finding aid. Finding aids represent the archive's objects at the collection level rather than the individual object level. Included in a finding aid are inventories of the objects in the collection, detailed descriptions of the collection's historical context and provenance, as well as subject headings, authority controlled access points, details on the physical condition of the objects, and notations linking the objects to a

Figure 4.25. Dublin Core General Elements

Dublin Core Metadata Element Set

- Contributor
- Coverage
- Creator
- Date
- Description
- Format
- Identifier
- Language
- Publisher
- Relation
- Rights
- Source
- Subject
- Title
- Type

physical location within the archive. In the web environment, finding aids use the *Encoded Archival Description* (EAD) as their encoding metadata scheme.

As noted in Chapter 3, EAD is a data structure that defines the elements to include in the finding aid. It is not a data content structure. Cultural heritage organizations rely on other archival content creation standards such as the ISAD (G) (*General International Standard Archival Description*), which is similar in scope to the ISBD described in Chapter 3. ISAD is designed to be used to create content in archival records or finding aids or to serve as the basis for the development of archival standards (ISAD, 2000). DACS (*Describing Archives: A Content Standard*) is the content creation archival standard accepted by most of the U.S. archival community. Figure 4.26 shows an example of a finding aid using EAD.

Museums have recently begun creating representations that allow access to their collections by public users rather than for internal use only. Metadata schemes, such as the CDWA (Categories for the Description of Works of Art), or content creation standards such as the CCO (Cataloging Cultural Objects) have been developed within museum collections. Refer to Chapter 3 for discussion of these standards.

Figure 4.26. EAD Finding Aid from the Library of Congress

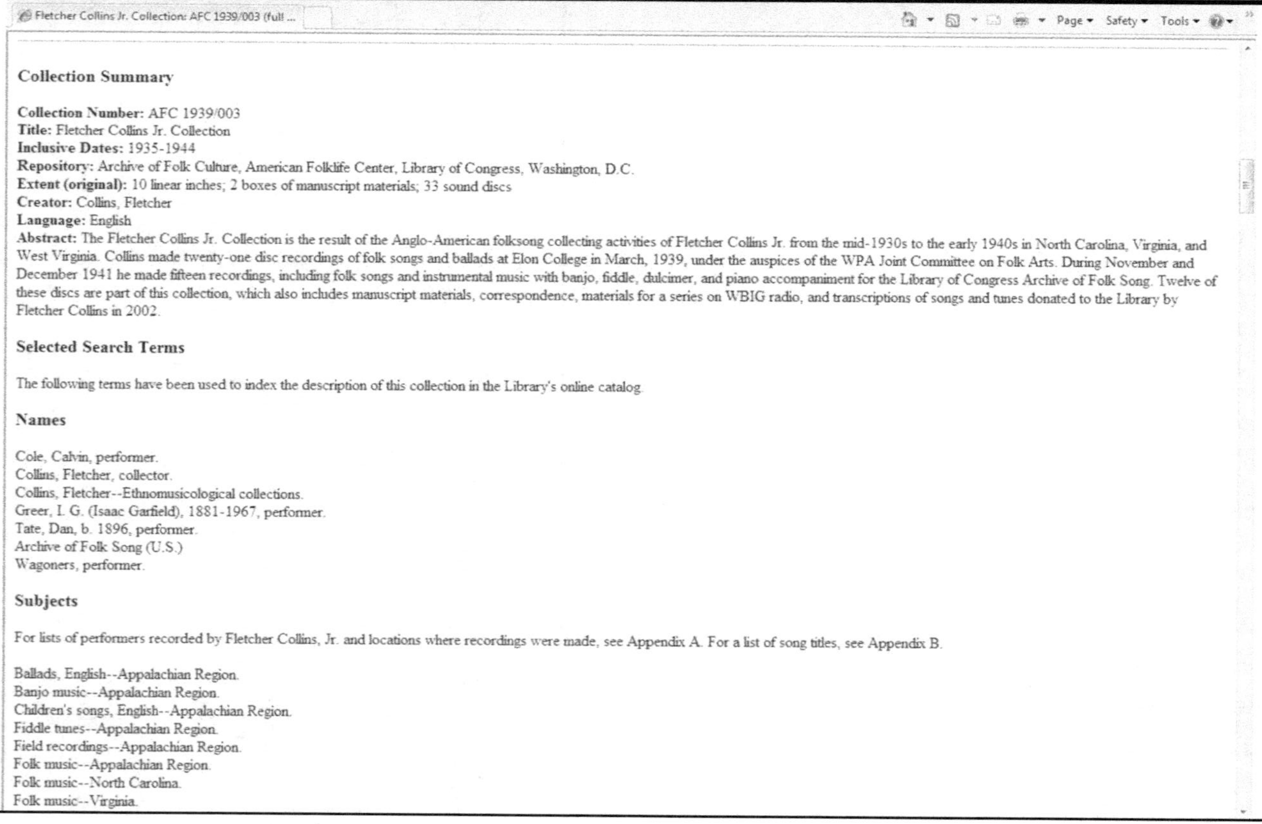

Collection Summary

Collection Number: AFC 1939/003
Title: Fletcher Collins Jr. Collection
Inclusive Dates: 1935-1944
Repository: Archive of Folk Culture, American Folklife Center, Library of Congress, Washington, D.C.
Extent (original): 10 linear inches; 2 boxes of manuscript materials; 33 sound discs
Creator: Collins, Fletcher
Language: English
Abstract: The Fletcher Collins Jr. Collection is the result of the Anglo-American folksong collecting activities of Fletcher Collins Jr. from the mid-1930s to the early 1940s in North Carolina, Virginia, and West Virginia. Collins made twenty-one disc recordings of folk songs and ballads at Elon College in March, 1939, under the auspices of the WPA Joint Committee on Folk Arts. During November and December 1941 he made fifteen recordings, including folk songs and instrumental music with banjo, fiddle, dulcimer, and piano accompaniment for the Library of Congress Archive of Folk Song. Twelve of these discs are part of this collection, which also includes manuscript materials, correspondence, materials for a series on WBIG radio, and transcriptions of songs and tunes donated to the Library by Fletcher Collins in 2002.

Selected Search Terms

The following terms have been used to index the description of this collection in the Library's online catalog.

Names

Cole, Calvin, performer.
Collins, Fletcher, collector.
Collins, Fletcher--Ethnomusicological collections.
Greer, I. G. (Isaac Garfield), 1881-1967, performer.
Tate, Dan, b. 1896, performer.
Archive of Folk Song (U.S.)
Wagoners, performer.

Subjects

For lists of performers recorded by Fletcher Collins, Jr. and locations where recordings were made, see Appendix A. For a list of song titles, see Appendix B.

Ballads, English--Appalachian Region.
Banjo music--Appalachian Region.
Children's songs, English--Appalachian Region.
Fiddle tunes--Appalachian Region.
Field recordings--Appalachian Region.
Folk music--Appalachian Region.
Folk music--North Carolina.
Folk music--Virginia.

Metadata Structures in Nonlibrary Settings

In corporate and other nonlibrary settings, the knowledge structures used to represent the collections are customized to suit the needs of the users as well as the unique characteristics of the specialized collection used in the corporate information environment. Taxonomies and ontologies are developed based on the unique characteristics of the information objects generated by the organization (i.e., white papers, corporate profiles, human resources records, client records and correspondence, e-mails, etc.). A corporate intranet, for example, provides access to the corporation's information objects and is accessible only by the corporation's employees. Corporate or special librarians, and/or knowledge managers (some of the current literature refers to these individuals as "ontologists" or "taxonomists"), develop knowledge structures designed around the unique information needs of the users and the information objects of the specialized collections. Chapter 5 presents further discussion and examples related to the use, development, and customized nature of taxonomies and ontologies within corporate contexts.

Controlled Vocabularies

Controlled vocabularies are one of the three forms of indexing languages that catalogers and indexers (in libraries) or record creators (in nonlibrary contexts) use to provide terminology that describes the subject-related content of information and knowledge resources. The other two indexing languages include *natural language*—terms derived directly from the resource itself, which are extracted by either a human or computerized automatic indexing program; and *free text*—terms entered at the discretion of the cataloger/record creator to more closely align with new terminology present in a discipline or domain or for language more commonly used by searchers. Controlled vocabularies are often used in bibliographic representations in conjunction with either or both natural language and free text. Controlled vocabularies can also be used by searchers of information retrieval systems as a source for search terms.

A new form of indexing language is emerging, that of *user-defined* or *user-contributed tags*, which is subject terminology that has been provided by users within Web 2.0–enabled bibliographic systems, databases, or other social networking environments. Chapters 6 and 7 will further explore this new form of indexing language and its potential uses within knowledge structures.

Controlled vocabularies are defined simply as authorized lists of subject terms that represent either the world of knowledge or the terminology within a specific discipline. Controlled vocabularies also include varying semantic relationships structured into the controlled vocabulary to resolve issues of synonymy and homography and to provide for broader or narrower representation. Semantic relationships may include equivalence (synonymy), hierarchical (broader and narrower terms), and associative (part of, related to).

These knowledge structures are developed and are used by the library and information science communities, but also by other disciplines such as education and in proprietary database systems that contain resources related to specific disciplines and that are designed for specific user groups, such as school-aged children. There are two types of controlled vocabularies: *subject headings lists* and *thesauri.*

Syndetic Structure within Controlled Vocabularies

Structured into the controlled vocabulary through the use of *syndetic structure* are the semantic relationships of (1) *equivalence* (designated using USE/UF), (2) *hierarchical* (BT/NT), and (3) *associative* (RT/RT). Other relationships may also be included, depending on the controlled vocabulary and its intended users, but the three relationships mentioned here are the most prevalent. Figure 4.27 shows how each relationship is structured into the controlled vocabulary entry for the term "cataloging" from the *Library of Congress Subject Headings* (LCSH).

The *equivalence relationship* indicates to the cataloger/record creator or searchers which terms are preferred or authorized for use in either a bibliographic record or as query terms in a search entered into an information retrieval system. In the example in Figure 4.27, the designator UF (USE FOR), indicates to the users that the term following UF "cataloguing" is not authorized for use. In some subject headings lists, such as the *Sears List of Subject*

Figure 4.27. Example from LCSH for Term "Cataloging" Showing Syndetic Structure

Cataloging (May Subd Geog) [R S D]
[Z693-695.83] [L S D]
UF Cataloguing ← equivalence relationship
BT Information organization — hierarchical relationship
Technical services (Libraries)
RT Books ← associative relationship
NT Collection level cataloging [R] — hierarchical relationship
Cooperative cataloging [R]
Copyright cataloging [R]
Corporate headings (Cataloging) [R]
Descriptive cataloging [R]
Library catalog management [R]
Minimal level cataloging [R]
Multiple versions (Cataloging) [R]
Names, Personal (Cataloging) [R]
Recataloging [R]
Retrospective conversion (Cataloging) [R]
Shelflisting [R]
Subject cataloging [R]
Uniform titles (Cataloging) [R]

Cataloging–Analytical entry [R S D]
[Z693.3.A52] [L S D]
UF Analytical entry (Cataloging)
Analytics (Cataloging)
Catalog analytical entries
Library catalog analytical entries
BT Cataloging of serial publications

Headings (Sears), this practice appears to be phasing out; the designator "See" is used to represent the equivalence relationship. In LCSH, preferred terms are also presented in bold type.

Terms following the BT or NT designators are also authorized for use and present the cataloger with additional terminology to use in representations or when searching for the concept in the system. BT and NT are used to designate the *hierarchical relationship* of broader (BT) or narrower (NT) terms in the structure of the controlled vocabulary.

Terms following the RT designators are also authorized for use and present the user with additional related terms. RT is used to represent the *associative relationship* within the syndetic structure. Terms may be related in the following ways (Lancaster, 1986: 46–47):

1. Between a "thing" and its applications or as the converse relationship of its application
   ADHESIVES
   RT BONDING
   BONDING
   RT ADHESIVES
2. Between an effect and a cause (and vise versa)
   BRITTLE FRACTURE
   RT HYDROGEN EMBRITTLEMENT
3. Between a "thing" and a property strongly associated with it
   RUBBER
   RT ELASTICITY
4. Between a raw material and a product
   KAOLIN
   RT CHINA
5. Between two complementary activities
   TEACHING
   RT LEARNING
6. Between certain opposites
   LIFE
   RT DEATH
7. Between an activity and a property associated with it
   BENDING
   RT PLASTICITY
8. Between an activity and an agent of that activity
   SMOKING
   RT CIGARETTES
9. Between an activity and a product of that activity
   WEAVING
   RT CLOTH
10. Between a thing and its parts (where not provided for in some other way)
    AIRPLANES
    RT FUSELAGE

The *associative* relationship also can be thought of as akin to the recommender features present in many commercial systems, such as Amazon's browsing feature, "Other people who purchased this title also purchased these titles," or, as restated by F.W. Lancaster (1986: 47–48), "It is likely that someone seeking information indexed under term A might also be interested in information indexed under term B."

The issue of homography, or the instance of when a word or concept is spelled in the same manner but can have multiple, different meanings, is resolved in controlled vocabularies by the use of explanatory "Scope Notes," as well as the addition of parenthetical qualifiers following the term. Figure 4.28 includes an example of both a Scope Note and a parenthetical qualifier applied to the term "Speech disorders" in the LCSH.

Principles of Controlled Vocabularies

There are two sets of principles that need to be considered when discussing controlled vocabularies: (1) those related to the *construction* of controlled vocabularies and (2) those related to the *application* of controlled vocabularies.

Principles Related to the Construction of Controlled Vocabularies

Principles related to the *construction* of controlled vocabularies are those that would be considered whenever a new controlled vocabulary is being developed or an existing controlled vocabulary is being adapted for use. The na-

Figure 4.28. Example of Scope Note and Parenthetical Qualifier in Entry for Term "Speech Disorders" from LCSH

Speech disorders (May Subd Geog) [R S D]
[RC423-428.5] [L S D]
Here are entered works on disorders of the physiological mechanisms required for the articulation, patterning, or productio
of speech. Works on disorders of the central neurological function affecting the reception, processing, or expression of
language are entered under Language disorders.
UF Defective speech
Disorders of speech
Speech, Disorders of [Former Heading]
Speech defects
Speech pathology
BT Communicative disorders
NT Aphasia [R]
Articulation disorders [R]
Cluttering (Speech pathology) [R]
Mutism [R]
Stuttering [R]
Tongue thrust [R]
Velopharyngeal insufficiency [R]
Voice disorders [R]

Scope Note

Parenthetical qualifier

Speech disorders--Treatment
USE Speech therapy [R]

Speech disorders, Grammatical
USE Agrammatism [R]

tional and international standards related to the construction of controlled vocabularies, as outlined in Chapter 3, provide very specific guidelines for:

1. concepts that are represented in the controlled vocabulary (e.g., things, materials, activities or processes, events or occurrences, properties of people, things, materials, or units of measure);
2. word form choice (e.g., use of nouns and avoidance of verbs, use of plurals for "count nouns" and use of singular for "non-count nouns," use of slang or jargon rules, use of abbreviations or acronyms rules);
3. devices to use to distinguish homographs (e.g., parenthetical qualifier and/or Scope Notes; and
4. form of the heading (e.g., use of inverted or direct headings).

There is also a set of generally accepted principles within the library and information science community, which include the following:

1. **Specificity**—or the "level of semantic depth found in a particular controlled vocabulary" (Taylor and Joudrey, 2009: 341). Words should be appropriate for the users and intended purposes of the controlled vocabulary. Semantic depth can include both the specificity of a word (how general or specific a word is), as well as the depth at which individual concepts are represented within the controlled vocabulary. In subject headings lists that have as their scope the entire world of knowledge and that have been designed for a homogenous user, concepts may be represented by the use of fewer terms, at a more general level. Thesauri, however, which have as a scope a specific domain, discipline, or context, may include many terms to represent various aspects of a concept, with terms that are more specific in nature. For example, LCSH has greater specificity of terms and depth of representations than Sears, which is designed for use by small to medium-sized libraries. Thesauri, such as *Medical Subject Headings* (MeSH), have even more terms to represent concepts, with the terms being of a more specific nature.
2. **Literary warrant**—terms of the controlled vocabulary should be derived from the published literature that it is designed to represent (Hulme, 1911; Lancaster, 1986). The controlled vocabulary should include terms that have been published and are being published currently in the literature (all information sources and formats). Literary warrant also speaks to the need for the controlled vocabulary to be continually revised and updated.
3. **User warrant**—terms of the controlled vocabulary should be included only if they are of interest to the user (Lancaster, 1986). The controlled vocabulary should include terms that are in current use and of interest to the user but also at the appropriate level of specificity for the user. Terminology occurring in the literature may be at a higher level of specificity than is appropriate for the user. To determine the appropriate level of specificity and terms to include in the controlled vocabulary, users' search terms can

be reviewed or users can be surveyed. User warrant also speaks to the need for the controlled vocabulary to be continually revised and updated.

4. **Direct entry**—"a concept should be entered into the controlled vocabulary using the term that names it, rather than treating that concept as a subdivision of a broader concept" (Taylor and Joudrey, 2009: 342). Terms of the controlled vocabulary should represent the concept at the most specific level that is appropriate for the use and users of the controlled vocabulary. For example, in LCSH, one might find the term "Education, Bilingual." It would be more appropriate to use the direct form of the term "Bilingual Education" to more closely align with the form users would use to search for the concept in the system.

Principles Related to the Application of Controlled Vocabularies

Principles related to the *application* of controlled vocabularies are those that would be considered when using a controlled vocabulary to provide subject access within an information retrieval system. The principles include:

1. **Specific entry**—the most specific term present in the controlled vocabulary that represents the subject of the information resource should be used rather than a more general term. Choosing a controlled vocabulary term that is most specific to the subject reduces the time a user must spend searching within a system. However, for less experienced and/or younger users, use of the more specific term may cause problems in retrieval. For example, specific entry dictates the use of the more specific term "poison arrow frogs" for describing a resource on this topic. Younger users, however, may use the less specific term "frogs" when searching and, as a result of more specific entry, may not find this resource.
2. **Co-extensive entry**—"the subject headings applied to a resource will cover all, but no more than, the concepts or topics covered in that resource" (Taylor and Joudrey, 2009: 344). More than one heading entry may be necessary in order to cover both or all subjects represented in the resource. It may be the case that the controlled vocabulary does not include a heading that covers the entire subject matter and only by using multiple headings can both concepts be represented.
3. **Number of terms to assign**—there are no specific rules that guide the number of terms to assign a resource. Local practice of the library or information organization may dictate the number of terms to assign to each resource. However, the headings assigned should adequately represent all concepts of the resource that are appropriate for both the user and the use of the collection.
4. **Concepts not present in the controlled vocabulary**—there should be a mechanism in place to propose the addition of terms to the controlled vocabulary. Concepts not represented within the controlled vocabulary should be represented with a general term until a more appropriate term has been added to the controlled vocabulary.

These principles for application of a controlled vocabulary illustrate the general uses of controlled vocabularies but do not show those of individual subject headings lists or thesauri. Each of these knowledge structures contains its own rules or guidelines for application.

Subject Headings Lists

Subject headings lists are controlled vocabularies that generally include as their scope the entire world of knowledge, organized in alphabetical and hierarchical arrangements, with semantic relationships displayed to direct the user (both cataloger/record creator and searchers) to terms that can be used to represent subject content within knowledge-organizing systems or for use in search queries. Subject headings lists are designed with a general homogeneous user in mind and may reflect both broad as well as specific terminology. Examples of subject headings lists include the *Library of Congress Subject Headings* (LCSH) and the *Sears List of Subject Headings* (Sears).

Library of Congress Subject Headings

Library of Congress Subject Headings (LCSH) has an enumerative scope, meaning it was designed to represent the subjects of the entire world of knowledge and is not limited to a specific domain or context. LCSH includes the three primary semantic relationships described in the previous section on controlled vocabularies and is updated on a weekly basis to add new terminology as well as to delete obsolete or inappropriate, outdated terminology. To review a list of weekly updates, visit the Library of Congress Acquisitions and Bibliographic Access Directorate website (www.loc.gov/aba/cataloging/subject/weekly lists). Figure 4.29 illustrates the structure of LCSH and the three semantic relationships of (1) equivalence (designated using USE/UF), (2) hierarchical (BT/NT), and (3) associative (RT/RT). LCSH also employs the use of Scope Notes and parenthetical qualifiers, as appropriate. The SA (See Also) designator instructs the cataloger about potential subdivisions that can be created. Subject heading entries in LCSH take many different forms, as shown in Table 4.1.

LCSH also includes provisions for the construction of subdivisions to the main topical and geographic headings by appending additional authorized headings to the end of the main heading. Construction of subdivisions, in most cases, provides a more specific subject heading than the main heading. The main heading may be subdivided by one or more of four kinds of subdivisions: topical, geographic, chronological, or form. Subdivisions are constructed following specific principles and citation order. There are two allowable citation orders for constructing subject headings that contain subdivisions:

A. Topic—Place (allowable only when the notation *May Subd Geog* follows the main heading)
    - Then you can add: Topic, Chronological Period, and Form subdivisions if appropriate.
    - You might also see Topic—Topic, etc.

Figure 4.29. Example of Subject Heading and Relationships for the Term "Computer Adventure Games" from LCSH

Computer adventure games *(May Subd Geog)*
[GV1469.22-GV1469.25]
UF Adventures and adventurers—Computer games
Adventure games, Computer
Games, Computer adventure
BT Adventure games
Computer games
SA *subdivision* Computer games *under subjects*
NT Island of Kesmai (Game)
Queen: The Eye (Game)

Fine arts
USE Art
Arts

Foreign relations
USE *subdivision* Foreign relations *under names of countries*
International relations

Games, Computer adventure
USE Computer adventure games

Table 4.1. Examples of Forms of Subject Headings in LCSH

Type of Subject Heading	Example of Subject Heading
Single Noun	Skating
Noun preceded by adjective	Administrative Law
Noun preceded by other noun used as adjective	Energy industries
Noun connected with another by preposition	Radioisotopes in cardiology
Noun connected with another by "and"	Libraries and society
Noun followed by parenthetical qualifier	Cluttering (speech pathology)
Phrase or sentence	Show driving of horse drawn vehicles
Inverted headings	Education, Bilingual
Proper name headings	(may use any proper name)
Geographic names	Oklahoma
Genre/topic terms	Animated films

B. Place—Topic (aspects of a place, e.g., history)
   - Then you can add Chronological Period and then Form if needed.
   - You can also check the Authority files to see which heading-subdivisions have been authorized for use.

As with any controlled vocabulary there are a set of principles and guidelines to follow to apply and/or construct subject heading entries with LCSH. The *Subject Cataloging Manual* provides users of LCSH with the guidelines for applying and constructing subject heading entries. Use of LCSH is a complex process that is guided by the *Subject Cataloging Manual*, the principles and rules developed by the Library of Congress for subject assignment, and also the local practices of a specific library or information organization. The general application principles outlined earlier in the controlled vocabularies section apply to the LCSH, as do others developed by Charles A. Cutter, which include the following:

1. **User and usage**—Cutter (1904: 7) believed that "the convenience of the public is always to be set before the ease of the cataloger. In most cases they coincide. A plain rule without exception is not only easy for us to carry out, but easy for the public to understand and work by." However, Cutter is often called into question regarding his idealization of a user. Miksa (1983: 74) recognizes that in Cutter's time users probably were relatively homogeneous and we could characterize a "typical user" and user habits. The Library of Congress's policy for establishing headings illustrates the principle of "user warrant" described as a general principle of controlled vocabularies. The Library of Congress's policy states that "User needs are best met if headings reflect current usage in regard to terminology. Thus terms in current use are selected in establishing new subject headings" (Chan, 2005: 20).
2. **Uniform headings**—in order for a system to represent what subjects a collection contains, uniform headings must be used to represent the same subject concept within the records of the system. Uniformity ensures consistency of entry and the collocation feature of a system.
3. **Unique headings**—each heading in a system should represent only one subject. This principle addresses the issue of homographs within controlled vocabularies. To minimize confusion of application of terms, devices such as parenthetical qualifiers are used to distinguish homographs from each other.
4. **Internal consistency**—within LCSH, maintaining consistency of form of headings is accomplished by the use of recurring patterns within the headings and heading-subdivision constructions. Internal consistency is difficult to achieve as is evident in Table 4.1, which illustrates the variety of different forms of headings present in LCSH. According to Lois Mai Chan (2005), no systematic effort, to date, has been made to revise existing headings to ensure a consistent structure and form.

The reader is referred to Chan (2005) for a comprehensive guide to both the application and construction of Library of Congress subject headings.

While the LCSH was originally designed for use by the Library of Congress, it is now considered the de facto standard for subject cataloging and indexing internationally. According to Lois Main Chan (2005: 3),

> LSCH has become an important subject access tool both within the Library of Congress [LC] and outside. Most of the cataloging records provided by major bibliographic utilities and services such as OCLC Online Computer Library Center . . . carry LC subject headings, and most of the individual libraries in the United States use them for subject cataloging. Furthermore, a number of commercial retrieval services such as DIALOG carry the LC MARC file. . . . Internationally, LCSH has also gained wide acceptance. Over the years, many libraries in other countries have adopted or adapted LCSH, using it as is or as a model for developing controlled vocabularies for use in their own catalogs.

Sears List of Subject Headings

The *Sears List of Subject Headings* (Sears), the second most commonly used subject heading list (Hoerman and Furniss, 2000), was designed by Minnie Earl Sears in 1923 to provide subject access in small and medium-sized libraries. Sears includes the three primary semantic relationships described previously and also includes the cross-reference of "See Also" to refer users to other terms that might be useful. It also employs Scope Notes to further clarify the specific meaning of terms and how they are used within Sears.

Sears differs from LCSH in many ways that make it appropriate for representing small or medium-sized collections or children's resources. For example, Sears contains fewer technical terms, prefers common names instead of scientific names, uses direct geographic subdivisions, and has converted inverted headings into direct forms (Miller, 1998; Abbas, 2005). Sears has continually been revised throughout the years and new enhancements and changes incorporated into its structure. For example, in the thirteenth edition of Sears, and in accord with a suggestion of the Cataloging of Children's Materials Committee of the American Library Association, many of the headings from the *Subject Headings for Children's Literature* were incorporated into Sears. With the publication of the fifteenth edition in 1994, the practice of inverted headings was discontinued, and all remaining inverted headings were converted to direct form headings at that time.

Like the LCSH, Sears subscribes to the principles outlined earlier for general controlled vocabularies of specific and coextensive entries and the use of direct entry for form of terms. However, where Sears differs from LCSH is in the number of entries that can be entered. Sears abides by the "Rule of Three" as follows: "As many as three specific subject headings in a given area may be assigned to a work, but if the work treats more than three subjects, then a broader heading is used instead and the specific headings are omitted" (Miller, 1998: 68).

Subject headings lists may not always be useful for all knowledge organizing systems. Discipline-specific structures have been developed in the form of thesauri, which will be detailed in the next section. There have also been efforts to develop or adapt an existing controlled vocabulary for a specific user group, namely, for children or younger users, including work by the Library of Congress to develop the Library of Congress's Annotated Card program, as described in Chapter 2. Figure 4.30 shows an example of how terminology from the LCSH has been adapted to suit representation of resources for younger users.

In the example in Figure 4.30, the Juvenile Subject Heading for the term "poison frogs" directs the user to this term and away from using the terms "poison arrow frogs" or "poison dart frogs," both of which might not be appropriate to effectively represent subject content for younger users. Few younger users would know the more specific species names of "poison arrow frogs" or "poison dart frogs"; therefore their search would prove ineffective. It is interesting, however, that the term "frogs" does not appear in the Juvenile Subject

Figure 4.30. Juvenile Subject Headings Entry for the Term "Poison Frogs"

Poison-arrow frogs
  USE Poison frogs [R]

Poison-dart frogs
  USE Poison frogs [R]

Poison frogs (May Subd Geog) [R]
  UF Dendrobatidae
    Poison-arrow frogs
    Poison-dart frogs

Police, Private
  USE Security guards [R]

Polyglot materials [R]
  UF Polyglot texts, selections, quotations, etc.

Polyglot texts, selections, quotations, etc
  USE Polyglot materials [R]

Portrait painters
  USE Artists [R]

Possessions, Lost and found
  USE Lost and found possessions [R]

Prayer-books
  USE Prayer books and devotions [R]

Headings, as this is probably the term that most younger users would associate with frogs, rather than the more descriptive "poison frogs."

A further effort by members of OCLC's Knowledge Organization research team has produced *Subject Headings for Children*, a list of approximately 20,000 LCSH subject terms. The list was compiled by searching OCLC's WorldCat database of bibliographic records. The list includes LCSH terms and some specially devised terms. Name headings from the Library of Congress's Name Authority File are also included. Reviews of the *Subject Headings for Children* indicate that the list is probably useful but still contains many inappropriate terms, such as "miscellanea," and doesn't incorporate terms in common use by children (Towsey, 1999; Abbas, 2005).

Thesauri

Thesauri, as mentioned previously, are generally designed for use within a specific discipline, occupation, or proprietary database system. During the mid-twentieth century numerous thesauri were developed for use by library and information professionals when cataloging/indexing resources within specific disciplines (e.g., education, medicine, law, social science, psychology, arts, anthropology, archaeology, criminal justice, engineering) or contexts (e.g., art museums, medical libraries, rare book or special collections). Thesauri do not include controlled terminology that represents the entire world of knowledge, but rather they capture the knowledge of the discipline, specific contextual environment, or profession that will be using the knowledge organizing system.

Thesauri generally include terminology that is derived from the discipline and its publications. The terminology also tends to be more specific in nature than that found in subject headings lists in order to meet the needs of the discipline or context for which the thesauri are focused. Thesauri contain structured semantic relationships similar to subject headings lists; however, the relationships that are included may be customized for the specific discipline. Examples of thesauri include the following:

1. *Medical Subject Headings* (MeSH): www.nlm.nih.gov/mesh/meshhome.html
2. *Thesaurus of ERIC Descriptors* (Education Resources Information Center): www.eric.ed.gov
3. *Art & Architecture Thesaurus* (AAT): www.getty.edu/research/conducting_research/vocabularies/aat
4. *Thesaurus for Graphic Materials I: Subject Terms* (TGM I): www.loc.gov/rr/print/tgm1

Classification Schemes

Knowledge structures within library and information science have as their primary goal to link users with the information and knowledge resources. Each structure provides users with a mechanism to access the information and knowledge resources of local and global collections in many contexts. Classification schemes, within bibliographic systems, have two primary functions:

1. Linking an item within the library or information organization's collection to the bibliographic record that represents it. This linking is accomplished through the class number (notation) that forms part of the call number assigned to the object.
2. Retrieval of the object by collocation, or the grouping together of objects classified into the same class or assigned the same notation. Collocation also enables browsing of the physical or digital collection by users.

Classification schemes, as we learned in Chapter 2, are based on principles from philosophy and cognitive science. How humans create categories and the categories they create inform classification schemes developed by library and information science such as the Library of Congress Classification (LCC), Dewey Decimal Classification (DDC), Universal Decimal Classification (UDC), and other less common schemes, for example, Bliss Classification (BC) and Colon Classification (CC). Classification schemes, like controlled vocabularies, represent what is known about the world of knowledge at a current time. Also, like controlled vocabularies, they are continually updated in an effort to reflect accurately the subjects present in the world.

There are two approaches present in classification schemes, *enumerative* and *faceted* (also referred to as analytico-synthetic). Traditionally, classification schemes followed the classical classification approach applied by Aristotle and later Linnaeus of dividing the world of knowledge into categories or classes. These classes were then further divided into subclasses (divisions) and further subdivision into sections. This top-down, deductive approach results in an enumerative scheme that attempts to represent the world of knowledge within its class structure. Both the LCC and DDC schemes are enumerative. According to Rowley and Hartley (2008: 177–178), enumerative approaches have the following limitations:

1. Successive subdivision of classes can usually only effectively cover one semantic relationship, the hierarchical relationship. Other semantic and syntactic relationships are difficult to represent. However, the DDC does include some associative relationships within its structure.
2. Successive subdivision of classes carries the temptation to continue to subdivide classes, ignoring the concept of literary warrant.
3. Repetition is also a problem in enumerative schemes. Subordinate topics have to be enumerated consistently, thereby increasing the size of the scheme.
4. Enumerative classification schemes permit only a limited amount of pre-coordination. For complex subjects, if the classification is being used for physical placement, only one class can be used. However, in the digital environment, multiple classes to represent all aspects of the complex subject may be used.

By contrast, faceted classification schemes such as the Colon Classification scheme, or the *Art & Architecture Thesaurus* (which also can be used for classification purposes), employ a bottom-up, inductive approach to classification. They do not attempt to represent the entire world of knowledge in predefined classes or in a predetermined order. They may, however, contain classes and other similar features of enumerative schemes. Faceted schemes generally group terms or concepts into a number of mutually exclusive categories, called *facets*, which may represent general characteristics of the objects within a collection. Within each facet, more specific characteristics are identified and expanded as the subject matter of the facet also changes. These divisions are called *foci*, *subfacets*, or *arrays*. Subjects and complex subjects, then, are classified by first determining the primary, secondary, tertiary, etc., facet(s). Further classification includes the application of specific foci (as applicable) to the subject matter. Complex subject classification is constructed by synthesis of the facets and foci.

Classification schemes have three components: (1) the *schedule*, in which the scheme is published; (2) *notation*, a code using numbers and/or alphabetic characters, as well as punctuation, used to denote the classification of the object using the scheme; and (3) an *index* to assist in the location of terms within the schedules and to link terms to classes. When classifying an object, the classifier will locate the subject of the object within the index, which points the classifier to the place in the schedule (or the class) in which the subject is contained. Once the class and any applicable subclass is determined, the notation assigned to that class/subclass will be appended to the object.

The DDC and LCC are the most well-known enumerative classification schemes in use. The DDC, according to Rowley and Hartley (2008), is the most widely used classification scheme in the world. It is used in over 135 countries and in national bibliographies in more than 60 countries. It has been translated into 30 different languages. Libraries of many types use the DDC. The following sections will examine the structure of the DDC and LCC as exemplars of enumerative schemes.

Dewey Decimal Classification Scheme

As noted in Chapters 2 and 3, the DDC was first published in 1876 by Melvil Dewey. Today, copyright for the DDC is held by the Online Computer Library Center (OCLC) but it continues to be updated by the Decimal Classification Editorial Policy Committee (EPC) at the Library of Congress. The DDC is published in both a print and an online version and is continually updated to reflect the changes of the world of knowledge.

In the DDC, basic classes are organized by disciplines or fields of study. The DDC is divided into ten *main classes*, which together cover the entire world of knowledge. Each main class is further divided into ten *divisions*, and each division into ten *sections*. These are the ten main classes of the DDC:

000	Computers, information & general reference
100	Philosophy & psychology
200	Religion
300	Social sciences
400	Language
500	Science
600	Technology
700	Arts & recreation
800	Literature
900	History & geography

Each main class includes 10 divisions, which results in 100 divisions. For example, the divisions under the 500 class Science include the following:

500	Science
510	Mathematics
520	Astronomy
530	Physics
540	Chemistry
550	Earth sciences & geology
560	Fossils & prehistoric life
570	Life sciences; biology
580	Plants (Botany)
590	Animals (Zoology)

Each division, in turn, can be further subdivided into 10 sections, resulting in 1,000 sections. For example, these are the sections in the 590 division:

590	Animals (Zoology)
591	Specific topics in natural history
592	Invertebrates
593	Marine & seashore invertebrates
594	Mollusks & molluscoids
595	Arthropods
596	Chordates
597	Cold-blooded vertebrates; fishes
598	Birds
599	Mammals

The DDC makes heavy use of various types of Notes to provide the classifier with additional information for constructing DDC notations. According to the DDC Introduction,

> Notes are important because they supply information in regard to order, structure, subordination, and other matters that is not obvious in the notational hierarchy or in the heading. Notes may appear in the record for a

> number or a span of numbers. Notes may also appear at the beginning of a table. Footnotes are used for instructions that apply to multiple subdivisions of a class, or to a topic within a class. (DDC, accessed 2010)

Additional types of Notes are defined in Table 4.2.

Notations are formed using Arabic numerals that represent the class and division, followed by a decimal point and the section number (as applicable).

Table 4.2. Notes within the DDC Scheme

There are different forms of notes used within the DDC. A sample of some of the most common are listed here.

Types of Notes	Definitions
(A) Notes That Describe What Is Found in a Class	*Definition notes* define the meaning of a term as it is used in the heading. *Number-built notes* give the source of built numbers included in the schedules and tables and explain how the number was built. You might occasionally find the built numbers included in the schedules or tables to provide additional information or to indicate exceptions to regular add instructions. *Variant-name notes* are used to show synonyms or near synonyms.
(B) Including Notes	*Including notes* identify topics that have placeholders in the schedule where the note is found. If the literature in this topic increases in the future, the topic may be assigned its own number.
(C) Notes That Describe What Is Found in Other Classes	*Class-elsewhere notes* help to point the classifier to interrelated topics under which to classify the topic. *See-also references* lead the classifier to related topics that might also be considered when classifying a topic.
(D) Notes That Explain Changes or Irregularities in the Schedules and Tables	"*Revision notes* warn users that there have been changes in the subdivisions of a class since the previous edition." "*Discontinued notes* indicate that all or part of the contents of a number have been moved to a more general number in the same hierarchy, or have been dropped entirely."

Source: www.oclc.org/dewey/versions/ddc22print/intro.pdf, pp. 14–21.

Synthesis or *building* within the DDC can be necessary if the specific subject is not included in the schedules. There are four sources for building in DDC: (1) Table 1 Standard Subdivisions; (2) Tables 2–6; (3) other parts of the schedules; and (4) add tables in the schedules.

One potential difficulty of classifying using the DDC is in first locating where a subject might be located within the schedules. In the online version of the DDC one can search or browse the schedules, the relative index, or classes. For example, Figure 4.31 illustrates how this seemingly simple search resulted in 14 potential areas to classify the subject "frogs," ranging from "Frogs—resource economics," to scientific classifications of frogs, to "Frogs as pets."

Figure 4.32 traces "Frogs—resource economics" down through the hierarchical class under the 300 class for Social Science.

Figure 4.33 traces "Dendrobatidae" or poison arrow frogs down through the 500 class to its specific classification of 597.877. Note also in this instance that some scientific knowledge (specifically the scientific name of the specific frog) is required to ascertain which division and section applies. One of the benefits of an online classification tool, such as the OCLC Web Dewey online scheme, is that finding correlations among the different schemes is possible through hyperlinking.

Figures 4.34 and 4.35 illustrate linking to the OCLC's authority record for the term "Dendrobatidae" and to the LCSH listing for the term.

Library of Congress Classification

As noted in Chapters 2 and 3, the LCC began publication in 1899 and was mostly complete by 1910. The scheme contains 21 main classes that are published in over 50 volumes. The LCC is published both in print format and in an online version available through Library of Congress's subscription-based service Classification Web. LCC was primarily developed to classify the Library of Congress's collection; however, its popularity has grown and it is used in many large academic and research libraries. According to Rowley and Hartley (2008: 212),

- The LCC is clearly tailored to the needs of the Library of Congress collections.
- The order of the classes is pragmatic in nature; every class exists for a specific purpose as subject specialists perceived of its use.
- The order and classes have been developed by subject specialists to meet the needs of an exceptionally large working collection.
- Each class was compiled independently and can be used as such.
- Classes are divided in a broadly hierarchical manner with little consistent application of either hierarchies or a facet structure, even within single classes.

Figure 4.31. Results of Search in DDC for the Term "Frogs"

14 records found searching for **ri: (frogs)** in **WebDewey**

View Record **View List** 1

Search Results

1.	B	333.95789	Frogs--resource economics
2.		584.73	*Hydrocharitales
3.		597.865	*Pipoidea
4.		597.87	*Bufonoidea
5.		597.877	*Dendrobatidae (Poison arrow frogs)
6.		597.878	*Hylidae (Tree frogs)
7.		597.89	*Ranoidea
8.	B	597.890994	Frogs--Australia
9.		625.163	Turnouts and crossings
10.	B	639.3789	Frogs as pets, . . .

View Record 1 **View List** 1

Figure 4.32. "Frogs—Resource Economics" Traced

Built Class Number: 333.95789
Segmented Number: 333.95/789
Caption: Frogs--resource economics

	Main Classes
300	Social sciences
330	Economics
331-333	Economics of labor, finance, land, energy
333	Economics of land and energy
333.7-333.9	Natural resources and energy
333.9	Other natural resources
333.95	*Biological resources
333.955-333.959	Specific taxonomic groups of animals
333.957	*Reptiles and amphibians
333.9578-333.9579	Amphibians, specific reptiles
333.9578	Amphibians--resource economics
333.95789	**Frogs--resource economics**

Terms

Relative Index Terms

Frogs--resource economics

Figure 4.33. "Dendrobatidae" Traced

Class Number: 597.877
Segmented Number: 597.87/7
Caption: *Dendrobatidae (Poison arrow frogs)

	Main Classes
500	Science
579-590	Natural history of specific kinds of organisms
580-590	Plants and animals
590	Animals (Zoology)
592-599	Specific taxonomic groups of animals
597	*Cold-blooded vertebrates Pisces (Fishes)
597.8	*Amphibia (Amphibians)
597.86-597.89	Anura (Salentia)
597.87	*Bufonoidea
597.877	***Dendrobatidae (Poison arrow frogs)**

Figure 4.34. OCLC Authority File Record for "Dendrobatidae"

Roman	|	Ref status	a	Mod rec		Name use	b
Govt agn	|	Auth status	a	Subj	a	Subj use	a
Series	n	Auth/ref	a	Geo subd	i	Ser use	b
Ser num	n	Name	n	Subdiv tp	n	Rules	n

010	sh 85036706
040	DLC ‡b eng ‡c DLC ‡d DLC
053	QL668.E233 ‡c Zoology
150	Dendrobatidae
450	Arrow-poison frogs
450	Poison-arrow frogs
450	Poison-dart frogs
450	Poison frogs
550	Anura ‡w g
550	Frogs ‡w g
670	Heselhaus, R. Poison-arrow frogs, 1992 ‡b (Poison-arrow, or Poison-dart frogs, family Dendrobatidae)
670	Britannica Micro. ‡b (arrow-poison frog)

Figure 4.35. Correlation to LCSH within the OCLC Classification Web

Dendrobatidae (May Subd Geog) [R S D]
[QL668.E233 (Zoology)] [L S D]
UF Arrow-poison frogs
Poison-arrow frogs
Poison-dart frogs
Poison frogs
BT Anura
Frogs
NT Colostethus [R]
Dendrobates [R]
Phyllobates [R]

Dendrobenthamia
USE Dogwoods [R]

Dendrobium (May Subd Geog) [R S D]
[QK495.O64 (Botany)] [L S D]
[SB409.8.D45 (Culture)] [L S D]
BT Orchids

Dendrobium industry (May Subd Geog) [R S D]
[SB409] [L S D]
BT Orchid industry

Dendrobius
USE Degus [R]

Dendrocereus
USE Cereus [R]

LCC is organized into 21 main classes:

A	General Works
B	Philosophy. Psychology. Religion
C	Auxiliary Sciences of History
D	World History and History of Europe, Asia, Africa, Australia, New Zealand, etc.
E	History of The Americas
F	History of The Americas
G	Geography. Anthropology. Recreation
H	Social Sciences
J	Political Science
K	Law
L	Education
M	Music and Books on Music

N	Fine Arts
P	Language and Literature
Q	Science
R	Medicine
S	Agriculture
T	Technology
U	Military Science
V	Naval Science
Z	Bibliography. Library Science. Information Resources (General)

Unlike the symmetry present in the DDC, each class is subdivided into an irregular number of subclasses that represent the specific subject area of the main class. However, this system of subdivision allows the LCC to provide more specific and enumerative coverage of subject areas than the DDC's more rigid structure. For example, under the Q class for Science, subclasses include the following:

Subclass Q	Science (General)
Subclass QA	Mathematics Subclass
QB	Astronomy Subclass
QC	Physics Subclass
QD	Chemistry Subclass
QE	Geology Subclass
QH	Natural history – Biology Subclass
QK	Botany Subclass
QL	Zoology Subclass
QM	Human anatomy Subclass
QP	Physiology Subclass
QR	Microbiology

Under the Subclass of QL for Zoology the structure is:

- Subclass QL (QL1–991) Zoology
  - QL1–355 General—Including geographical distribution
  - QL360–599.82 Invertebrates
    - QL461–599.82 Insects
  - QL605–739.8 Chordates. Vertebrates
    - QL614–639.8 Fishes
    - QL640–669.3 Reptiles and amphibians
    - QL671–699 Birds
    - QL700–739.8 Mammals
  - QL750–795 Animal behavior
    - QL791–795 Stories and anecdotes
  - QL799–799.5 Morphology
  - QL801–950.9 Anatomy
  - QL951–991 Embryology

Unlike the DDC, LCC makes little use of Notes within the schedules. Notation using LCC requires less synthesis than the DDC because of the more specific nature of the scheme. For example, the LCC classification for the subject "Dendrobatidae" is **QL668.E233**. Figure 4.36 traces this term through LCC's class structure. This figure also illustrates the depth of classification possible with LCC. For example, LCC shows the classifications for 25 specific species of frogs, whereas DDC includes broad categories of frogs and only specifically classifies a few species. More specific classification is also possible by using a series of tables but only when instructed to do so by directions within the schedule. Use of the Library of Congress's Cutter table also provides for more specific classification if needed for geographic location, topical subdivisions, chronological periods, and names. Guidelines for application of Cutter numbers are provided in the *Subject Cataloging Manual: Shelflisting*.

Colon Classification Scheme

The CC is a faceted classification scheme developed by S.R. Ranganathan and published in 1933. The sixth edition was published in 1963 and represented Ranganathan's continued refinement of the original scheme. Each class is broken down into its basic elements based on specific characteristics, called *facets*. Ranganathan (1967) identified five fundamental categories, referred to as PMEST:

- P (Personality)—the focal or most specific subject
- M (Material or Matter)—a component
- E (Energy)—an activity, operation, or process
- S (Space)—a specific or generic place or location, and
- T (Time)—a chronological period, year, a season, etc. (Taylor and Joudrey, 2009: 387)

Figure 4.36. Classification of "Dendrobatidae" in LCC

Zoology--Chordates. Vertebrates--Reptiles and amphibians--Systematic divisions--Amphibians--By order and family, A-Z--Ecaudata (Anura; Salientia; frogs; toads)--Dendrobatidae

QL668.E22	Atelopodidae [H R L D S]
QL668.E224	Bombinatoridae [H R L D S]
QL668.E225	Brevicipitidae [H R L D S]
QL668.E227	Bufonidae (Toads) [H R L D S]
QL668.E23	Centrolenidae (Glass frogs) [H R L D S]
QL668.E233	Dendrobatidae [H R L D S]
QL668.E235	Discoglossidae [H R L D S]
QL668.E24	Hylidae (Tree frogs) [H R L D S]
QL668.E244	Hyperoliidae [H R L D S]
QL668.E255	Leiopelmatidae [H R L D S]
QL668.E257	Leptodactylidae (Robber frogs) [H R L D S]

Table 4.3 provides the 21 main classes of the CC.

Notation using CC, according to Lois Mai Chan (2007: 433), is "extremely mixed and complex. It combines Arabic numerals, capital and lower case letters, some Greek letters, brackets, and certain punctuation marks." In formulating a class number, certain punctuation marks are used as facet indicators to show the nature of the element being presented, for example, the (,) is the connecting symbol for the Personality facet; the (;) is the connecting symbol for the Matter facet; the (:) is the connecting symbol for the Energy facet; the (.) is the connecting symbol for the Space facet; and the (') is the connecting symbol for the Time facet. Construction of a classification notation using CC is a very complex task and results in a lengthy, often unwieldy notation, as this example from Chan (2007: 435) illustrates:

> Research in the cure of the tuberculosis of lungs by X-Ray, conducted in India in 1950's results in a notation of: L,45;421:6;253:f.44'N5. The CC classification breaks down to:

Table 4.3. Colon Classification Classes

z Generalia	HX Mining
1 Universe of Knowledge	I Botany
2 Library science	J Agriculture
3 Book science	K Zoology *(same facet schedule as I Botany)*
4 Journalism	L Medicine *[organ]:[problem],[cause]:[handling]*
B Mathematics	M Useful arts
C Physics	N Fine arts
D Engineering	O Literature
E Chemistry	P Linguistics
F Technology	Q Religion
G Biology	R Philosophy
H Geology	S Psychology
H1 Mineralogy	T Education
H2 Petrology	U Geography
H3 Structural Geology	V History
H4 Dynamic Geology	W Political science
H5 Stratigraphy	X Economics
H6 Paleontology	Y Sociology
H7 Economic Geology	Z Law
H8 Cosmic Hypothesis	

Source: Ranganathan, 1967.

L	Medicine
45	Lungs
421	Tuberculosis
6	Treatment
253	X-Ray
f	Research
44	India
N5	1950

While not widely used for physical classification within libraries, the CC scheme has served as the basis for classification schemes developed by e-commerce.

Knowledge Structures within Social Sciences

Structures for representing knowledge within the social sciences are more of an ad hoc or informal nature than those utilized by either natural science or library and information science disciplines. However, that said, some taxonomies developed within social science contexts have stood the test of time and have been revised to adapt to new understandings by the discipline. For example, a well-known taxonomy in education is Bloom's Taxonomy of Educational Objectives (Bloom's Taxonomy) developed by Bloom in 1956. This taxonomy is a hierarchical structure representing six levels of thinking and learning skills that range from basic learning objectives such as knowledge of content through higher-order learning such as synthesis, evaluation, and creativity. Bloom's Taxonomy formed the basis for early work on the development of instructional objectives for classes and curricula (Bloom and Krathwohl, 1956). Figure 4.37 shows the conceptual representation of Bloom's Taxonomy.

The original taxonomy has been revised to reflect new understandings within the discipline related to cognitive domains; the effect of affective domain on learning; and the psychomotor domain effect on skill acquisition. Figure 4.38 shows the revision by Krathwohl, Bloom, and Masia (1964) to incorporate the effect of the affective domain into the original taxonomy.

Structures for organizing knowledge within the social sciences include informal classification schemes, typologies, and taxonomies that represent data gathered within specific scientific studies and within very specialized contexts. Kenneth Bailey (1994: 5–10) identifies the following forms of classification used within social sciences:

1. **Conceptual classification**—a typology or taxonomy used to represent type concepts rather than empirical cases.
2. **Taxonomies**—used in this context to represent empirical entities, most often used by ethnologists or ethnobotanists.
3. **Numerical taxonomy** (quantitative classification)—usually a computerized method for constructing taxonomies, including for example, cluster analysis and pattern analysis.

Figure 4.37. Bloom's Taxonomy

Source: Bloom and Krathwohl (1956: 19); www.techdis.ac.uk/resources/files/Blooms%20taxonomy.png.

Figure 4.38. Bloom's Taxonomy Revised to Illustrate Affective Domain

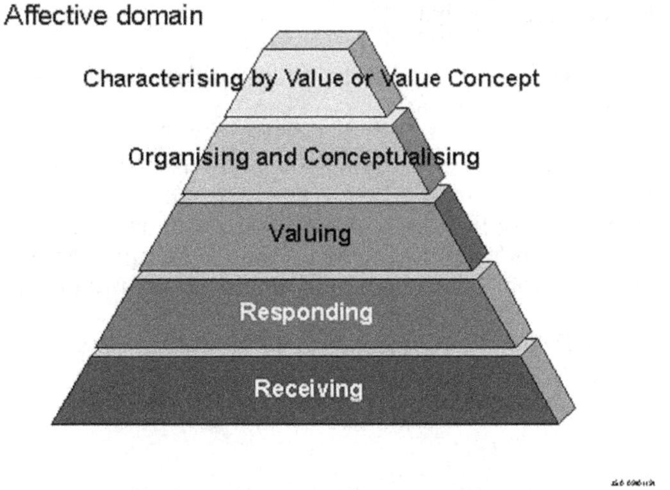

Source: Krathwohl, Bloom, and Masia (1964: 35); www2.selu.edu/Academics/Faculty/rhancock/bloomaff.gif.

4. **Synchronic classification**—most classification in social science is synchronic or cross-sectional, meaning it occurs at a single point in time.
5. **Diachronic classification**—classification of relationships shown over a period of time. Phyletic relationships, such as those shown in studies related to evolution, are diachronic.

Classification within the social sciences serves a management function but also, more importantly, a descriptive function. While developing classifications, typologies, and taxonomies allows social scientists to manage huge amounts of data, an additional very important role for classification, the research utility of classification, should not be downplayed. According to Kenneth Bailey (1994: 12–15) advantages of classification include the following:

1. Description—provides a researcher with exhaustive means to represent arrays of types or taxa present in the study data.
2. Reduced complexity—taxonomies and typologies allow huge masses of data to be condensed into small numbers of types or taxa.
3. Classification allows researchers to recognize similarities among cases and to group similar cases together for analysis.
4. Classification allows researchers to recognize dissimilarities among cases and to group similar cases together for analysis.
5. Representation of an exhaustive set of dimensions on which types are based.
6. Comparisons of typologies and taxa.
7. Inventory and management of types.
8. Display of relationships in the data which potentially leads to hypotheses about these relationships.

Some of Bailey's (1994: 15–16) disadvantages of classification within the social sciences include the following:

1. They *are* descriptive, rather than explanatory or nonexplanatory. Some researchers tend to stereotype the descriptive nature of classification in negative terms, rather than understand its necessity related to explanation.
2. Classification may be static rather than dynamic. Many research approaches in social science are synchronic (static) rather than diachronic (dynamic).
3. Unmanageability—classifications may be unmanageable and not useful for very large, complex data sets.
4. Typologies are often dependent upon the logic of classes, rather than using continuous data.

Knowledge structures within the social sciences therefore serve a management role, but also a descriptive function, providing researchers with a framework for displaying, filtering, and organizing data for analysis and synthesis. The structures used include mechanisms developed in an ad hoc basis for a specific study or data analysis, for example, typologies or taxonomies developed by anthropologists to represent the basic-level terms used by a population to name plants and animals in their environment (folk classification). Conceptual classification is necessary for both its descriptive and explanatory functions. While knowledge structures are of a more informal nature in the social sciences, there are long-standing taxonomies (e.g., Bloom's Taxonomy) that have utility beyond the original use.

Conclusion

This chapter presented an overview of the knowledge structures in use within a sample of academic disciplines, including biology, zoology, library and information science, and social science. Specific examples of knowledge structures illustrated the principle functions and the roles the structures play within the discipline. Examples of how the knowledge structures have translated into applications available in the digital environment were also presented to add to our understanding of how digital knowledge structures provide new avenues for research and education within the disciplines, provide global solutions for the dissemination of ideas, and enable more widespread access to collections, thereby ensuring more collaboration within and across disciplines.

In the next chapter our focus will shift to exploring how people organize their personal spaces and the knowledge structures they develop in order to function effectively in personal and work-related situations.

Thought Exercises

1. Compare and contrast the principle functions for knowledge structures within academic disciplines. Give specific examples. Take into consideration what each discipline could learn from the other's use of knowledge structures.
2. Do you think that knowledge structures used and developed by the different disciplines have changed much through the years? Explain your answer. What changes do you think are needed that have NOT occurred?
3. Brainstorm the advantages and disadvantages of developing digital knowledge structures. Make a list of all of the advantages/disadvantages and then note how the digital environment has added to/detracted from the traditional knowledge structure.
4. Controlled vocabularies and classification schemes have been developed to aid users in finding information. Write about the last time you looked for information. Give details about (1) purpose of the search, (2) which systems you used, (3) what knowledge structures were used by the systems, and (4) any knowledge structures you used to aid in your searching. Ex-

plain your answer in depth, keeping in mind the functions of bibliographic subject access tools (controlled vocabularies and classification schemes).

References

Abbas, June. 2005. "Creating Metadata for Children's Resources: Issues, Research, and Current Developments." *Library Trends* 54, no. 2: 303–317.

"Approved Lists of Bacterial Names." 1980. *International Journal of Systematic Biology* 30: 225–420.

Bailey, Kenneth D. 1994. *Typologies and Taxonomies: An Introduction to Classification Techniques*. Thousand Oaks, CA: Sage.

Bloom, B.S., and D.R. Krathwohl. 1956. *Taxonomy of Educational Objectives: The Classification of Educational Goals by a Committee of College and University Examiners. Handbook I: Cognitive Domain.* New York: Longman, Green.

Botanicus. "About." 2009. Available: www.botanicus.org/about.aspx (accessed June 4, 2010).

Chan, Lois Mai. 2005. *Library of Congress Subject Headings: Principles and Application*. Westport, CT: Libraries Unlimited.

———. 2007. *Cataloging and Classification: An Introduction*. Lanham, MD: Scarecrow Press.

Classification Bank. 2009. "Introduction—ClassificationBank." Available: www.ubio.org/index.php?pagename=clsbank (accessed June 7, 2010).

Cutter, Charles A. 1904. *Rules for a Dictionary Catalog*, 4th ed., reprinted 1962. Washington, DC: Government Printing Office.

DDC. "Introduction." Available: www.oclc.org/dewey/versions/ddc22print/intro.pdf (accessed June 4, 2010).

Dublin Core Metadata Initiative. 2009. "Dublin." Dublin Core Metadata Initiative. Available: dublincore.org (accessed June 4, 2010).

EOL. 2009a. "FAQs." Available: eol.org/content/page/faqs (accessed June 4, 2010).

———. 2009b. "Help Build EOL." Available: eol.org/content/page/help_build_eol (accessed June 4, 2010).

GBIF. 2009a. "About." Available: www.gbif.org/index.php?id=269 (accessed June 4, 2010).

———. 2009b. "Data Portal." Available: data.gbif.org/welcome.htm (accessed May 13, 2010).

Hoerman, Heidi Lee, and Kevin A. Furniss. 2000. "Turning Practice into Principles: A Comparison of the IFLA *Principles Underlying Subject Heading Languages (SHLs)* and the Principles Underlying the *Library of Congress Subject Headings* System." *Cataloging & Classification Quarterly* 29, no. 1/2: 31–52.

Hulme, E.W. 1911. "Principles of Book Classification." *Library Association Record* 13: 354–358.

International Association for Plant Taxonomy. 2006a. "Preamble." In *International Code of Botanical Nomenclature Online*. Vienna: International Association for Plant Taxonomy. Available: ibot.sav.sk/icbn/no%20frames/00003Pre.htm (accessed June 4, 2010).

———. 2006b. "Principles." In *International Code of Botanical Nomenclature Online*. Vienna: International Association for Plant Taxonomy. Available: ibot.sav.sk/icbn/no%20frames/Contents.htm (accessed June 4, 2010).

International Commission on Zoological Nomenclature. 1999. "Preamble." In *International Code of Zoological Nomenclature*. Canberra, Australia: International Commis-

sion on Zoological Nomenclature. Available: www.iczn.org/iczn/index.jsp?nfv=true&booksection=preamble (accessed June 4, 2010).
International Society for Horticultural Science. 2009. *International Code of Nomenclature for Cultivated Plants*. Available: www.ishs.org/sci/icracpco.htm (accessed June 4, 2010).
International Union of Microbiological Societies. 1992. "Principles." In *International Code of Nomenclature of Bacteria*. Available: www.ncbi.nlm.nih.gov/bookshelf/br.fcgi?book=icnb&part=A717 (accessed June 4, 2010).
ISAD. 2000. *General International Standard Archival Description*. Ottawa: International Council on Archives.
Krathwohl, D.R., B.S. Bloom, and B.B. Masia. 1964. *Taxonomy of Educational Objectives. The Classification of Educational Goals—Handbook II: Affective Domain*. New York: McKay.
Lancaster, Frederick, W. 1986. *Vocabulary Control for Information Retrieval*, 2nd ed. Arlington, VA: Information Resources Press.
LINNE. "Introduction." 2009. Available: www.flmnh.ufl.edu/linne (accessed June 4, 2010).
LSID. "Homepage." 2009. Available: lsids.sourceforge.net (accessed June 4, 2010).
Mayr, Ernst, and Peter D. Ashlock. 1991. *Principles of Systematic Zoology*. New York: McGraw-Hill.
McNeill, John, and Nicholas Turland. 2006. "Preface." In *International Code of Botanical Nomenclature Online*. Vienna: International Association for Plant Taxonomy. Available: ibot.sav.sk/icbn/no%20frames/00002Preface.htm (accessed June 4, 2010).
Miksa, Francis. 1983. *The Subject in the Dictionary Catalog from Cutter to the Present*. Chicago: American Library Association.
Miller, J. 1998. "Sears List of Subject Headings." In *Cataloging Correctly for Kids: An Introduction to the Tools*, 3rd ed. (pp. 67–70), edited by S. Zuiderveld. Chicago: American Library Association.
NameBank. "Introduction—NameBank Separates Fact from Fiction." Available: www.ubio.org/index.php?pagename=nb_facts_opinions (accessed June 7, 2010).
NCD. "Homepage." 2009. Available: www.tdwg.org/activities/ncd (accessed June 4, 2010).
Pyle, Richard. 2009. *ZooBank User's Instruction Guide*. International Trust for Zoological Nomenclature. Available: zoobank.org/docs/ZooBankInstructions.pdf (accessed June 7, 2010).
Pyle, Richard L., and Ellinor Michel. 2008. "ZooBank: Developing a Nomenclatural Tool for Unifying 250 Years of Biological Information." *Zootaxa* 1950: 39–50.
Ranganathan, S.R. 1967. *Prolegomena to Library Classification*, 3rd. ed. London: Asia Publishing House.
Ride, W.D.L. 1999. "Introduction." In *International Code of Zoological Nomenclature*. Canberra, Australia: International Commission on Zoological Nomenclature. Available: www.iczn.org/iczn/index.jsp?nfv=true&booksection=introduction (accessed June 7, 2010).
Rowley, Jennifer, and Richard Hartley. 2008. *Organizing Knowledge: An Introduction to Managing Access to Information*, 4th ed. Burlington, VT: Ashgate.
Sneath, P.H.A. 2003. "A Short History of the Bacteriological Code." International Committee on Systematics of Prokaryotes. Available: www.the-icsp.org/misc/Code_history.htm (accessed June 7, 2010).
Speers, Larry, and James L. Edwards. 2008. "International Infrastructure for Enabling the New Taxonomy: The Role of the Global Biodiversity Information Facility

(GBIF)." In *The New Taxonomy* (pp. 87–94), edited by Quentin D. Wheeler. Boca Raton, FL: Taylor & Francis Group.
Taylor, Arlene, G., and Daniel N. Joudrey. 2009. *The Organization of Information*, 3rd ed. Westport, CT: Libraries Unlimited.
TDWG. "Darwin Core." 2009a. Available: www.tdwg.org/standards/450 (accessed June 7, 2010).
———. "Homepage." 2009b. Available: www.tdwg.org/about-tdwg (accessed June 7, 2010).
Towsey, M. 1999. "Subject Headings for Children." *Catalogue and Index* 131: 9–10.
Wilson, E.O. 2003. "The Encyclopedia of Life." *Trends in Ecology and Evolution* 18: 77–80. Available: eol.org/content/page/article_eol_wilson_2003 (accessed June 7, 2010).
Wilson, Patrick. 1983. "The Catalog as Access Mechanism: Background and Concepts." *Library Resources & Technical Services* 27 (January): 4–17.
ZooBank. 2009. "Instruction Guide for ZooBank Web Interface." Available: www.zoobank.org/docs/ZooBankInstructions.pdf (accessed June 7, 2010).

Websites Noted in Text

ClassificationBank. Available: www.ubio.org/index.php?pagename=clsbank (accessed June 7, 2010).
Department of Education. 2009. *Thesaurus of ERIC Descriptors*. Available: www.eric.ed.gov (accessed June 7, 2010).
Encyclopedia of Life. Available: eol.org (accessed June 7, 2010).
GBIF. Available: www.gbif.org (accessed June 7, 2010).
GBIF Data Portal. Available: data.gbif.org/welcome.htm (accessed June 7, 2010).
International Society for Horticultural Science. 2009. *International Code of Nomenclature for Cultivated Plants*. Available: www.ishs.org/sci/icracpco.htm (accessed June 7, 2010).
ITIS. Available: www.itis.gov (accessed June 7, 2010).
J. Paul Getty Trust. *Art & Architecture Thesaurus* (AAT). Available: www.getty.edu/research/conducting_research/vocabularies/aat (accessed June 7, 2010).
Library of Congress. 1995. *Thesaurus for Graphic Materials I: Subject Terms*. Available: www.loc.gov/rr/print/tgm1 (accessed June 7, 2010).
———. 2003. Understanding MARC Bibliographic: Machine Readable Cataloging. Available: www.loc.gov/marc/umb (accessed June 7, 2010).
———. 2004. Understanding MARC Authority Records: Machine Readable Cataloging. Available: www.loc.gov/marc/uma (accessed June 7, 2010).
———. 2009. *Acquisitions and Bibliographic Access Directorate*. Available: www.loc.gov/aba/cataloging/subject/weeklylists (accessed June 7, 2010).
———. 2010. MARC 21 Format for Bibliographic Data. Available: www.loc.gov/marc/bibliographic (accessed June 7, 2010).
NameBank. Available: www.ubio.org/index.php?pagename=nb_facts_opinions (accessed June 7, 2010).
National Library of Medicine. 2009. *Medical Subject Headings*. Available: www.nlm.nih.gov/mesh/meshhome.html (accessed June 7, 2010).
Official Lists and Indexes of Names in Zoology. 2009. Available: www.nhm.ac.uk/hosted_sites/iczn/lists&indexes.pdf (accessed June 7, 2010).
TDWG. 2009a. Available: www.tdwg.org (accessed June 7, 2010).

———. 2009b. "Biodiversity Information Projects of the World Database." Available: www.tdwg.org/biodiv-projects/projects-database (accessed June 7, 2010).

ZooBank. 2009. Available: www.zoobank.org/Default.aspx (accessed June 7, 2010).

Part II

Personal Structures for Organizing Knowledge

5

Structures for Organizing Knowledge in Personal and Professional Contexts

Focus Points

- How do people "naturally" organize knowledge in their personal spaces?
- How do people organize knowledge in professional spaces?
- What forms of knowledge organizing structures are used in both contexts?
- What role(s)/functions do structures for organizing knowledge play in both personal and professional contexts?
- How can we apply what we know about personal and professional structures for organizing knowledge into designing formal knowledge organizing structures?

Introduction and Scope of the Chapter

In Chapter 4 the formal and informal structures for organizing knowledge within a diverse sample of academic disciplines, as well as the principles underlying the development of the structures and their practical applications, were examined. While the structures for organizing knowledge within each discipline contain some commonalities, it is also evident that each structure is designed with a particular use and specific user community in mind. In this chapter, we will shift focus away from the academic use and development of structures for organizing knowledge and will begin to explore how lay people organize knowledge in both personal and professional contexts. Chapter 5 will address these questions:

1. How do we organize knowledge in our personal and professional contexts so that it makes sense and is useful?

2. What forms of knowledge-organizing structures are used in personal and professional contexts, and do differences or similarities exist within the form(s) and use(s) within these two contexts?
3. What role(s) do categories, ontologies, taxonomies, and other structures play in the process of organizing?
4. What do we need to know (and what do we *already* know) about human information interactions and organizing behaviors in order to design useful structures for organizing knowledge?

To explore these questions, Chapter 5 is organized into two sections: the first focuses on structures for organizing knowledge within personal contexts, and the second focuses on professional contexts, such as the workplace. Each section includes an examination of the areas of research that can help us better understand how people organize their personal and professional spaces. From the research, we can begin to identify the forms being used as well as the roles or functions they provide in organizing knowledge.

Knowledge Structures and Knowledge Spaces within Personal Contexts

Defining Personal Knowledge Spaces

Let's begin this section with a thought exercise. Take a moment and think about the knowledge that you use in your everyday life. Now focus this exploration on only your personal, nonwork-related knowledge use and personal knowledge spaces. What kinds of objects (either in a physical form or in a mental representation) do you include? What forms do they take? Say, for example, you consider your personal knowledge space as your home office. What knowledge-bearing objects do you organize, store, and use in your daily life? *How* is this knowledge organized, stored, or used? What role does each play? Your home office probably has a computer that holds files of both personal and professional (work-related) nature. These files might be organized in folders on your desktop for easy access or on your computer hard drive. The files may contain personal letters, picture collections, music libraries, to-do lists, craft projects, home contacts, and documents generated to keep your personal life organized, such as tax documents, bills to pay, passwords to access online accounts, etc. Your computer might also have a calendar function and an e-mail program that contains e-mail messages arranged individually or in folders. The files might have been generated by you or by many others in your household.

You might also have shelves of books in your home office that are related to work or to personal interests or that are part of a larger personal collection. Your knowledge space might also include a filing cabinet that holds records necessary for keeping your personal life organized, including, for example, files containing receipts of bills paid, product information, documents that show achievements of your family members, contact lists, warranties, bank statements, medical records and receipts, pension and retirement information, children's art projects, school report cards, and vehicle registration, insurance, and maintenance schedules. The walls of your home office might have calendars, dry erase boards, bulletin boards, announcements, schedules, or messages to remind you of something posted on them.

Now let's expand this knowledge space out beyond the confines of the office walls into the rest of the house. You might have additional collections of books housed within the rooms they are used in, such as cookbooks in the kitchen, children's books in the family room or library, or personal collections of books within each family member's room. Along with books, you might have collections of other sorts, such as music and movie collections in various formats and on multiple genres, and photograph collections. Your personal collections might also include clothes in the closets, artifacts found while excavating the local quarry for fossils, antiques collected and inherited from others, knickknacks given as gifts, tools for various home improvement projects or gardening, and stores of other items in the attic or basement.

All of these items may not seem to be knowledge-bearing objects at first, but, when considered as a whole, they all represent the knowledge of the individual and/or the members of the household collectively. In Chapter 1, knowledge was defined as the resulting product of the processing of information through synthesis, internalization, analysis, and reduction. In addition, Rowley and Hartley (2008: 6) point to the "added ingredients" many authors include as necessary in the processing of information into knowledge, including (1) contextual information, values, experiences, and rules; (2) perception, skills, training, common sense, and experience; (3) information, expert opinion, skills, and experience; and (4) information combined with understanding and capability. Plotkin's (1994) view holds that "knowledge is what gives our lives order and that 'knowing is living and surviving'" (as cited by O'Connor, Kearns, and Anderson, 2008: 8–9). The "user template of meaning or understanding" proposed by O'Connor, Kearns, and Anderson can be used to characterize the personal knowledge store or knowledge space of an individual (or household). The information objects contained in the personal space combined represent the personal knowledge of the individual. Each user's template is "constructed by a complex network of experiences, ideas, images, emotions, and knowledge" (O'Connor, Kearns, and Anderson, 2008: 18). The template also is constructed with the tacit knowledge of individuals of the intentional process or procedures they have set up to encounter information, such as monitoring specific newspapers, browsing the new nonfiction shelf at the library, signing up for e-mail alerts from websites, etc. (personal communication with B.C. O'Connor, December 2, 2009).

Each of the objects in the personal collections, whether housed in physical or digital form, is an artifact of a person's life. These artifacts were created or gathered because of a specific situation or experience, and there might be emotions or memories associated with them. Each serves a role or function in the personal context, and the artifacts are organized and maintained so that each can be referred to as needed to keep individuals informed, to entertain, as reminders or remembrances, or to just conduct life's daily activities. For the purposes of this chapter's exploration, the resulting personal collection described in the earlier scenario is defined as a *personal knowledge space.* Figure 5.1 illustrates this idea further.

Research Focused on Personal Knowledge Organization

Research that informs us about personal knowledge spaces and the structures used to organize the knowledge or information within them is limited. Few studies have focused on personal knowledge organization spaces in the home environment. The majority of work has explored personal knowledge organization in work-related contexts. Because of the nascent nature of research on personal knowledge spaces, it is not possible to determine if personal knowl-

Figure 5.1. Representation of Personal Knowledge Space

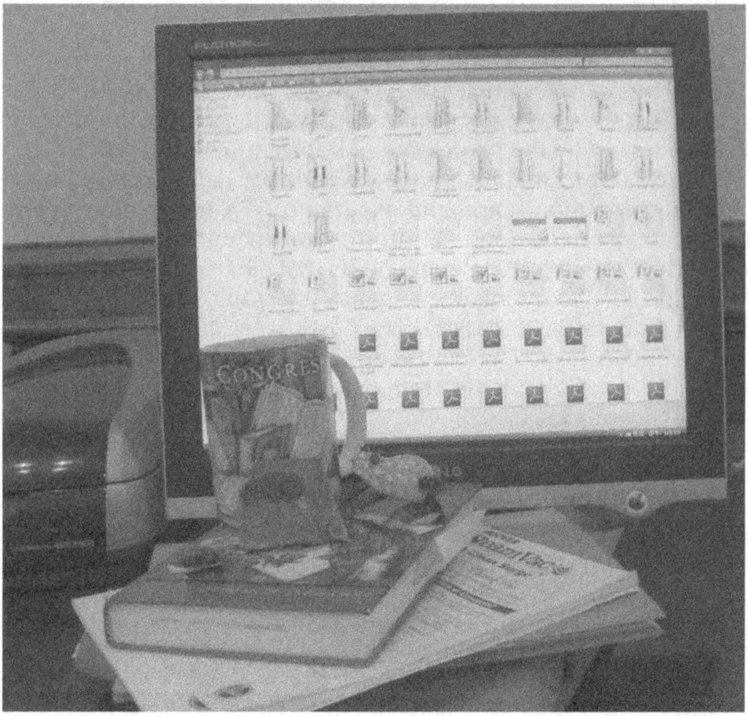

edge organization in nonwork-related contexts mirrors that of work-related contexts. With these limitations in mind, for the purposes of this exploration, home and work-related environments will be addressed separately.

Four primary areas of research have addressed the issue of how people organize their personal information. These areas include research focused on (1) human information behavior (HIB), (2) knowledge organization and classification (KO), (3) human–computer interaction (HCI), and (4) personal information management (PIM).

Tom Wilson (2000: 49) defined information behavior as "the totality of human behavior in relation to sources and channels of information, including both active and passive information seeking and information sharing, and use of information." Studies related to how people seek or search for information (referred to as "information-seeking studies") are an area of HIB research that potentially can add to our understanding of how people organize their personal knowledge spaces. According to Donald Case (2006), between January 2001 and December 2004, more than 2,000 potentially relevant studies related to HIB were published in the field of library and information science. Case (2002: 295) presents a useful framework for understanding the breadth and depth as well as diversity of research covered by HIB researchers:

- Information seekers by occupation (e.g., scientists, managers)
- Information seekers by role (e.g., patient or student)
- Information seekers by demographics (e.g., by age or ethnic group)
- Theories, models, and methods used to study information seekers.

Using this framework, it is evident that studies about information seeking tend to focus on the range of technologies (analog and digital) used by specific users in defined contexts as they seek information to satisfy an information need. However, information-seeking research is not necessarily focused on *how* people organize the information once they find it. For this reason, information-seeking studies will not be addressed here unless relevant to how people organize information once found. Furthermore, HIB studies have focused on personal knowledge spaces in the *work environment* rather than in the home, and no parallels between home and work environments have been proposed. As a result, the studies from HIB will be discussed in the section focused on knowledge organization in professional contexts.

Knowledge organization (KO) research focuses on, for the most part, understanding the effectiveness of structures for organizing knowledge (such as controlled vocabularies and ontologies, metadata schemes and database and/or XML field structures, and classification schemes or taxonomies) for helping people find information resources. One area of focus within KO research has sought to understand specific work-related domains or communities of practice within which people conduct work and how knowledge organization systems should be structured for discovery of knowledge resources in order to facilitate the work process. Other areas within KO research focus on the effectiveness of interactions between people and existing structures for organizing knowledge (MARC records, Dewey Decimal and Library of Congress Classification schemes, subject headings, etc.) within library contexts. While KO practitioners and researchers have been developing knowledge structures for many years (as examined in earlier chapters), there exists a very small body of research that has investigated users' success in using these structures to find information and knowledge resources. The goal of KO research is to inform the development of standards for representation of objects within systems, but also the design of those structures themselves.

Research into the interaction between people and computers (referred to as "human–computer interaction" [HCI]) is an interdisciplinary approach from both information science and computer science that can also help us understand more about how people organize their personal and professional knowledge spaces. More specifically, personal information management (PIM) is an intersection of library and information science, cognitive psychology, HCI, database management, and information retrieval. PIM has been characterized as the methods by which individuals handle, categorize, and retrieve information (Thomas, Meech, and Macredie, 1996). PIM has further been defined as

> both the practice and the study of the activities people perform to acquire, organize, maintain, retrieve, use, and control the distribution of information items such as documents (paper-based and digital), Web pages, and email messages for everyday use to complete tasks (work-related and not) and to fulfill a person's various roles (as parent, employee, friend, member of community, etc.). (Jones and Teevan, 2007: 3)

Research in PIM has focused on both paper-based and digital-based information that people acquire, organize, and maintain. The organization of work-related paper files in file cabinets and bookcases and on desktops has been explored by a few, as will be outlined later in the section on structures for organizing professional knowledge spaces. PIM research related to digital information organization has focused on (1) how files are organized on work computers, (2) how e-mail is organized to enable refinding and use, and (3) how people organize web-based information, such as websites and bookmarks.

The general goal of HCI and PIM research is to improve on, or to design, more user-centered technologies that can be used in either everyday personal or professional contexts. Even in the rich research area of PIM, little empirical research has been conducted into *how* people organize their paper-based and digital information (empirical studies). Much of the literature cites earlier studies, most conducted with small sample sizes, and then presents a new prototype the authors have designed or the results of the use of the new prototype (prototypical design) (Boardman and Sasse, 2004). The latter of these two types of studies does little to increase our understanding of how people organize information in knowledge spaces beyond explaining how a small sample of individuals use the specific prototype. The following section will present research findings from KO, HCI, and PIM as related to the organization of personal nonwork-related knowledge spaces.

Organization of Personal Knowledge Spaces in the Home Environment

Brush and colleagues (2005: 2035) emphasize the importance of the "home" as an environment to study. They point out that one aspect of home life that is understudied is the "considerable time and effort put into the practical business of managing and running a household's events, movements, routines, etc." Furthermore, "'Home,' as it were, transcends place and involves an amalgam of activities. . . . '[H]ome' exists in the so very mundane grocery-shopping lists pinned to bulletin boards and used while at the store. Even the quick call to the plumber, while at work, falls under the auspices of 'home'" (Brush et al., 2005: 2036). O'Brien and Rodden (2000: 293) point out that "households incorporate domestic technologies into the complex set of routines, rights, and obligations constituted in and through the social organization of the household; indeed we find that these technologies are *accommodated* within this social organization."

Reviewing the research related to organization of personal knowledge spaces in the home environment, two central themes are present: (1) group social dynamics present in the home and the artifacts developed to assist in organizing activities (also of interest is the role these artifacts play in the social order of the family); and (2) specific forms of collections within the home environment and the structures used to organize the collections. Research in this area has also begun looking at why people keep specific types of collections, e.g., photo collections, and the role this keeping plays.

In home and work-related contexts, researchers use methods adapted from anthropology, for instance, ethnographic approaches (such as participant observation, interviews, keeping diaries of interactions within the research environment) to study individual and group knowledge organization. It is also important to note that the research has focused primarily on the family as a unit of analysis rather than on single-person households.

Artifacts and Collections as Structures for Organizing Knowledge

From our thought exercise earlier, it is evident that many different artifacts (organizing structures) are developed in the course of organizing personal knowledge spaces. Artifacts might include, for example, to-do lists, grocery lists, calendars, white erase boards of activities, files of papers or digital files, notebooks of events, and phone numbers. The artifacts that are used to organize a household can be both rudimentary and complex. They can be paper based or digital. They can be ad hoc, or they can be what Alex Taylor and Laurel Swan (2005: 642) refer to as "artful design," meaning that the artifacts continually are redesigned to fit the role they play, but also to integrate with other artifacts, or "organizing systems" (Taylor and Swan, 2005: 641) of the home as needed. Crabtree, Hemmings, and Rodden (2002) and Crabtree and Rodden (2004) have uncovered patterns of domestic routines within the home by studying what they refer to as "activity centers," such as kitchen tables where homework is done, the week's menu is planned, or family schedules are reviewed and put onto a calendar; or the locations where mail is handled and distributed. Learning the domestic routines has enabled them to make suggestions for where to situate technology within the home and to determine how to integrate technology with the existing organizing structures used by the family.

A small body of research has examined the artifacts produced to organize a home environment. Artifacts studied include calendars, charts, notebooks, notice boards, and lists used by families.

Calendaring Systems

Crabtree, Hemmings, and Mariani (2003) and Plaisant and colleagues (2006) have examined the forms and roles that calendaring systems play in domestic routines. Plaisant and colleagues (2006), in preparation for developing a calendaring system, surveyed 401 individuals about their use of calendars and found that most participants used more than one calendar, with only 17 percent using only one calendar. Many users share multiple calendars with others and use computer or PDA calendars, but paper-based calendars are still heavily used. Also of interest was that the majority of sharing took place with others in their household. Some of the most common problems with using calendars people reported include that they had too many calendars to maintain, that synchronizing their contents was difficult, and that the calendar did not have not enough space to write all of their notes (Plaisant et al., 2006: 323).

Lists, Charts, Notebooks, and Notice Boards

Taylor and Swan (2004, 2005) used case studies to explore the development, forms, and roles that lists (to-do lists, task or chore lists, grocery lists, etc.), charts, notebooks, and notice boards have within organizing structures of the home. Taylor and Swan's work illustrates the importance of lists as structures for organizing knowledge in the home. They view lists, charts, and notice boards as "central to the complex and dynamic arrangements involved in organizing the home" (Taylor and Swan, 2004: 542). These artifacts not only help organize, plan, and coordinate the complex activities, tasks, and routines of the multiple people of the home but they also serve as navigation devices, spatial maps, and schedules. They play a central role in keeping a family organized and outlining social order and responsibility. Taylor and Swan's research confirms findings by Crabtree and Rodden regarding the importance of "activity centers" and the artifacts used in conjunction with these centers. They observed the various and ingenious ways that lists, charts, notebooks, and notice boards were used and organized. A summary of their general findings follows:

- Structures for organizing activities need to be flexible and "artful," meaning they can be easily adapted to fit the needs of the family, as well as take into account the limitations and affordances of their physical media.
- These structures must also be easily integrated into other "organizing systems" present in the home, such as activity centers.

- Organizing structures are not static and are continually being redesigned to fit the changing needs of the family.
- These structures were very personalized, idiosyncratic, and people go to great lengths to devise their own organizing structures. (Taylor and Swan, 2005: 647)

Unfortunately research centered in the home has not yet explored other artifacts of personal knowledge organization spaces, such as files housed either in file cabinets or on computers, with the exception of the Williams, John, and Rowland (2009) study outlined in the next section. Also, how people organize, use, and keep digital photograph collections is an area of interest that is receiving more attention currently. What is known about personal file organization is in the context of the workplace (e.g., Malone, 1983; Case, 1986; Kwasnik, 1989; Mander, Salomon, and Wong, 1992) and will be presented in the section on personal organization in professional contexts.

Digital Files

Little published research examines how personal digital files are organized in the home environment. Research has instead focused on organization of personal files in the workplace. As noted earlier, it is not clear if parallels can be made between home and work-related organization of knowledge, which necessitates the need for study in the home environment. The area of personal information management within personal digital collections is gaining much interest. In the context of a study to learn more about how people develop, organize, and maintain personal collections, Williams, John, and Rowland (2009) and Williams and colleagues (2008) describe their Digital Lives project, an ongoing research project in the United Kingdom that is examining the personal and work-related digital collection building and digital collections of various professionals, including politicians, architects, authors, playwrights, scientists, knowledge managers, lecturers, and digital artists. Using a "digital information cycle" approach to exploring the development, use, organization, and maintenance of digital information, Williams, John, and Rowland (2009: 348–356) outline these phases of the digital information cycle:

- **Obtaining information**: actively seeking it; passively seeking or receiving it; actively creating it themselves; and passive creation of information
- **Information creation**: socialization from individual or group interaction; externalization of information; combination from separate explicit knowledge and systemic explicit knowledge; and internalization
- **Short-term information management**: immediate retention decisions such as keeping, leaving, and ignoring
- **Document and task management**: grouping, naming, or organizing; integration of documents with other documents and systems; and refinding of organized documents

- **Long-term personal archiving, preservation, and disposal**: decisions on keeping and why; and when to and criteria for deleting documents.

Findings from their study as related to knowledge organization within personal contexts, as reported (Williams et al., 2008), include the following:

1. While the study was focused on both work and nonwork contexts, unless asked specifically, participants did not readily include discussion of nonwork-related digital information in their accounts.
2. There was little division between work and home computers; however, organization of documents reflected the separation of work and leisure.
3. No obvious patterns of file organization and storage have emerged at this point in the study, other than
   a. that files are stored in hierarchies and folders that reflect either chronological creation or topic;
   b. many people also put the date manually as part of the file name;
   c. collections appeared to grow organically, meaning that folders were not routinely moved to less visible areas on the computer (from desktop to Documents folder, for example); and
   d. file and folder structures were replicated.
4. E-mail accumulated unintentionally. It took less effort to keep e-mails than to review and delete them.
5. The main motivating force behind moving files from an active use location to an archive is due to the need to change to a new computer.
6. Decisions to archive are based on
   a. value placed on the artifact professionally, academically, or emotionally;
   b. the possibility that the document might be useful in the future; and
   c. having a backup for a hard-copy artifact.

Digital E-mail Files

Williams and colleagues (2008) reported on how personal e-mail accumulates unintentionally mostly because of the effort required to review and delete e-mails within a collection of e-mail. Other researchers have extensively studied the organization of and refinding issues associated with work-related e-mail and will be discussed in the section on organizing knowledge in professional spaces. David Elsweiler, Mark Baillie, and Ian Ruthven (2008), however, conducted a nonwork-related study with students and the role memory plays in e-mail refinding. Of particular relevance to how individuals organize this form of digital information are the attributes of the e-mail messages that were remembered by participants when refinding e-mails within their own personal e-mail collections. They reported the frequencies of remembrance of each attribute and the percentages as follows (Elsweiler, Baillie, and Ruthven, 2008: 16):

1. the most frequently remembered attribute was the topic of the email (85.1%)
2. reason the email was sent was second (80.9%)
3. sender of the email (77.1%)
4. temporal information, such as date (57.5%)
5. other recipients (46.8%)
6. links or URLs (21.8%)
7. attachments (12.8%)
8. images (2.1%).

Elsweiler, Baillie, and Ruthven also employed a set of filing strategies categories developed earlier by Whittaker and Sidner (1996) while examining work-related e-mail refinding. These categories include *nonfilers*, individuals who do not use folders and leave all e-mail messages in their inboxes; *frequent filers*, who use folders to organize their e-mail collections; and *spring cleaners*, who make use of folders but clean up and organize their e-mails only periodically. Using these three categories of filing strategies, Elsweiler, Baillie, and Ruthven found that nonfilers remembered the most for all attributes with the exception of "other recipients," followed by spring cleaners, and then filers. For the "other recipients" attribute all three groups remembered with high similarity, with the filer group being the lowest (Elsweiler, Baillie, and Ruthven, 2008: 22).

Other conclusions of the Elsweiler, Baillie, and Ruthven (2008: 30) study include the following:

- participants generally demonstrated good ability to remember their e-mails
- the most frequently remembered attributes were semantic based (the topic of the e-mail and the reason the e-mail was sent)
- the attributes that tended to be remembered changed in different scenarios
- the temperature of the task, the filing strategy of the participant, the participant's experience, the size of their collection, and their preferred method of refinding all had influence on the attributes that were remembered

The study conducted by Civan and colleagues (2008) looked at the efficacy of using folder structures to organize e-mails compared with using tags as labels for the e-mails. According to Civan and colleagues (2008: 2), "folders follow a 'put this here' model that agrees well with the way we organize objects in our physical world. Put the keys on the table, put the tax return in the 'tax' folder, [while] tags follow a different model. The information isn't 'put' anywhere . . . instead the representation (labels) comes to the information item." Their findings (Civan et al., 2008) indicate the following:

- Placing files into folders provided control over their information by helping people to get items out of their way.
- Keeping files required both the cognitive effort of choosing a category and/or label for the file and the physical effort of assigning label(s) and moving the file to a folder.
- Clutter from too much visible information disrupted attention and tasks. Hiding information by placing files in folders reduces clutter but also causes people to forget where items were placed.
- Participants found folders better for refinding than tags; however, most participants found that labels provided greater flexibility than folders by offering multiple paths back to an e-mail.
- Folders offered visual cues to refinding an e-mail, while tags gave a semantic cue, such as summary of the content or category; labels also offer opportunities for serendipitous encounters.
- Better support for information organization may need to include a combination of both folders and tags.

Digital Photo Collections

Studies in library and information science have a long history of looking at how users might represent photographs and how to provide subject access to photograph collections. Studies such as those of O'Connor, O'Connor, and Abbas (1999) and Hastings (1995) asked users to assign subject terms to digital photographs from either the researcher's collection or a museum collection. While these studies are useful for learning more about how users might represent the subject content of photographs, they do not illustrate actual practice by individuals within their own collections. Other research into users' representation of photographs, such as Neil's (2008) research on representation of photographs by journalists, takes place in professional contexts. In a 2005 essay, Neil Beagrie noted the need to study personal digital libraries, including photographic collections, as a way to inform archivists about potentially unique archiving needs should personal collections become part of national collections or institutional repositories. Marshall (2007) has begun studying the keeping habits within personal photograph archives. Social sharing websites such as Flickr and YouTube are increasingly the choice for users to share and store digital photo collections. These websites represent a rich environment for studying personal information representation and organization of nonwork-related photographic and video collections.

Physical Collections

No research to date has focused specifically on how personal collections, such as personal book collections, or other collections within the personal knowledge space are organized. Attention has been given to collection building, or *why* people develop collections (Basbanes, 1999), but not to *how* people organize personal collections. For example, do individuals organize their collections based on structures they already have experience using, such as Library of Congress or Dewey Decimal classification schemes? Do they create databases to represent their books like information professionals do in libraries? If so, how are these systems structured? Are they similar to bibliographic systems used in libraries or in special collections? What can we learn from individual representation strategies that can be incorporated into bibliographic systems or controlled vocabularies? These are questions we need to explore. The new social sharing and social bookmarking technologies of Web 2.0, such as LibraryThing and Delicious, may make it possible to learn more about how individuals organize their personal collections within knowledge spaces. Findings related to how people are organizing their personal collections in Web 2.0 environments and ideas for further research in this area will be addressed later in Chapters 6 and 7.

Learning more about how personal knowledge is organized, and the structures used to do so, is an area of research that needs to be developed. Most of the studies in this area, specifically in HCI or PIM, have the goal of developing digital products or tools that can be used to organize personal collections. Studies from KO have focused specifically on how people might label their photographs within collections, but they have not explored actual practice *within* personal collections. While studies of personal knowledge organization in work-related environments can provide some understanding of how people organize print-based and digital files, we cannot draw parallels or assume similarities between the two contexts without research to support these assertions. Also, the studies conducted in the home environment, as outlined here, include very small sample sizes, and their findings should not be generalized to larger contexts.

Knowledge Structures and Knowledge Spaces within Professional Contexts

Defining Professional Knowledge Spaces

Let's begin this section with another thought exercise. Think about the routines and tasks of your daily work-related life. What types of tasks do you complete? What knowledge sources do you use to complete each task? What technologies do you use? What documents do you create as a result? The list is probably fairly long. For example, in the course of reviewing morning e-mail, you might be alerted to meetings you need to attend. The e-mail might also include one or more attached files to review. Or, you might be reminded to complete a task for a committee you are on or a project that needs your attention. You might also have a request for further information from a client or student. Each of these different routines or tasks no doubt facilitates the use, finding or refinding, synchronizing between different technologies, and assimilation of different files to accomplish the task. Each task requires you think about *where* you might have stored the file that contains the information you need. Is it on this computer or on a USB drive? Is it in hard copy in your file cabinet? Is it attached to an e-mail? *What* is the file or folder name?

This thought exercise illustrates daily work-related issues that are at the heart of personal organization of knowledge spaces. Your office space, including your desktop, computer, file cabinets, personal collection of resources housed on both bookcases and computer hard drives or multiple technical devices, as well as other resources that might be spread around the larger work space, such as company file cabinets or the company library, represent your *personal work-related knowledge space*. It should be noted at this point that the literature on PIM refers to this concept as *personal space of information* (or PSI) (Jones and Teevan, 2007; Jones, 2008).

Organizing your personal work-related knowledge space includes the issues of (1) work habits, (2) strategies for organizing resources, (3) technology use, (4) cognitive-related issues, and (5) temporal factors such as time and spatial location. Effective personal work-related knowledge organization requires an understanding of individual strategies for accomplishing tasks, the resources available and how they are used/reused, how those knowledge resources are organized, and the factors that affect organization of knowledge resources.

Research Focused on Professional Knowledge Organization

Research that focuses on the organization in personal work-related knowledge spaces and the structures used to organize the knowledge within them is quite broad. Multiple studies have explored personal knowledge organization in work-related contexts. As noted in the earlier section on personal knowledge spaces in nonwork-related environments, there are four primary areas of research that have addressed the issue of how people organize their personal information. These areas include research focused on (1) human information behavior (HIB), (2) knowledge organization and classification (KO), (3) human computer interaction (HCI), and (4) personal information management (PIM). Each of these research areas approaches this issue from a different but interrelated perspective. For example, HIB researchers have focused on paper-based knowledge organization within office spaces of academic researchers. Their research traces the information use cycle, beginning with *how* academics seek and find resources and *what* resources academics might use to find information during the process of creating new knowledge. Little research in this area has focused on issues related to the strategies, tools, and structures they use for organizing that knowledge. However, this area of research is growing as a result of efforts of both HIB and KO researchers to develop discipline-specific and institutionwide repositories and the standards for metadata schemes and digital curation of these knowledge sources.

KO researchers have employed what is referred to as "domain analysis" (Hjorland, 2002) as a means of understanding the unique discipline-specific or domain-specific information needs and practices of a community. What KO researchers learn about the community's common work practices, information needs, use of resources, and discipline/domain-specific language use informs the development of taxonomies and ontologies for organizing knowledge within the specific domain or community of practice. KO domain analysis has been conducted within various disciplines, professions, and work-related contexts. The findings, while helpful for developing taxonomies and ontologies for use within the specific domain/disciplinary context, may not necessarily be extended beyond that community of practice. Furthermore, no effort to date has been made to synthesize these findings and draw parallels across domains or disciplines that might be useful in our exploration of structures for organizing knowledge spaces. KO domain analysis has also not focused on learning more about the strategies used by individuals within specific domains/disciplines to organize their work-related knowledge.

HCI and PIM researchers, as noted earlier in the section introducing the research areas that study organization of personal knowledge spaces, have focused on how individuals in work and nonwork-related contexts acquire, organize, and maintain both paper-based and digital information. The organization of work-related paper files in file cabinets and bookcases and on desktops has been explored by a few, but the majority of PIM research is related to digital information organization and has focused on (1) how files are organized on work computers, (2) how e-mail is organized to enable refinding and use, and (3) how people organize web-based information, such as websites and bookmarks. As noted earlier, the objective of HCI and PIM research is to develop new user-centered technologies, or enhance existing ones, that can be used in either everyday personal or professional contexts. However, as Boardman and Sasse (2004: 583) point out, there are few current empirical studies being conducted into *how* people organize their paper-based and digital information. Much of the literature references earlier empirical studies and then presents a new prototype the authors have designed or reports the results of the use of a new prototype (prototype design studies). Prototype design studies do little to help us understand more about how people organize information in either personal or professional knowledge spaces beyond explaining how a small sample of individuals use the specific prototype.

The following section will present research findings from HIB, KO, HCI, and PIM as related to the organization of work-related personal knowledge spaces. For lack of a more cohesive structure, the section will be divided based on the medium of the knowledge sources being organized (paper based and digital). This section will be limited to the empirical studies and will not include those related to specific prototypes. It also will not attempt to include all studies conducted in every domain/discipline or profession.

Research on Paper-Based Knowledge Organization

Organization strategies used by individuals within work-related environments have been studied within various professional environments (Malone,

1983; Mander, Salomon, and Wong, 1992; Kidd, 1994; Whittaker and Hirschberg, 2001) and with academics (Case, 1986, 1988, 1991; Kwasnik, 1989, 1991). From each of these studies we have learned much about work habits, organization strategies, and cognitive and temporal factors that affect how knowledge resources are organized. These findings are described here.

Malone (1983) was one of the first to study how people organize paper-based resources in their work environment. He conducted a series of interviews with professional and clerical office workers in an effort to learn not just *how* or *what* strategies they used to organize their work resources but also *why* and *which* factors affected their organization strategies. The resulting categories of strategies for organizing work-related knowledge spaces and the reasons for these strategies have been used by other researchers as a framework or model for categorizing personal information management and organization strategies. For example, Malone (1983: 101–104) characterized workers' use of their office spaces (desktops and available spaces in their offices, such as chairs, floor space, and bookshelves) into two categories of strategies for organizing knowledge spaces: (1) filers and (2) pilers:

> *Filers* rely heavily on files and precisely organized piles arranged primarily on their desktops. They tend to have neater offices and every space has a specific purpose, such as shelves for organizing books, file cabinets for housing files, etc.
>
> *Pilers,* on the other hand, organize their information in loosely stacked piles of mixed content. They tend to have messier offices and use most available space (chairs, tables, floor space, etc.) to store the piles of information. Pilers, as a result, seem to have a more difficult time retrieving or refinding information.

Malone (1983: 105) also explains that files and piles are units of desk organization or "ways of collecting groups of elements into larger units." For example, files are the units being organized and are usually labeled and arranged in some order. Piles, on the other hand, are the units being organized but they are not labeled or arranged in any specific order, other than, perhaps, order of receipt or chronological. They might also be organized based on topic or project.

Malone also points out two specific functions of desk organization that are referred to in most PIM research: (1) the finding or refinding function and (2) the reminding function. Malone discovered that the reason why people organize information is so that they can refind it for use at a later date and that how and where they locate the information serves a reminding function.

Malone also proposed that certain cognitive and temporal factors affect choices for organizing strategies. For example, the decision to leave an information item in a pile or on the desktop may reflect the cognitive factor of the difficulty a person experiences when trying to determine how to classify something or what category or folder to place it in. Kwasnik (1989, 1991) also discusses this issue in her work. When Malone examined the file systems used by the individuals in the study, he saw that temporal and spatial factors were evident. For example, many of the classifications were based on chronological attributes, such as date, time used, or event associated with. Recency of use of a file also determined where the file might be located within the office space. Other attributes used related to author, title, or project name.

As noted earlier, the models of strategies used to organize knowledge spaces developed as a result of Malone's study have been cited by and built upon by numerous PIM researchers. Mander, Salomon, and Wong (1992) validated and explored additional reasons why people are either pilers or filers. Their study examined the organizing strategies of professionals working at a computer company, including managers, clerical, human resources, and technical departments. Not only does their research support Malone's findings but it also points out that "recency" of use and spatial organizing factors impact how information is organized. For example, piles enable users to visually browse piles to locate needed sources. Files do not allow this visual finding mechanism. Also frequently accessed information tended to be located nearer to a workspace so that it could be used as needed (Mander, Salomon, and Wong, 1992: 627–628). Kidd's (1994) research further illustrates the spatial factors related to organizing strategies. In her study of knowledge workers, she characterizes information that knowledge workers have not yet internalized as being kept on either a desktop or on the floor of the office space. This "temporary holding pattern" indicates their reticence to file the information away, as well as a fear of being unable to locate it again for future use (Kidd, 1994: 187). Locating the information in piles or folders kept on or near the desktop served as cues for reminding as well. Knowledge workers were also hesitant to label files or folders (if used) until they had internalized the information (Kidd, 1994: 190).

Whittaker and Hirschberg (2001) extend the findings of Malone (1983), Mander, Salomon, and Wong (1992), and Kidd (1994) but also add some intriguing reasons for why people keep paper-based documents as well as identify cognitive and attentional factors for deferring classification and/or filing of documents. For example, people acquire extraneous paper for three reasons: (1) lack of time to read and process new information; (2) inability to gauge the future utility of the information; and (3) information overload from the large amount of information they encounter. These factors lead to deferment of evaluating the information and classifying it or otherwise organizing it into folders. People also keep paper-based information because of its affordances. Paper can be more easily available and better supports the reminding function (Whittaker and Hirschberg, 2001: 164–168).

The Case (1986, 1991) and Kwasnik (1989, 1991) studies of academic organizing strategies report many of the same strategies and rationales for keeping and organizing paper-based documents. As reported by Case (1986), the difficulty of categorizing information led to the piling strategy being used by social scientists, and the spatial location of piles served a reminding function. Case also notes that while organizing strategies of academics may not differ from those in the professional environment, where they do differ is in the amount of storage needed by academics.

Kwasnik's research of academics adds the interesting dimension of context to what is known about paper-based organizing strategies in academic and professional environments. Her research into the factors related to classification decisions identified that frequency of use and kinds of uses for the document were critical factors in classification decisions. A document's use or intended purpose is often the first factor upon which it is classified. Her research also indicates that we choose categories that have the most usefulness but that also require the least cognitive effort to devise (Kwasnik, 1989: 209–210).

Research on Digital Knowledge Organization

Each of the empirical studies on how people organize paper-based resources in their work-related knowledge spaces serves as the foundation for further study within the digital environment. Much of what we know about personal knowledge organization within digital environments comes from PIM research and is focused on (1) how files are organized on work computers, (2) how e-mail is organized to enable refinding and use, and (3) how people organize web-based information, such as websites and bookmarks.

One of the first papers published that investigated how digital information was organized in work-related spaces was by Deborah Barreau and Bonnie A. Nardi in 1995. Their concurrent research projects were the first to report findings related to how individuals organize their work-related documents using personal computers. From 1995 forward, the literature of HCI and PIM contains numerous studies of both empirical and prototypical focus. Because of the sheer volume of this literature and the variety of approaches taken to extend the findings of earlier studies, no attempt to detail individual research projects will be attempted. Instead, the general overall findings of PIM related specifically to the organization of work-related knowledge spaces will be outlined. The reader is also pointed to two very comprehensive resources in PIM that further explain the state of current research in this area: Jones and Teevan (2007) and Jones (2008). The Further Readings section of this chapter also lists many of the studies that the reader might find useful.

While PIM includes the entire spectrum related to the information cycle (acquiring or finding, keeping, organizing and maintaining, and refinding, as well as issues related to securing information), this section will focus on only the organizing and maintaining functions of PIM. As we saw in our thought exercise for this section, we acquire and use various forms of information for different tasks within our daily activities. Deciding how to organize this information, as outlined in the studies in the section on paper-based organization, can be based on many different factors. Primary to organizing is the idea that we will need to refind/reuse the information at a later time and most likely for a specific use or purpose. Jones (2008: 125) characterizes "information organizing" as

> decisions made and actions taken in the selection and implementation of a scheme to relate the information items in a collection to anticipated needs. Decisions can include (1) How should items in this collection be named? (2) What set of properties make sense for and help to distinguish the items in this collection from one another? (3) How should items within this collection be grouped? Into what piles or folders?

Jones (2008: 126) further explains the connection between organizing and maintaining as

> decisions made and actions taken relating to the preservation and upkeep of personal information. Decisions include how information is stored (where? in what formats? in what kinds of storage? backed up how?), how information is updated or corrected, and what happens to older information (e.g., is it deleted or archived?).

Upon review of the PIM literature related to organizing of information, several key points are evident:

- People vary greatly in their approaches to organizing information. Even within the same work environment or discipline, their approaches and organizing strategies may differ. People employ a variety of structures that are available through the technology they are using to store the information. For example, they might use hierarchies or taxonomies in which folders containing various knowledge objects in various formats are structured. They may employ multiple hierarchical structures within one computer and also may or may not replicate these same structures on various computers or USB drives.
- Challenges related to organizing strategies are greater when multiple devices and software applications are used. For example, if multiple computers or USB drives are used to store files, then synchronizing and refinding specific files is more difficult.
- People may not keep information with a specific purpose in mind. As illustrated by the studies of paper-based systems, there are many factors (cognitive, temporal, attentional) that affect whether or not people keep information as well as their organizing strategies. Not every knowledge source kept and organized has a specific purpose or use. Filing may be an attempt to reduce a distracting file or resource from one's desktop (physical or personal computer).
- Each organizing strategy (filing or piling) has limitations and advantages. The cognitive effort required to file away or to organize the piece of information may be greater than not organizing it. When organizing information, it is necessary to determine what folder to put it in, to decide what to label the file and folder, and to develop or work within existing personal or shared structures for organizing knowledge. Also, hiding the information

may detract from the refinding and reminding functions of the knowledge object. As the personal information stored grows in size, refinding a specific file may become more difficult. Alternative strategies of using tagging or labels may allow visual browsing, but then, as the volume of loosely organized information increases, browsing also becomes problematic.

- Organizing and maintaining decisions can be based on various criteria, including, for example, (1) the belief that we will be able to find/refind it for future use or that it will still exist in some form we have access to (Jones, 2008: 135); (2) the value we place on the information, for example, (a) is it precious, irreplaceable; (b) is it extremely difficult to replace; (c) is it part of a larger collection that is used frequently (photograph collections, recipes, reference materials); and (d) is it necessary for a specific project or task we are working on? (Jones, 2008: 160).

A further intriguing dimension hinted about by Jones (2008) is the sense-making ability afforded by personal knowledge structures. Recall the discussion at the beginning of this chapter related to the definition of *personal knowledge spaces*, as well as O'Connor, Kearns, and Anderson's (2008: 18) "user template of understanding." Jones (2008: 136–138) proposes that

> an organizational scheme (e.g., tags or folders) should meaningfully reflect our needs for information as used in the various projects we are trying to complete, the decisions we need to make, and the roles and obligations we need to fulfill. Keeping according to such a scheme affects our memories and even our understanding of the items we keep. . . . The visual structure we impose on information (even if only a basic folder hierarchy) can serve to highlight key relationships among the information items in a collection. Organizational structure can help us to make sense of our information and its applications.

The structure(s) we employ for organizing personal information in both work and nonwork-related environments may reflect how we conceptually think about and structure the routines, tasks, projects, etc., that we are engaged in on a daily basis and also over a lifetime. These structures may also allow us to discover new connections or ideas previously not noticed. They may serve as reminders of other tasks to complete or may illustrate history related to projects, collections, family, and work-related events.

Findings outlined in the earlier discussion on organizing strategies and issues related to work-based personal information not only inform interface and system design but also provide us with a more in-depth understanding of how individuals organize their own knowledge spaces, their rationale(s) for keeping and organizing knowledge objects, and the cognitive, temporal, and attentional factors that influence organizing strategies and behaviors. The studies also indicate the primary ways and attributes used by individuals to represent their knowledge objects.

Taxonomies and Ontologies Developed for Professional Use

Additional structures for organizing knowledge in work-related contexts include taxonomies and ontologies that have been developed for use within a specific corporation, industry, discipline, or community of practice. Taxonomies, as defined by Rowley and Hartley (2008: 223), "typically provide a set of categories with hierarchical and other relationships specified between the categories." In a corporate setting, taxonomies may serve multiple organizing and sense-making functions. According to Gilchrist (2001: 101), a taxonomy serves the functions of (1) navigating through various resources of the organization; (2) providing tools for representing documents of the organization, and (3) serving as a sense-making tool or visual representation of the knowledge base of the organization. Ontologies are likened to controlled vocabularies developed for use by a specific domain, discipline, or community of practice. They contain the "explicit formal specifications of the terms in a domain and the relationships between them" (Rowley and Hartley, 2008: 225). However, where they differ from controlled vocabularies is in the diverse ways that they are constructed or represented. For example, instead of using a strict hierarchical structure for showing relationships, the ontology may be structured using a nonlinear graphic delineating the terms and relationships using facets.

As noted earlier, KO researchers conduct a "domain analysis" as a means of understanding the unique discipline-specific or domain-specific information needs and practices of a community. KO domain analysis has been conducted within various disciplines, professions, and work-related contexts. For example, Bowker and Star (1999) relate work they have conducted in the area of mental health classification. Bowker's 2005 book, *Memory Practices in the Sciences*, details the development of knowledge-organizing systems within geology and cybernetics.

In the area of digital curation, library and information studies researchers are developing customized metadata schemes and ontologies to use for bringing interdisciplinary projects in biodiversity, geology, and other sciences together in interconnected knowledge systems such as digital discipline-specific and institutional repositories (Palmer, Teffeau, and Newton, 2008). Results that HIB and KO researchers learn about the community's common work practices, information needs, use of resources, and discipline/domain-specific language use inform the development and implementation of customized metadata schemes, taxonomies, and ontologies for organizing knowledge within the specific domain or community of practice. For example, many of the works in the biodiversity community outlined in Chapter 4 are examples of efforts to develop discipline-specific ontologies and taxonomies. Furthermore, in the bioinformatics domain, researchers have developed ontologies to represent specific species' genomic coding. The Open Biological and Biomedical Ontologies (OBO) Foundry, which is a "collaborative experiment involving developers of science-based ontologies who are establishing a set of principles for ontology development with the goal of creating a suite of orthogonal interoperable reference ontologies in the biomedical domain" (OBO Foundry, 2010b), provides access to multiple ontologies through its website. The mission of the OBO Foundry, as stated on its website,

> is to support community members who are developing and publishing ontologies in the biomedical domain. It is our vision that a core of these ontologies will be fully interoperable, by virtue of a common design philosophy and implementation, thereby enabling scientists and their instruments to communicate with minimum ambiguity. (OBO Foundry, 2010a)

The Ontology Research Group (ORG; org.buffalo.edu) of the New York State Center of Excellence in Bioinformatics & Life Sciences, at the State University of New York at Buffalo, conducts ontology research in a variety of disciplines, ranging from the critical review and reconstruction of what people refer to as "ontologies" and ontology-based applications in the biomedical domain, to creating and maintaining software to support information retrieval, such as natural language processing and other applications in scientific domains.

The European Bioinformatics Institute (EBI; www.ebi.ac.uk), part of the European Molecular Biology Laboratory (EMBL), manages databases of biological data including nucleic acid, protein sequences, and macromolecular structures. The EBI's mission states that there is an ongoing, and growing, need to collect, store and curate bioinformatics information in ways that allow its efficient retrieval and exploitation. The EBI's Ontology Lookup Service (OLS; www.ebi.ac.uk/ontology-lookup) provides bioinformatics researchers with a centralized area to find ontologies related to their work.

There are many widely used taxonomies for industry that have been standardized, for example, the International Standard Industrial Classification Taxonomy (ISIC; unstats.un.org/unsd/cr/registry/regcst.asp?Cl=2) and the North American Industry Classification System (NAICS; www.ntis.gov/products/naics.aspx.

Browsing the website for the Taxonomy Warehouse (www.taxonomywarehouse.com) illustrates the wide and diverse variety of taxonomies and ontologies used within various different industries, domains, and communities of practice. Figure 5.2 illustrates the categories of taxonomies, thesauri, and ontologies available from the Taxonomy Warehouse.

Figure 5.3 shows the Commerce & Industry Category list on Taxonomy Warehouse, and Figure 5.4 shows the detailed information given by the WAND Industrial Equipment and Supplies Taxonomy.

SKOS (Simple Knowledge Organization), as outlined in Chapter 3, is an initiative underway in the Semantic Web community to develop specifications and standards to support the use of knowledge organization systems (KOS) such as thesauri, classification schemes, subject headings systems, and taxonomies within the framework of the Semantic Web. Although it is not developing ontologies, SKOS is formulating standards for the construction of ontologies and other knowledge organization systems (W3C, 2008).

Figure 5.2. Categories of Taxonomies, Thesauri, and Ontologies from the Taxonomy Warehouse

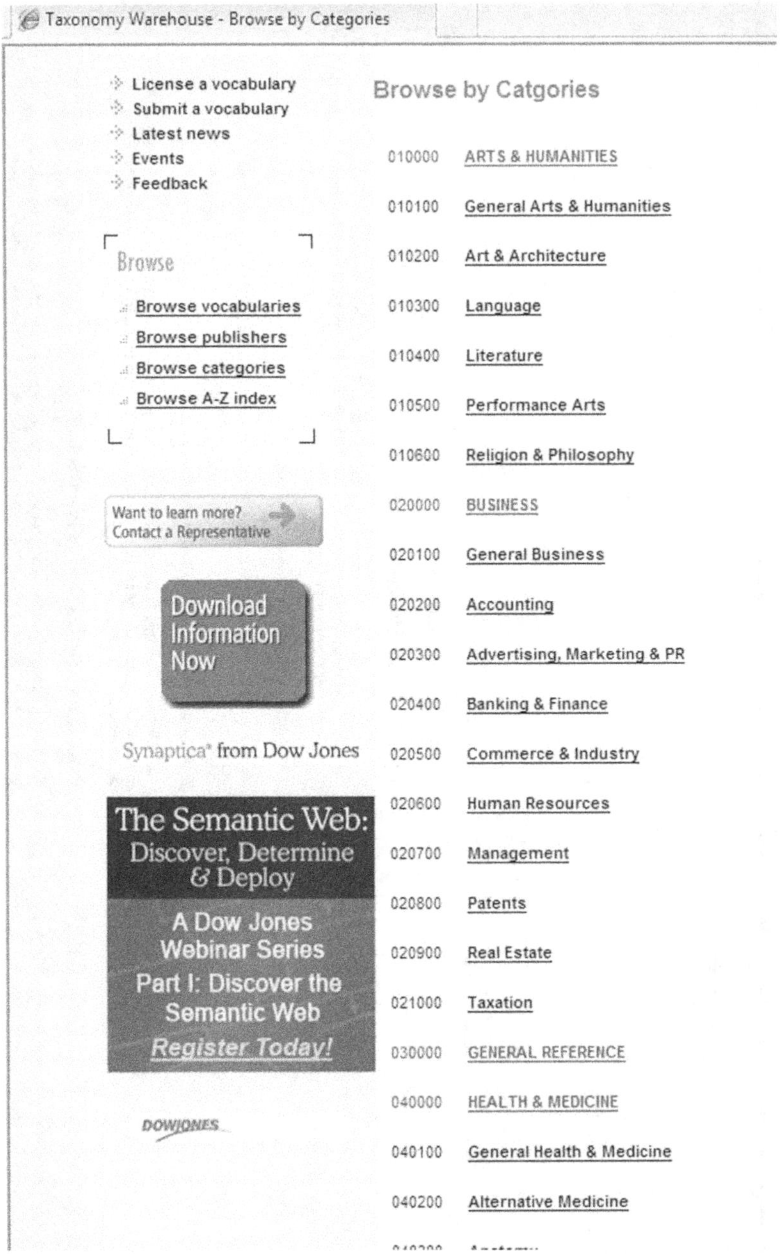

Figure 5.3. Commerce & Industry Category on Taxonomy Warehouse

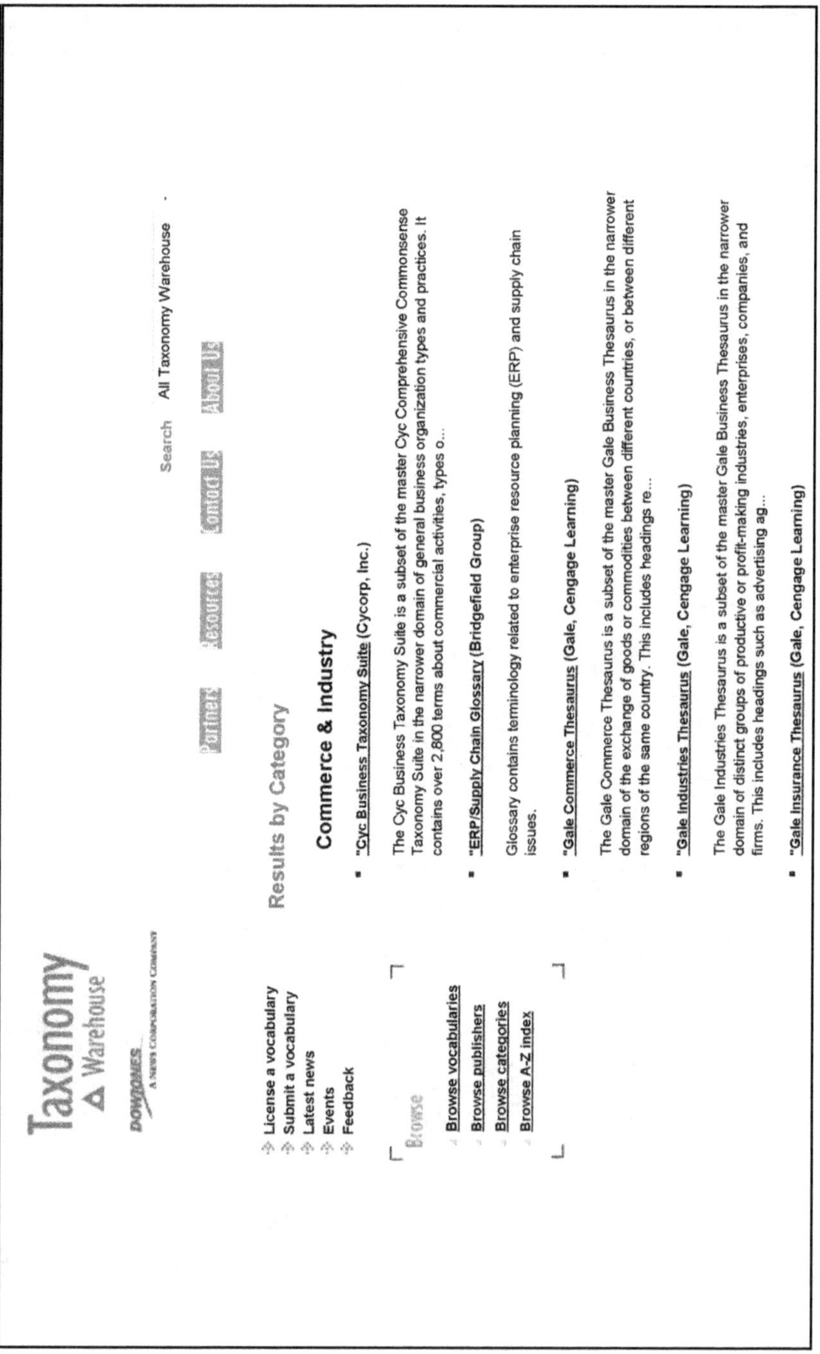

Figure 5.4. Vocabulary Details of the WAND Industrial Equipment and Supplies Taxonomy

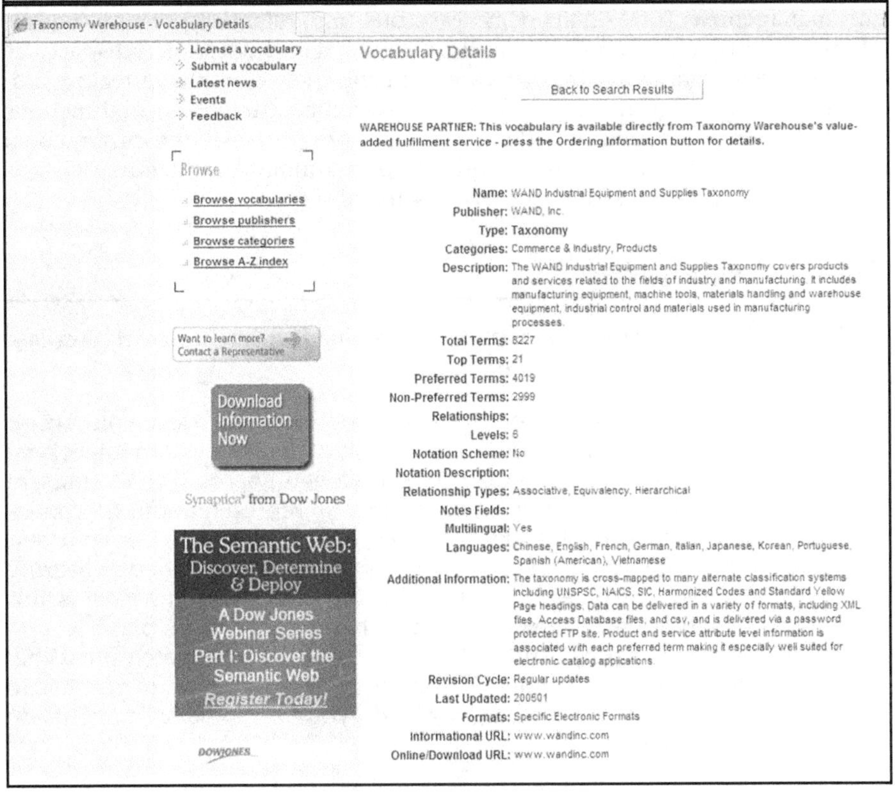

Conclusion

In this chapter we explored the following questions:

- How *do* we organize knowledge in our personal and professional contexts so that it makes sense and is useful?
- What forms of knowledge-organizing structures are used in personal and professional contexts, and do differences or similarities exist within the form(s) and use(s) within these two contexts?
- What role(s) do categories, ontologies, taxonomies, and other structures play in the process of organizing?
- What do we need to know (and what do we *already* know) about human information interactions and organizing behaviors in order to design useful structures for organizing knowledge?

Research from the areas of human information behavior (HIB), knowledge organization (KO), human–computer interaction (HCI), and personal information management (PIM) helped increase our understanding of how people "naturally" organize knowledge in their personal and professional spaces as well as which organizing strategies are used and the factors that affect organization of knowledge resources. We also examined the role(s) or functions structures for organizing knowledge play in both personal and professional contexts. Last, the development and use of taxonomies and ontologies as knowledge-organizing structures was discussed.

Thought Exercises

The Thought Exercises for this chapter are contained within the text, but in case you missed them, they are repeated here:

1. Take a moment and think about the knowledge that you use in your everyday life. Now focus this exploration on only your personal, nonwork-related knowledge use and personal knowledge spaces. What kinds of objects (either in a physical form or in a mental representation) do you include? What forms do they take? Say, for example, you consider your personal knowledge space as your home office. What knowledge-bearing objects do you organize, store, and use in your daily life? *How* is this knowledge organized, stored, or used? What role does each play?
2. Think about the routines and tasks of your daily work-related life. What types of tasks do you complete? What knowledge sources do you use to complete each task? What technologies do you use? What documents do you create as a result?

References

Barreau, Deborah, and Bonnie A. Nardi. 1995. "Finding and Reminding: File Organization from the Desktop." *SIG CHI Bulletin* 27, no. 3: 39–43.

Basbanes, Nicholas. 1999. *A Gentle Madness: Bibliophiles, Bibliomanes, and the Eternal Passion for Books*. New York: Henry Holt.

Beagrie, Neal. 2005. "Plenty of Room at the Bottom? Personal Digital Libraries and Collections." *D-Lib Magazine* 11, no. 6 (June). Available: www.dlib.org/dlib/june05/beagrie/06beagrie.html (accessed June 4, 2010).

Boardman, Richard, and M. Angela Sasse. 2004. "'Stuff Goes into the Computer and Doesn't Come Out': A Cross-tool Study of Personal Information Management." In *Proceedings of ACM SIGCHI Conference* (pp. 583–590). New York: ACM Press.

Bowker, Geoffrey C. 2005. *Memory Practices in the Sciences*. Cambridge, MA: MIT Press.

Bowker, Geoffrey C., and Susan Leigh Star. 1999. *Sorting Things Out: Classification and Its Consequences*. Cambridge, MA: MIT Press.

Brush, A.J., Leysia Palen, Laurel Swan, and Alex S. Taylor. 2005. "Designs for Home Life." In *Proceedings of the SIGCHI Conference on Human Factors in Computing Systems, Extended Abstracts* (pp. 2035–2036). New York: ACM Press.

Case, Donald O. 1986. "Collection and Organization of Written Information by Social Scientists and Humanists: A Review and Exploratory Study." *Journal of Information Science* 12: 97–104.

———. 1988. "How Do Experts Do It? The Use of Ethnographic Methods as an Aid to Understanding the Cognitive Processing and Retrieval of Large Bodies of Text." In *Proceedings of the 11th Annual International ACM SIGIR Conference on Research and Development in Information Retrieval* (pp. 127–133). New York: ACM Press.

———. 1991. "The Collection and Use of Information by Some American Historians: A Study of Motives and Methods." *Library Quarterly* 61, no. 1: 61–82.

———. 2002. *Looking for Information: A Survey of Research on Information Seeking, Needs, and Behavior*. San Diego: Academic Press.

———. 2006. "Information Behavior." In *Annual Review of Information Science and Technology* (pp. 293–327), edited by Blaise Kronin. Medford, NJ: Information Today.

Civan, Andrea, William Jones, Predrag Klasnja, and Harry Bruce. 2008. "Better to Organize Personal Information by Folders or by Tags? The Devil Is in the Details." *Proceedings of the 2008 Annual Meeting of the American Society for Information Science and Technology* 45, no. 1: 1–13.

Crabtree, A., T. Hemmings, and J. Mariani. 2003. "Informing the Design of Calendar Systems for Domestic Use." In *Proceedings of the 8th European Conference on Computer Supported Cooperative Work* (pp. 125–128). New York: Kluwer Academic Publishers.

Crabtree, Andy, Terry Hemmings, and Tom Rodden. 2002. "Pattern-based Support for Interactive Design in Domestic Settings." In *Proceedings of the Conference on Designing Interactive Systems: Processes, Practices, Methods, and Techniques* (pp. 265–276). New York: ACM Press.

Crabtree, Andy, and Tom Rodden. 2004. "Domestic Routines and Design for the Home." *Computer Supported Cooperative Work* 13, no. 9: 191–220.

Elsweiler, David, Mark Baillie, and Ian Ruthven. 2008. "Exploring Memory in Email Refinding." *ACM Transactions on Information Systems* 26, no. 4, Article 21: 1–36.

Gilchrist, A. 2001. "Corporate Taxonomies: Report on a Survey of Current Practice." *Online Information Review* 25, no. 2: 94–102.

Hastings, S. 1995. "An Exploratory Study of Intellectual Access to Digitized Art Images." *Proceedings of the Fifty-ninth Annual Meeting of the American Society for Information Science* 32: 3–8.

Hjorland, Birger. 2002. "Domain Analysis in Information Science: Eleven Approaches—Traditional as Well as Innovative." *Journal of Documentation* 58, no. 4: 422–462.

Jones, William. 2008. *Keeping Found Things Found: The Study and Practice of Personal Information Management*. New York: Morgan Kaufmann Publisher.

Jones, William, and Jaime Teevan, eds. 2007. *Personal Information Management*. Seattle: University of Washington Press.

Kidd, Alison. 1994. "The Marks Are on the Knowledge Worker." In *Proceedings of the ACM SIGCHI Conference on Human Factors in Computing Systems* (pp. 186–191). New York: ACM Press.

Kwasnik, Barbara H. 1989. "How a Personal Document's Intended Use or Purpose Affects Its Classification in an Office." In *Proceedings of the 12th Annual International ACM SIGIR Conference on Research and Development in Information* (pp. 207–210), edited by Nick Belkin and C.J. van Rijsbergen. New York: ACM Press.

———. 1991. "The Importance of Factors That Are Not Document Attributes in the Organization of Personal Documents." *Journal of Documentation* 47, no. 4: 389–398.

Malone, Thomas W. 1983. "How Do People Organize Their Desks? Implications for the Design of Office Information Systems." *ACM Transactions on Office Information Systems* 1, no. 1: 99–112.

Mander, Richard, Gina Salomon, and Yin Yin Wong. 1992. "A 'Pile' Metaphor for Supporting Casual Organization of Information." In *Proceedings of the ACM SIGCHI Conference on Human Factors in Computing Systems* (pp. 627–634). New York: ACM Press.

Marshall, Cathy. 2007. "How People Manage Personal Information over a Lifetime." In *Personal Information Management* (pp. 57–75), edited by William Jones and Jaime Teevan. Seattle: University of Washington Press.

Neil, Diane. 2008. "News Photographers, Librarians, Tags, and Controlled Vocabularies: Balancing the Forces." *Journal of Library Metadata* 8, no. 3: 199–219.

OBO Foundry. 2010a. "About." Available: www.obofoundry.org/about.shtml (accessed May 17, 2010).

———. 2010b. "Homepage." Available: www.obofoundry.org (accessed May 17, 2010).

O'Brien, Jon, and Tom Rodden. 2000. "At Home with the Technology: An Ethnographic Study of a Set-Top-Box Trial." *ACM Transactions on Computer–Human Interaction* 6, no. 3: 282–308.

O'Connor, Brian C., Jodi Kearns, and Richard Anderson. 2008. "Background Concepts and Models." In *Doing Things with Information* (pp. 1–20). Westport, CT: Libraries Unlimited.

O'Connor, B.C., M. O'Connor, and J. Abbas. 1999. "User Reactions as Access Mechanism: An Exploration Based on Captions for Images." *Journal of the American Society for Information Science* 50, no. 8: 681–697.

Palmer, Carole, Lauren Teffeau, and Mark Newton. 2008. "Strategies for Institutional Repository Development: A Case Study of Three Evolving Initiatives." *Library Trends* 57, no. 2: 142–167.

Plaisant, Catherine, Aaron Clamage, Hilary Browne Hutchinson, Benjamin B. Bederson, and Allison Druin. 2006. "Shared Family Calendars: Promoting Symmetry and Accessibility." *ACM Transactions on Computer–Human Interactions* 13, no. 3 (September): 313–346.

Plotkin, Henry C. 1994. *Darwin Machines and the Nature of Knowledge*. Cambridge, MA: Harvard University Press.

Rowley, Jennifer, and Richard Hartley. 2008. *Organizing Knowledge: An Introduction to Managing Access to Information*, 4th ed. Burlington, VT: Ashgate.

Taylor, Alex, and Laurel Swan. 2004. "List Making in the Home." In *Proceedings of the 2004 ACM Conference on Computer Supported Cooperative Work* (pp. 542–545). New York: ACM Press.

———. 2005. "Artful Systems in the Home." In *Proceedings of the 2005 SIGCHI Conference on Human Factors in Computing Systems* (pp. 641–650). New York: ACM Press.

Thomas, P., J.F. Meech, and R.D. Macredie. 1996. "Information Management Using Integrated Information Appliances." In *Digital Media and Electronic Publishing* (pp. 64–76), edited by Rae Earnshaw, Huw Jones, and John Vince. London: Academic Press.

W3C. 2008. "SKOS." Available: www.w3.org/2004/02/skos/intro (accessed May 17, 2010).

Whittaker, Steve, and Julia Hirschberg. 2001. "The Character, Value, and Management of Personal Paper Archives." *ACM Transactions on Computer–Human Interaction* 8, no. 2 (June): 150–170.

Whittaker, S. and Sidner, C. 1996. "Email Overload: Exploring Personal Management of Email." In *Proceedings of CHI'96 Conference on Computer Human Interaction* (pp. 276–283). New York: ACM Press.

Williams, Pete, Katrina Dean, Ian Rowlands, and Jeremy Leighton John. 2008. "Digital Lives: Reports on Interviews with the Creators of Personal Digital Collections." *Ariadne* no. 55 (April). Available: www.ariadne.ac.uk/issue55/williams-et-al (accessed December 3, 2009).

Williams, Peter, Jeremy Leighton John, and Ian Rowland. 2009. "The Personal Curation of Digital Objects: A Lifecycle Approach." *Aslib Proceedings: New Information Perspectives* 61, no. 4: 340–363.

Wilson, Tom D. 2000. "Human Information Behavior." *Informing Science* 3, no. 2: 49–55.

Further Readings

Barreau, Deborah. 2008. "The Persistence of Behavior and Form in the Organization of Personal Information." *Journal of the American Society for Information Science and Technology* 59, no. 2: 307–317.

Bergman, Ofer, Ruth Beyth-Marom, and Rafi Nachmias. 2008. "The User-Subjective Approach to Personal Information Management Systems Design: Evidence and Implementations." *Journal of the American Society for Information Science and Technology* 59, no. 2: 235–246.

Hicks, B.J., A. Dong, R. Palmer, and H.C. McAlpine. 2008. "Organizing and Managing Personal Electronic Files: A Mechanical Engineer's Perspective." *ACM Transactions on Information Systems* 26, no. 4, Article 23: 1–40.

Khoo, Christopher S.G., Brendan Luyt, Caroline Ee, Jamila Osman, Hui-Hui Lim, and Sally Yong. 2007. "How Users Organize Electronic Files on Their Workstations in the Office Environment: A Preliminary Study of Personal Information Organization Behavior." *Information Research* 11, no. 2 (January). Available: informationr.net/ir/12-2/paper293.html (accessed June 4, 2010).

Lansdale, M. 1988. "The Psychology of Personal Information Management." *Applied Ergonomics* 19, no. 1: 55–66.

Whittaker, Steve, and Candace Sidner. 1996. "Email Overload: Exploring Personal Information Management of Email." In *Proceedings of the ACM SIGCHI Conference* (pp. 276–283). New York: ACM Press.

Websites Noted in Text

European Bioinformatics Institute. 2010. "About the EMBL-EBI." European Bioinformatics Institute, European Molecular Biology Laboratory. Available: www.ebi.ac.uk/Information/About_EBI/about_ebi.html (accessed June 4, 2010).

International Standard Industrial Classification Taxonomy. 2009. United Nations Statistics Division. Available: unstats.un.org/unsd/cr/registry/regcst.asp?Cl=2 (accessed May 17, 2010).

North American Industry Classification System. 2009. Office of Management and Budget's Economic Classification Policy Committee. Available: www.ntis.gov/products/naics.aspx (accessed May 17, 2010).

Open Biological and Biomedical Ontologies Foundry. 2010. Available: www.obofoundry.org (accessed June 4, 2010).
Ontology Research Group. 2010. Available: org.buffalo.edu (accessed June 4, 2010).
Taxonomy Warehouse. 2009. Dow Jones. Available: www.taxonomywarehouse.com (accessed May 17, 2010).

Part III

Socially-Constructed Structures for Organizing Knowledge

6

Social Knowledge-Organizing Behaviors and Socially-Constructed Structures for Organizing Knowledge: Research and Discussion

Focus Points

- What are the different forms of social networking, social bookmarking, and/or social cataloging sites being used on the web?
- What functions and/or roles do these social sites provide for users?
- What are the potential uses of tagging and the resulting folksonomy(ies) being developed by users of social networking sites?
- What can library and information science and related disciplines and practitioners learn from the development and use of these socially-constructed structures for organizing knowledge?

Introduction and Scope of the Chapter

Throughout earlier chapters of the book, traditional (classical) structures for organizing knowledge have been examined, and, with the use of exemplars, these structures have been explored in some depth. In Chapter 2 the historical and interdisciplinary foundations for many current classification and knowledge-organizing structures illustrated how the design and application of these systems was directly dependent on the current literature and thinking of the discipline for which it was developed as well as on other social and economic factors present at the time. In Chapter 4 the formal and informal structures for organizing knowledge within a diverse sample of academic disciplines, as well as the principles underlying the development of the structures and their practical applications, illustrated further how the structures for organizing knowledge within academic disciplines represent their understandings of the world and vary significantly in order to meet the needs of the discipline. We also saw that while the structures for organizing knowledge within each discipline contain some commonalities, it is evident that each structure is designed with a particular use and specific user community in mind. In Chapter 5, focus shifted to how individuals organize their own personal knowledge spaces in both home and work-related contexts. Research from the areas of human information behavior (HIB), knowledge organization (KO), human–computer interaction (HCI), and personal information management (PIM) helped increase our understanding of how people "naturally" organize knowledge in their personal and professional spaces, as well as the organizing strategies used and the factors that affect organization of knowledge resources.

In this chapter we will turn our attention to an examination of social organizing activities and the resulting socially-constructed structures for organizing knowledge that are emerging in Web 2.0 services, such as Flickr, Delicious (formerly known as del.icio.us), CiteULike, and LibraryThing. Social networking, bookmarking, and cataloging sites are services on Web 2.0–enabled websites that allow users to organize, describe, share, and, in some cases, such as photo, music, and video sharing sites, to upload objects from their personal knowledge spaces into online repositories (such as Flickr for photos and short videos and YouTube for videos). Brian O'Connor (1996), and as further explained by O'Connor, Kearns, and Anderson (2008), envisioned what he called the "Community Memory Interface," which was not unlike the Flickr social bookmarking site. In this social space, users could collaborate to describe the knowledge resources housed on the system.

Sites like Flickr began with the goal of providing online users with a place to store their personal photo collections and to make them available to their friends and family. However, because of the nature of these social sites, they became more collaborative, with user communities forming around similar interests, events, and geographic locations and within specific sites. Furthermore, the tagging function on social networking, bookmarking, and cataloging sites allowed users to create short representations of their personal objects, bookmarks, and other media in their personal knowledge spaces for their own use. However, as these sites became more popular, and more objects were represented using tags and commenting, their collaborative nature also afforded for the development of not just *individual* tagging and resulting folksonomies but also collaborative and sitewide folksonomies.

To the library and information science and computer science communities, tags, and the folksonomies that are developed as a result of the tagging activities of users, represent a potential means to supplement knowledge-organizing systems, such as controlled vocabularies (e.g., subject headings lists and thesauri) or as a means to infuse information retrieval systems with additional keywords that are more up-to-date, directly from the users' own terminology, and of wider global applicability. In other words, because the users themselves used the terms to describe their own resources, the terms are said to be more user centered or meaningful to the users, thereby use of these tags will afford more effective retrieval of resources in information retrieval systems such as library OPACs, online databases, and web-based services. However, as socially-constructed knowledge structures are relatively recent phenomena, we have much to learn about the potential uses of tags and folksonomies, as well as the social structures being developed by the users of the social networking, bookmarking, and cataloging sites.

This chapter will first introduce online social networking, bookmarking, and cataloging sites and the social taxonomic behaviors taking place within them. Second, a framework for examining the research and perspectives on tagging, bookmarking, and social sharing behaviors will be presented and discussed, along with research related to social construction of structures for organizing knowledge.

Introduction to Social Networking, Bookmarking, and Cataloging Sites

Definitions

To begin this section, it is perhaps necessary to define some of the terms related to social approaches for developing structures for organizing knowledge. As this topic is a fairly new area of research and application, some of the more prevalent terms and concepts are presented here, along with some alternate terms that are also present in the literature.

- **Folksonomy(ies)**: The set of terms and phrases resulting from the individual and/or collaborative tagging activities within a social bookmarking, social networking, or social cataloging site. Folksonomies can be used as a source for tags users can add to describe their resources, as well as a means to retrieve other items tagged with the same tag, through the use of visual displays of the tags called "tag clouds." Alternate terms include "unstructured vocabularies," "nonhierarchical ontologies," "nonhierarchical taxonomies," "tag sets," "tag clouds," and "emergent ontologies." The term "folksonomy" was coined by Thomas Vander Wal (2006). Presently the majority of the literature appears to have settled on the term "folksonomy (ies)."
- **Library 2.0**: The application of Web 2.0 technologies, applications, and philosophies within the library context to improve or provide new services to user communities. There are no alternate terms for this concept, although some of the literature is beginning to use "Library 3.0" and beyond. The term was coined by Michael Casey in 2005 on his blog "LibraryCrunch."

- **OPAC**: A library's online public access catalog that provides access to the services and collections of a library. OPACs can use either proprietary or open source software. There are no alternate terms for this concept.
- **Social bookmarking site**: Website that provides users with the means to organize, describe, and share their resources (e.g., web bookmarks, photographs, and videos) with others. Sites like Delicious, Diigo, and Flickr are examples. Alternate terms include "social networking," "social classification," "social cataloging," "social media sharing," and "social sharing site."
- **Social cataloging site**: Website that provides users with the means to organize, catalog, and share their personal collection of resources, namely, books, DVDs, and audio CDs, with others. Social cataloging sites often include portions of existing library bibliographic records as the basis for the records created by users, along with user-contributed content such as tags, reviews, and other comments. Sites like LibraryThing, Goodreads, Stashmatic, and Shelfari are examples. Alternative terms include "social networking," "social media sharing," "social bookmarking," and "social sharing sites."
- **Social networking site**: Website or application that provides users with a platform to set up personal spaces online to share information, music, software applications, etc. Social networking software may include other Web 2.0 technologies like blogs, wikis, and social bookmarking. Technorati, MySpace, and Facebook are examples. Alternate terms include "social bookmarking," "social sharing," "social media sharing," "social cataloging," and "social classification sites."
- **Tagging**: The act of providing a term or set of terms, referred to as a "tag" or "tags," to describe resources in a social bookmarking, social networking, or social cataloging site. Tags can also be used to sort, retrieve, and find/refind the resources by the tagger or others that use the site. The resulting "tag clouds" available on many social sites show users the tags they used, the tags used by others, and the most popular tags used by users of the site. Alternative terms include "descriptors," keywords," "user-generated descriptors," "user-contributed content," "user-defined descriptors," "social classification," and "ethnosocial classification," among others. Presently the majority of the literature uses the terms "tag(s)" and "tagging."
- **Web 2.0**: Using the Internet and World Wide Web as a network platform. Web 2.0 refers to a suite of devices, protocols, standards, and applications of technologies present in social networking, sharing, and cataloging websites. Web 2.0 philosophies include rethinking how software is developed and distributed and enabling more human connections through conversations, collaboration, participation, and exchange of ideas and technologies. Within the library context, the term "Library 2.0" is often used.

History of Social Networking, Bookmarking, and Cataloging Sites

According to Louise Spiteri (2008), since 2004, social software applications have continued to increase in popularity and use. At present, the Wikipedia entry for Lists of Media Sharing Sites lists 14 media sharing sites, 41 social bookmarking sites (Wikipedia, 2009a), and approximately 27 social cataloging sites (Wikipedia, 2009c).

Social networking, social bookmarking, and social cataloging sites actually have a relatively short history. The Wikipedia (2009b) entry for Social Bookmarking states that

> the concept of shared online bookmarks dates back to April 1996 with the launch of itList, the features of which included public and private bookmarks. Within the next three years, online bookmark services became competitive, with venture-backed companies such as Backflip, Blink, Clip2, ClickMarks, HotLinks, and others entering the market.

Another example of an early social bookmarking service, Slashdot, developed in 1997, allowed users to contribute links and sites to news stories. Delicious, a social bookmarking service for storing, organizing, sharing, and finding (and refinding) web bookmarks, was founded by Joshua Schachter in 2003 and acquired by Yahoo! in 2005. Delicious pioneered tagging and also is credited with coining the term "social bookmarking" (Wikipedia, 2009b). Further sites such as Furl (in 2004) and a host of others (Simpy, Spurl, Raw Sugar) were developed during 2003–2004 (Abbas, 2010: 453). CiteULike and Connotea, social bookmarking sites focused more on organizing and sharing journal articles for an academic audience, also were developed in 2004. The year 2004 also saw the first use of the term "Web 2.0" by O'Reilly and Battele (O'Reilly, 2005).

In 2005, LibraryThing, Flickr, and other social bookmarking sites were made available on the web. Users were encouraged to organize and tag their own collections of books, photos, and bookmarks and to tag and comment on other users' collections as well. Also of importance, in 2005 the Steve.Museum consortium tagging project began to explore the use of user-generated tags within online museum collections. The Steve.Museum Project illustrates one of the first large-scale research efforts to learn more about the feasibility of using user-contributed tags to index images on the museums' websites (Abbas, 2010). The term "Library 2.0" was also coined in 2005 by Michael Casey (Casey and Savastinuk, 2006).

In 2006, another significant development was the PennTags project at the University of Pennsylvania. The University of Pennsylvania library OPAC was opened up to the university community, and users were invited to tag or comment on library resources within the library's OPAC using a homegrown system developed by the University of Pennsylvania. Also in 2006, library integrated system vendors began to integrate tagging, faceted, and visual search and classification into library OPACs (Abbas, 2010). Many of the social cataloging sites, such as Goodreads or Shelfari, were started in 2006.

From 2007 to the present, libraries have begun integrating user-contribution features into their library OPACs. For example, in January 2007 SOPAC was developed by Ann Arbor District Library, which incorporates tagging, commenting, and reviews into the library's OPAC. In May 2007 LibraryThing for Libraries (LTFL) was launched. Libraries can connect their OPACs to LibraryThing using specialized software that allows users to provide tags to library resources. Danbury (CT) Library was the first library to go live with LTFL in 2007, and many other public and academic libraries have followed suit. For example, in July 2010, the LTFL website listed a total of 1,672 libraries and library consortia that were using LTFL to provide LibraryThing tags within their library OPACs (LibraryThing for Libraries, accessed 2010). Also of significance, in 2008, was the decision by the Library of Congress to add a photo collection of about 3,000 items to Flickr. The Library of Congress has also solicited the public for assistance in tagging the photos (Oder, 2008). In October 2008, Hadro reported that the OCLC WorldCat bibliographic database began integrating item tagging functionality into the catalog (Hadro, 2008).

Examples of Social Bookmarking and Social Cataloging Sites

In this section we will look at a few exemplars of social bookmarking and social cataloging sites, the features they include, and their resulting folksonomies. Social networking sites (such as MySpace and Facebook) will no longer be included in our discussion. While they may include Web 2.0 features such as tagging and commenting, their goal is to provide a platform to set up personal spaces online for individuals to communicate with others. These sites are not usually designed for individuals to organize, describe, and catalog personal collections. As Delicious, Flickr, and LibraryThing have been the focus for much of the research discussed later in this chapter, these social sites will be used as exemplars.

Social Bookmarking Sites: Delicious and Flickr

As noted earlier, Delicious was founded in 2003 by Joshua Schachter. Delicious pioneered the idea of tagging and is also credited with coining the term "social bookmarking." It was acquired by Yahoo! in 2005. Delicious's Help page defines the site's functions as both individual and collaborative: (1) a place to save your bookmarks online, (2) a place to share the bookmarks with other people, and (3) a place to see what other people are bookmarking. Delicious points to many of the issues discussed in Chapter 5 related to personal information management (PIM)—those of finding/refinding information found on the web, keeping track of the "good stuff" you find online, and having access to your bookmarks from multiple devices and locations. Contrary to what we learned in Chapter 5 about how people organize their own collections, Delicious sees folders as "the old way to organize your bookmarks." Tags and tagging instead are touted as means for user collections to naturally emerge and grow, and tags also allow a user's own bookmarks to be part of many collections rather than in just one folder (Delicious, "Help," accessed 2010).

Delicious also emphasizes the sharing features of its site, as well as the discovery or serendipitous opportunities that are possible by viewing both the new "freshest" bookmarks and the most popular or "hottest" bookmarks others have gathered, which will naturally "bubble up" to the top-rated sites as more people access and bookmark the sites. Figure 6.1 shows a screen capture of the "hottest" bookmarks on June 6, 2010. The boxes to the right of the bookmark indicate the number of people who have bookmarked and tagged the site in their collections. There is also a sidebar on the right side of the screen that shows the most popular tags at that point in time on the site.

Tags and tagging are considered important activities within Delicious, and the site encourages the use of tags for both organizing (labeling) your bookmarks and searching your own or others' bookmarks. The result of tagging activities is the "tag cloud" or folksonomy that develops as site members tag their bookmarks. Figure 6.2 shows an example of a tag cloud of Delicious' popular tags. The interactive tag clouds can be used as a source to gather tags for your own tagging, but the main function of the Delicious tag cloud, and tag search box available on each page, is to provide a visual search feature so that by clicking on the desired tag, users can find other bookmarks that have the same tag.

Figure 6.1. Delicious Popular Bookmarks

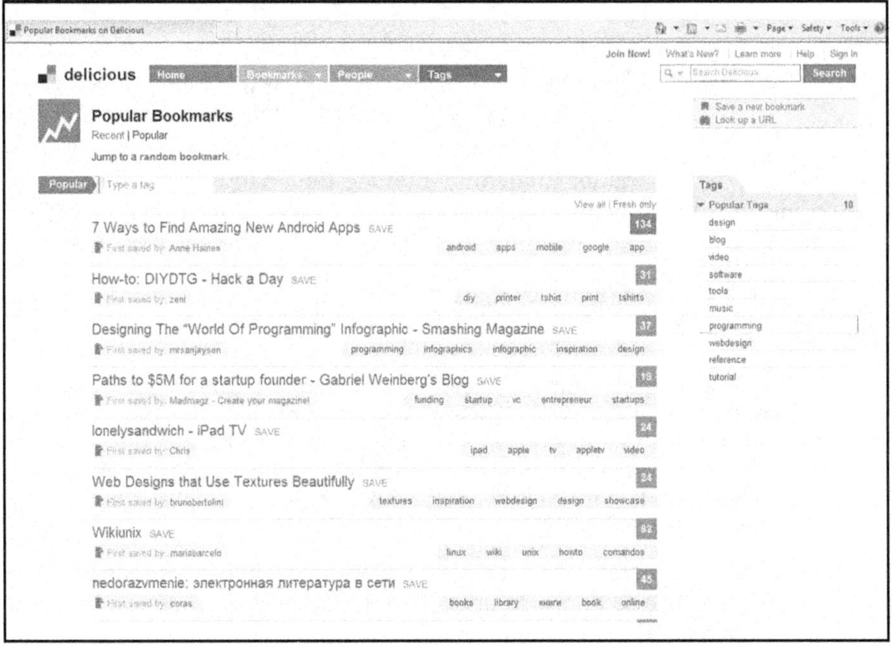

Figure 6.2. Delicious Tag Cloud: Popular Tags

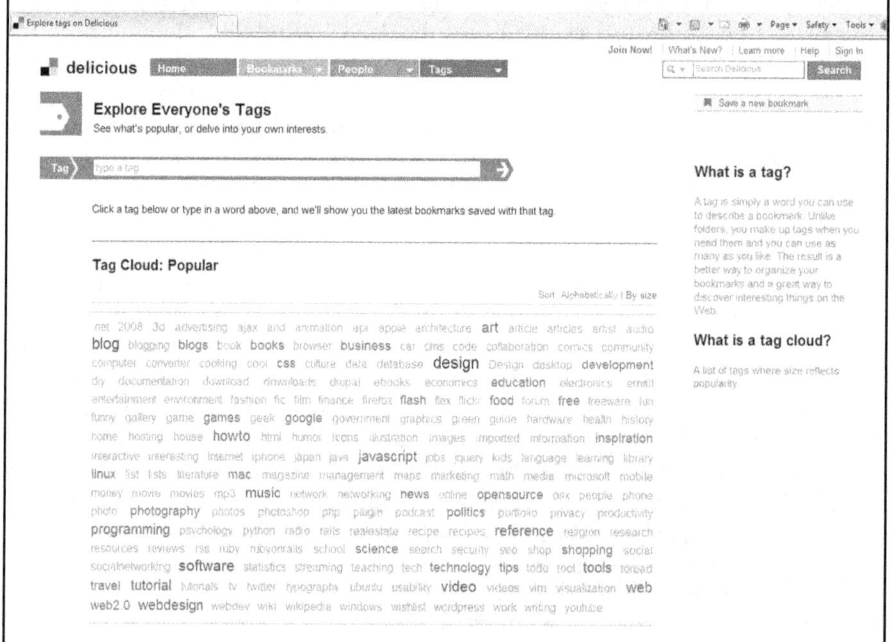

Flickr was developed in 2005 as a place where people could upload, save, organize, and share their personal image collections. Flickr's About page lists two goals for the site: (1) to be a place for people to share images and videos with the people who matter to them by making the images and videos available online and available through multiple devices and (2) to enable new ways of organizing photos and videos by allowing others to help you organize your photos and videos through the use of tags and comments (Flickr, 2009). Flickr speaks to the natural way that people like to interact with photos in the following statement:

> Part of the solution is to make the process of organizing photos or videos collaborative. In Flickr, you can give your friends, family, and other contacts permission to organize your stuff—not just to add comments, but also notes and tags. People like to ooh and ahh, laugh and cry, make wisecracks when sharing photos and videos. Why not give them the ability to do this when they look at them over the internet? (Flickr, 2009)

Flickr provides members with space online to organize their photos and videos into collections, sets, and photostreams. During the upload process, Flickr captures metadata related to the digital creation of the image, such as date, resolution, type of camera, and any special setting used. This information is also added to the photo's descriptive metadata. Once a photo is uploaded, users can add tags, comments, and notes to describe the photo. They can also choose who has access to the objects (anyone, friends and family, or contacts), as well as different levels of copyright for each photo or video. Figure 6.3 shows the features available in Flickr for organizing and describing a photo.

As shown in Figure 6.3, Flickr provides users with helpful, simple, and easy-to-use ways to describe their photos or videos. Users can add tags, comments, and notes to their objects. The interface provides a link to the user's own tag cloud and helpful instructions on how to form tags. Two views of personal tag sets are available to each user: (1) the traditional tag cloud (see Figure 6.4) and (2) a "big list" of tags in alphabetical order (see Figure 6.5).

Flickr further acknowledges the usefulness of the resulting metadata (tags, comments, notes) developed while objects are organized for both searching and describing collections. "And as all this info accretes as metadata, you can

Figure 6.3. Flickr Features for Describing an Image

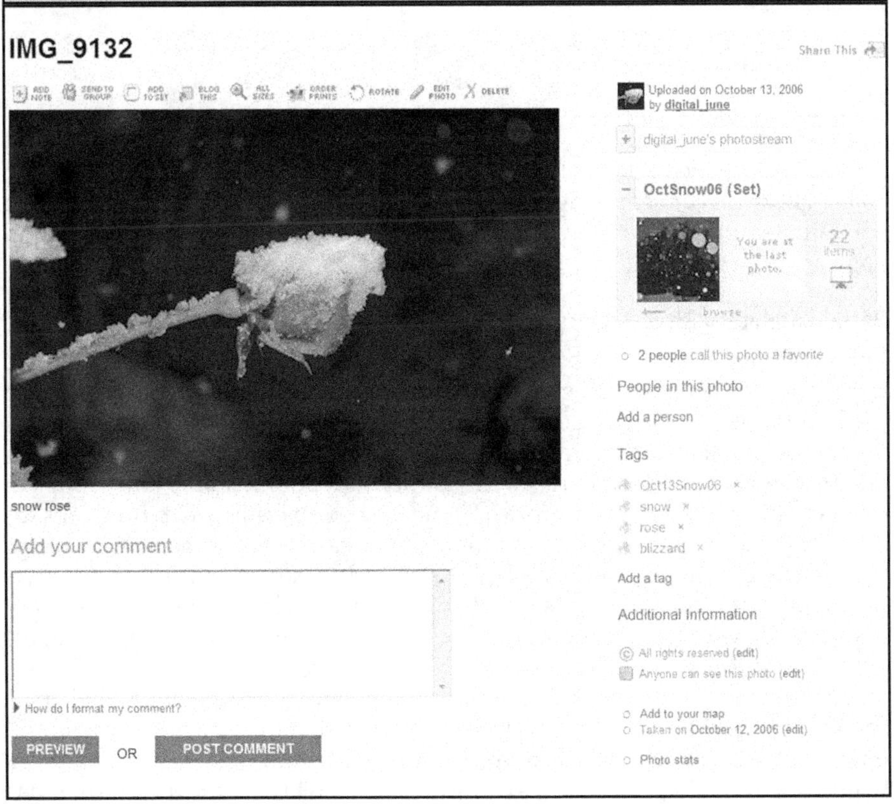

Figure 6.4. Personal Tag Cloud in Flickr

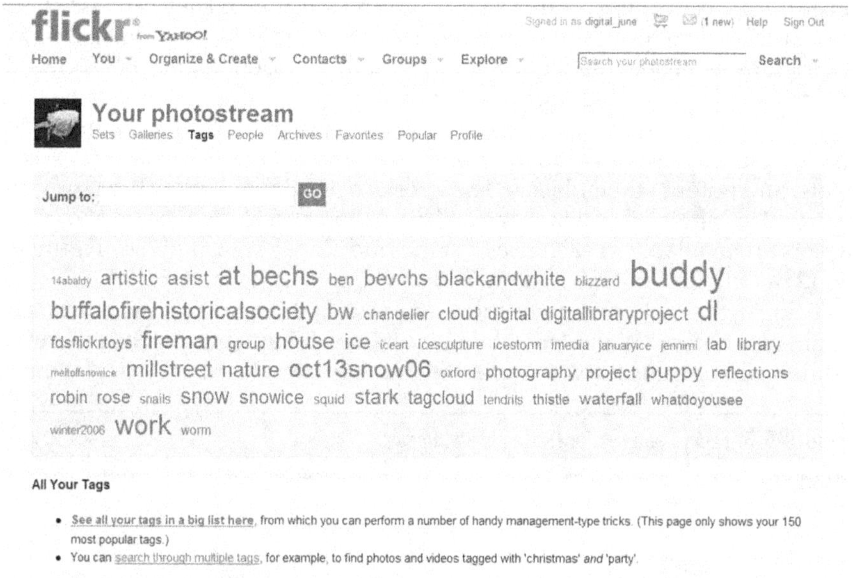

find things so much easier later on, since all this info is also searchable" (Flickr, 2009). Flickr makes searching by using tags even easier for users by providing a helpful feature for searching using multiple tags on each person's Tag Cloud page.

Social Cataloging Sites: LibraryThing

LibraryThing was created by Tim Spaulding in 2005 and remains one of the most popular social cataloging and social networking sites for organizing books. LibraryThing provides an online space for users to organize the books in their personal collections as well as to share the records for their books with others, to write reviews and recommendations for books, and to join groups of others with similar interests. LibraryThing's About page lists two functions for the site: (1) to help people catalog their books easily and to be able to access their catalog from anywhere and (2) to provide a social space that connects people with the same interests by allowing users to "check out other people's libraries, see who has the most similar library to yours, swap reading suggestions and so forth" (LibraryThing for Libraries, accessed 2010).

LibraryThing not only allows users an online place to organize their personal libraries of books, but it also integrates existing Library of Congress bibliographic records, as well as Amazon's records and those from more than 80 libraries around the world. Users can add their own tags to the records and use

Figure 6.5. Personal Tag "Big List" in Flickr

Your photostream

Sets Galleries Tags People Archives Favorites Popular Profile

	Tag	Entered as	On		
1	14abaldy		1 item	Edit	Delete
A	artistic	artistic	5 items	Edit	Delete
	asist	ASIST	5 items	Edit	Delete
	at	At	35 items	Edit	Delete
B	bechs	BECHS	29 items	Edit	Delete
	ben	Ben	1 item	Edit	Delete
	bevchs	BEVCHS	6 items	Edit	Delete
	blackandwhite	Blackandwhite	5 items	Edit	Delete
	blizzard	blizzard	1 item	Edit	Delete
	buddy	Buddy	88 items	Edit	Delete
	buffalofirehistoricalsociety	BuffaloFireHistoricalSociety	17 items	Edit	Delete
	bw	b&w	6 items	Edit	Delete
C	chandelier	chandelier	1 item	Edit	Delete
	cloud	cloud	1 item	Edit	Delete
D	digital	digital	1 item	Edit	Delete
	digitallibraryproject	digital library project, digitallibraryproject	2 items	Edit	Delete
	dl	DL	35 items	Edit	Delete

the Library of Congress and Dewey systems to classify their collections. A full record of a book added to LibraryThing, once aggregated by LibraryThing, includes not only the user's record and tags but also system-generated and collaboratively developed information about (1) how many users also have the book, (2) popularity ratings, (3) members who recently added the book, (4) a tag cloud with all users' tags representing the book, (5) recommendations for other similar books to read generated by LibraryThing's recommender system, (6) member recommendations and reviews, (7) published reviews from multiple sources, and (8) LibraryThing's "Common Knowledge" fields, which give users the opportunity to add additional descriptive information about the book, including, for example, series information, canonical title, people/characters mentioned in book, important events or places mentioned, and dedications. As shown in Figure 6.6, LibraryThing has, in effect, merged traditional

Figure 6.6. Three Threads Merged in the LibraryThing Record Structure

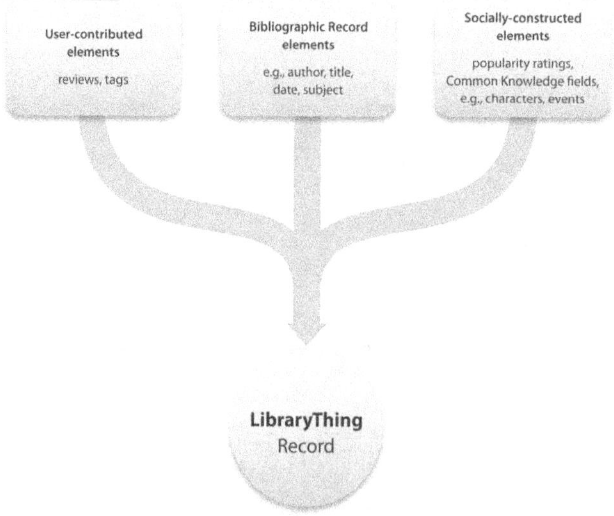

library structures for organizing knowledge (subject headings, bibliographic records, classification schemes) with personal, user-defined features (tags, reviews, additional attributes for describing the books, etc.), and socially-constructed, collaborative elements, such as the Common Knowledge elements, into one system for organizing and representing personal knowledge collections (books). Figure 6.7 shows an example of a partial record for a book cataloged in LibraryThing.

LibraryThing also provides views that will appeal to many different users' ways of organizing and displaying information. For example, Figure 6.8 shows the interactive Details view of the record, which surprisingly resembles a paper catalog card, with a few additions such as Reviews and Languages. Users can click on the hyperlinked author name, subject headings, member reviews, and classification notations links to find other related books and to find other members who also own the book. LibraryThing also includes a page with various images of cover art for the book that were uploaded by users.

Studying the activities of individuals and communities within each of the social sites described earlier in this chapter begins to illustrate the ways in which people choose to organize objects from their personal knowledge spaces, keeping in mind the limitations and features provided by each service. The activities and collections present in these social sites can help us gain a more in-depth understanding of what terms (tags) users naturally use to represent the attributes of their objects and those they choose not to use. The collections and their representations can also provide insights into the attributes users want to use to describe their objects, again keeping in mind the limita-

Figure 6.7. LibraryThing Record for the Book *Everything Is Miscellaneous*

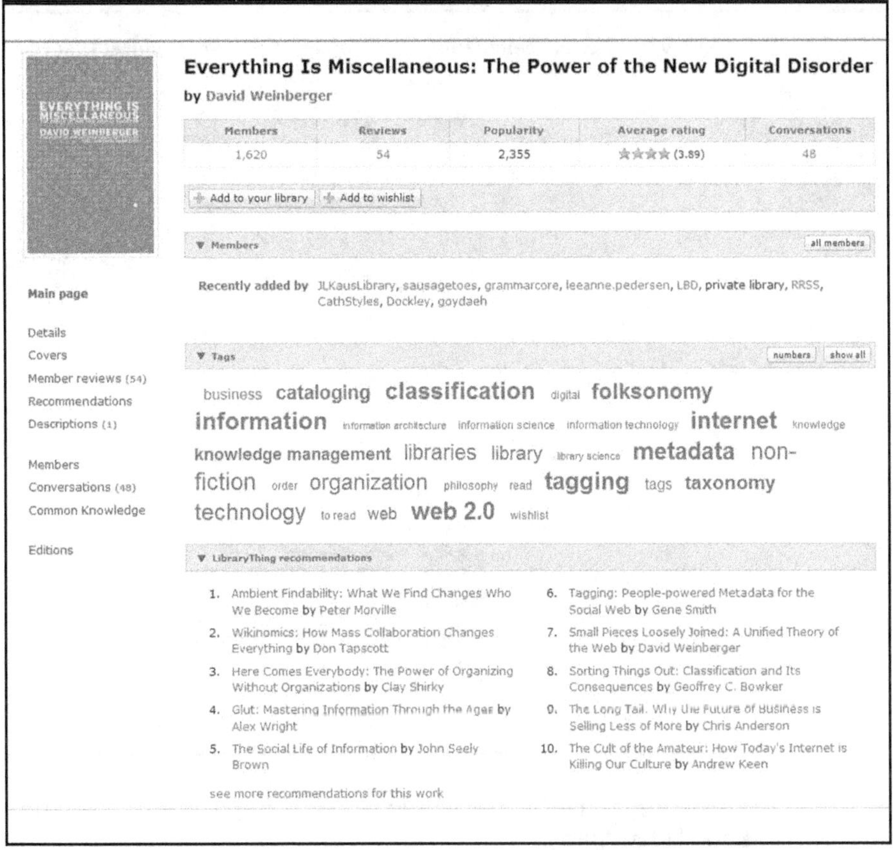

tions and features of the various social sites that are available to them. It is also evident by looking at the different structures of each of these social sites that the function and/or goal outlined by each site informs the system design and features available to users. For example, Delicious states that tags and tagging are the best way to describe and organize bookmarks and that by using tags users' collections will emerge naturally. Delicious does not support organizing bookmarks by any other feature, while Flickr takes a "shoe box collection" approach to how people traditionally have organized paper-based collections of personal photographs and allows users to create sets and collections.

Much is being discovered about users and their natural organizing behaviors, the terms and attributes they choose to use to represent their personal collections, and the motivations they have for organizing collections, but the picture is still very incomplete. The next section will outline various frameworks for learning more about these issues, as well as present the research and

Figure 6.8. LibraryThing Details View for the Book *Everything Is Miscellaneous*

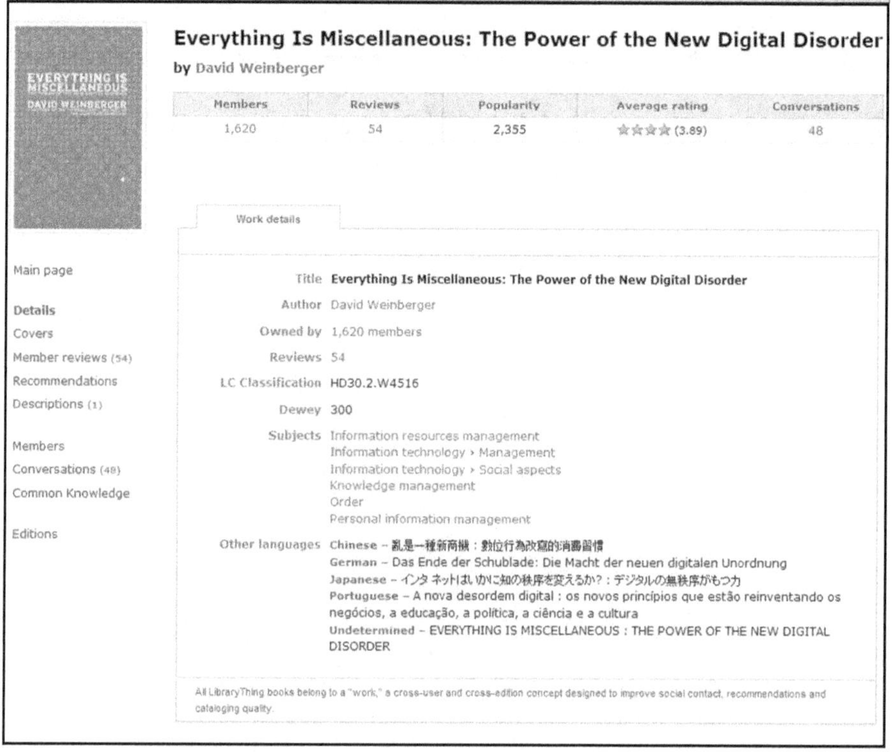

discussion focused on social knowledge-organizing behaviors and socially-constructed knowledge spaces.

Research Related to Social Knowledge-Organizing Behaviors and Socially-Constructed Knowledge Spaces

As described in the beginning of this chapter, social bookmarking and cataloging sites have been available in some form since 1996, with most of them being developed in 2003–2005. Spiteri (2008) observes that since 2004 folksonomy research has experienced remarkable growth. She further brings to our attention that folksonomy research is very interdisciplinary in nature and that fields such as library and information science (and the subfields of classification and knowledge organization and information behavior), computer science, human–computer interaction, information architecture, semiotics and semantics are engaged in folksonomy research.

As with any new technology, there is a period of exploration during which early adopters of the technology put it through its paces, discover any underlying bugs and/or issues, compare it to existing technologies and/or practices and standards, and make suggestions for changes. During this period, new ideas for use, often those not thought of by developers, are also uncovered. Wider adoption of the technology affords a larger audience to explore the technology and to adapt it to their specialized uses, as well as constant refinement and extension of the technology to other applications and contexts. The web and Web 2.0 technologies bring yet another dimension to this process—including users and user-contributed ideas into the development, application, and refinement stages.

Reviewing the research and practice-based literature on the uses of social bookmarking and social cataloging sites reveals similar patterns of adoption, exploration, development, and refinement. As social sites become more popular, more users begin using them, enhancements are made, and users adapt them in various ways to meet their specific organizing behaviors and needs. This Adoption/Development/Use Cycle, as shown in Figure 6.9, and the research conducted during each stage may be characterized as follows:

1. Early Exploration: including (a) learning more about how each site is used by individuals and communities; (b) tagging activities and user studies on what motivates users to tag; (c) how users are using tags for both describing and searching; (d) nature of tagging and resulting folksonomies (form or properties inherent in tags, positive and negative qualities of tags); and (e) comparison of tags and/or folksonomies with existing controlled vocabularies, subject headings lists, thesauri, ontologies, and taxonomies.
2. Application: including (a) feasibility studies for integrating folksonomies and other Web 2.0 features, such as tagging and commenting in library OPACs or designing OPACs that include these features; (b) integration of

Figure 6.9. Adoption/Development/Use Cycle

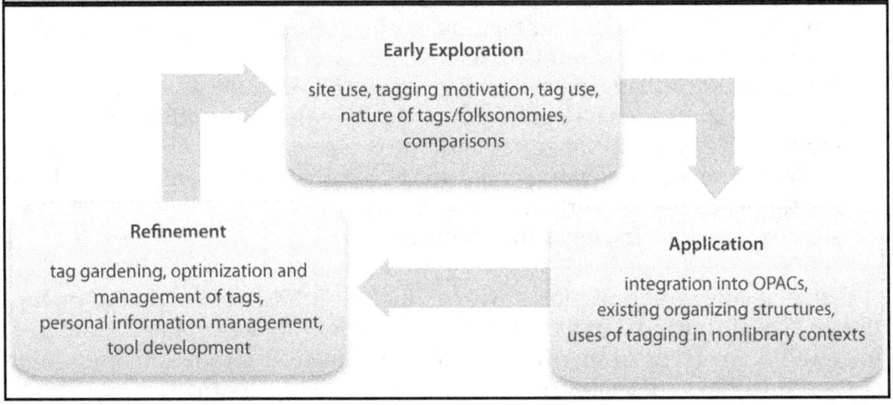

quality tags into existing structures for organizing knowledge, such as controlled vocabularies, as sources of new terms; and (c) uses of tagging and Web 2.0 features in nonlibrary contexts, such as museums, archives, and business intranets.
3. Refinement: including (a) tag gardening, tag maintenance, or automatic extraction of tags to form ontologies and taxonomies; and (b) development of tools for personal information management integrating tagging practices and tagging maintenance into these tools.

The research questions and methods for exploring the different issues identified earlier vary and are still being refined as more research is conducted. Studies have focused on the tags and resulting folksonomies and on the nature and quality of the most popular tags or collective folksonomy of either one or a few of the social sites. Other studies have taken traditional library and information science knowledge representation and information retrieval approaches such as co-occurrence and frequency analysis of tags and extent of match studies between folksonomies and controlled vocabularies such as *Library of Congress Subject Headings* (LCSH) and *Medical Subject Headings* (MeSH). However, as Trant (2008: 2) notes, "this is a new area of research, where theoretical perspectives and relevant research methods are only now being defined."

Trant presents a useful framework for categorizing the research and for analyzing social organizing behaviors and structures presented in the literature. Trant (2008) characterizes the literature as focused in three areas:

1. **The folksonomy itself** (and the role of tags in indexing and retrieval), including studies on tag usefulness in retrieval; the quality of tags and folksonomies; vocabulary control and evolution of tags/folksonomies; vocabulary analysis comparing tags to existing controlled vocabularies; patterns or structure present in tags and folksonomies; tag spaces as ontologies; and economics of tagging
2. **On tagging** (and the behavior of users), including studies on tagging behaviors and motivations for tagging, such as sense making, personal information management, and task related
3. **Nature of social tagging systems** (or sociotechnical frameworks), including the use of tags as navigational/retrieval tools and methods of processing tags to create folksonomies and ontologies for use in other systems or contexts; the role of ranking and expert-contributed tags within social systems; and using network analysis theories to study underlying relationships between users, tags, and resources

Trant's framework does not, however, include studies beyond 2007 or capture all aspects outlined in the Application and Refinement stages. An important addition to Trant's framework would be to include studies on integration of tags and Web 2.0 features such as reviews and comments into library

OPACs and other structures for organizing knowledge. Much of this work has been done after 2007. For the purposes of our discussion on the topic of social organizing behaviors and social structures for organizing knowledge, this chapter will present only the research related to the Exploration stage and Trant's "folksonomy itself" and "on tagging" focus areas. Some studies may be referenced in more than one section as they cover multiple areas of research. Furthermore, research and related discussion on the Application and Refinement stages and Trant's "nature of social tagging systems" will be addressed in Chapter 7. The reader is also referred to Trant (2008) for a more comprehensive review of research related to other areas of social bookmarking and cataloging sites that are not pertinent to socially-constructed structures for organizing knowledge.

Research Related to Exploration of Tags and Social Structures for Organizing Knowledge

Learning More about Site Use and Tagging Activities

As little was known about how the sites were being used by individuals and the communities, users' motivation for tagging, or about the role of tagging and folksonomies within the site, the earliest studies into social bookmarking and cataloging sites focused on taggers' use of the sites and their tagging activities. For example, Adam Mathes (2004), in a paper originally written as part of the requirements of a master's class in LIS, provides the first review and survey of social tagging and folksonomy systems. Mathes reviews and compares the tagging behaviors of users on Flickr and Delicious and notes the strengths of folksonomies, such as their use for serendipitous finding and as a means to track trends or interests of users, or what are referred to as "desire lines" by Merholz (2004). Mathes (2004) also presents his assertions on why folksonomies "work," citing the low cognitive costs to entering tags felt by individual taggers; a tight feedback loop; and the ability of users to share tags within the site. Unfortunately, while Mathes presents very useful conclusions, his study is often criticized for little or no explanation of his methodology, sampling, or research questions. He also admits that his observations are not based on quantitative analysis of the folksonomies (Spiteri, 2006).

Golder and Huberman (2006) conducted one of the first studies that looked at the structure of collaborative tagging within the Delicious site. Their study examined user activity, the types of tags, and the frequencies of their use within Delicious over a period of four days. They identified seven primary functions of tagging bookmarks:

1. Identifying what (or who) the bookmark is about
2. Identifying what it is (is the object a blog or a website?)
3. Identifying who owns it

4. Refining categories (that have already been established within Delicious, such as serving as a qualifier to existing categories)
5. Identifying qualities or characteristics (such as emotive connotations of funny, scary, etc.)
6. Self-reference (referring to the relationship of the bookmark to the tagger)
7. Task organizing (the bookmark's relationship to a specific task)

Other useful insights from Golder and Huberman (2006) related to tagging activities and what motivates people to tag included aspects of personal information management (PIM) related to (1) sense making and (2) refinding or rediscovery of bookmarks and websites. Kipp's (2006, 2007) work supports the PIM-related role of tags in task-related organization. While Golder and Huberman's (2006) study presents very useful findings, because of its narrow focus on only one social site and small sample size, its findings are not very generalizable to other social sites and tagging activities.

Marlow and colleagues (2006) present a case study of use of Flickr. They focused on the nature and role of relationships within the site and the impact these relationships had on tagging activities and taggers. For example, they see system design and attributes and user incentives as important variables into whether or not people will provide tags. Marlow and colleagues (2006) also identified characteristics of tagging systems, such as (1) tagging rights (who was allowed to tag and what they could tag); (2) tagging support (viewing other tags or having tags suggested); (3) how tags were aggregated by the system; (4) type of materials to tag; (5) source of materials (from user, web, or system); (6) resource connectivity (links to tags to use); and (7) social connectivity (links between users) that may serve as motivating factors to users related to tagging activities.

Ying and colleagues (2009) used tagging data gathered between 2005 and 2007 from Delicious, Flickr, and YouTube to determine if it was possible to profile a social bookmarking site by examining the tags used by users of each site. Using the UTO crawler developed by Torunski (2008), they harvested the tags used in each site during the three-year period. In total they reviewed around 1 million bookmarks, 2.8 million taggers, and 9.3 million tags from Delicious; around 300,000 photographs, 150,000 taggers, and 1.4 million tags from Flickr; and around 500,000 videos, 200,000 taggers, and 1.35 million tags from YouTube (Ying et al., 2009). Their analysis provided an average range of tagging per object (2.74 in YouTube to 9.31 in Delicious); the average number of tags assigned (3.33 in Delicious to 8.79 in Flickr); and the average number of objects tagged (0.36 in Delicious to 2.84 in YouTube). Using frequency analysis of tags, they determined that only 1,363 of the 648,368 unique tags (0.2 percent) were assigned more than 1,000 times each, while 357,028 (55 percent of all tags) were assigned only once.

Reviewing the popular tags in each site allowed them also to determine the stability of the tags/folksonomy of the site. For example, in Delicious, 85 percent of the top 20 tags are stable across 2006 and 2007, indicating a shared vocabulary (folksonomy) may be developing. They also note the more frequently used attributes that users like in Flickr, such as date, locations, colors, and seasons, and that Flickr users frequently use informal tags or more personal tags. This finding is not surprising given the goals we cited earlier for both Delicious and Flickr; one encourages collaboration and sharing, and the other is more for personal use. YouTube's most frequently used tags also point to the goal of the site—for entertainment related to subjects like music, videos, humor, sex, and girls. Last, the Ying and colleagues (2009) study supports findings reported by Marlow and colleagues (2006) that tagging rights within each site have "created differences not only in the role tags play in each system but also in the nature of the tags that are assigned" (Ying et al., 2009).

Nature of Tags, Tagging, and Folksonomies

Research conducted to discover more about the nature of tags, tagging, and folksonomies includes studies focused on determining the form or properties inherent in tags and the positive and negative qualities of tags. Also included are studies related to vocabulary control issues and evolution of tags and folksonomies.

It should be noted at this juncture that many of the studies included in this section build on past research methods, findings, and rationales used by researchers focused on knowledge organization, vocabulary control and development, and information retrieval. The idea of using user-contributed or -generated terminology or keywords is not a new idea within the field and much of the research predates the World Wide Web and the emergence of Web 2.0 and Library 2.0. Image retrieval researchers concerned with better access to rich collections of images in contexts such as libraries, archives, art history departments, and newspapers have been exploring the use of user-generated descriptors (user-contributed content) since the mid 1990s. Examples of image retrieval and other areas of research into the use of user-generated content include (1) Hastings (1995), who had users apply their own descriptions to a collection of Caribbean paintings; and O'Connor, O'Connor, and Abbas (1999), who explored the gathering and application of user-defined/supplied descriptors for personal photographs; (2) Ornager (1997) and Neal (2006), who examined how newspaper journalists requested and searched for images by using captions in newspaper databases; (3) Greenberg (2001), who examined user-supplied descriptors for business and medical applications; (4) Abbas (2001, 2005, 2007), who explored the vocabulary problem in digital libraries and systems designed for youth and proposed the use of users' most frequently used search terms as user-defined descriptors to build controlled vocabularies; and (5) Reuter and Druin (2004), who had children supply descriptors for digital picture books in the International Children's Digital Library.

Researchers and developers of structures for organizing knowledge have long realized that knowledge organization structures are not, and should not be, static. These structures are continually updated, and research to determine if they work has been prevalent through the years (Abbas, 2007). In addition, controlled vocabularies have often been criticized as being out-of-date, containing arcane, discriminatory, Anglo-centric terminology (Olson, 2002). Library and information science researchers have conducted studies that show that users don't understand how to use subject headings (Markey, 1984b; Drabenstott and Vizine-Goetz, 1990) or that the words users choose for searching do not match subject headings (called "extent of match" studies) (Taylor, 1984; Carlyle, 1989; Doyen and Wheeler, 1989; Lester, 1989; Abbas, 2001).

Kipp's (2006, 2007) research represents the first extent of match studies conducted within social sites. Kipp compared the vocabulary of users, authors, and catalogers in the CiteULike social site. Her 2007 study expanded this research to include both CiteULike and the PubMed database. At this point no extent of match research focused on the overlap between nontag search terms and tags within social bookmarking and cataloging sites has been conducted. This gap may be due to the assumption that tags are the main device used by users to search within social bookmarking and cataloging sites, although this assumption has also not been investigated.

Other research related to issues about the nature of controlled vocabularies, vocabulary control and development, and the effective use of controlled vocabularies includes what are called "inter-indexer consistency" studies. These studies compare the index terms (controlled vocabulary or cataloging terms) assigned to information objects by different professional catalogers and/or indexers. These studies, conducted since the 1960s, are exemplified by Zunde and Dexter (1969), Cooper (1969), Markey (1984a), Chan (1989), Reich and Biever (1991), Sievert and Andrews (1991), Tonta (1991), Giral and Taylor (1993), and Leininger (2000), to name a few, who each examined inter-indexer consistency in different subject domains and systems. Their findings point to the need for continual refinement of structures for organizing knowledge, namely, controlled vocabularies, as well as development and proper application of standards for cataloging/indexing using these structures. Wolfram, Olson, and Bloom (2009) continue this tradition as the first researchers to examine inter-indexer consistency within social bookmarking sites, using CiteULike as their test bed. Their findings indicate no significant differences in tagging consistency among the tags related to the three topic areas (science, social science, and social software) they studied. They have also pointed out issues they encountered in conducting consistency studies within social bookmarking and cataloging sites, such as difficulties in identifying individual taggers and system design features and limitations, such as tagging rights.

Much of the tagging literature focusing on the nature of tags and the resulting folksonomies highlights the problems of tagging and folksonomy development and use. The limitations, as reported by Mathes (2004), Bates (2006), Gordon-Murnane (2006), Golder and Huberman (2006), Guy and Tonkin (2006), Peterson (2006), MacGregor and McCulloch (2006), and Spiteri (2006), include that tags are:

- sloppy,
- imprecise,

- redundant,
- nonsensical,
- ambiguous,
- for single use,
- contain misspelling,
- often applied inaccurately,
- contain no synonym or homonym control,
- contain both plurals and singular forms,
- are of informal or personal nature (me, my, naming specific individuals),
- have no hierarchical structure, and
- lack precise retrieval.

Also it should be noted that limitations of the tagging software within the sites allow for odd constructions of tags when more than one word was used. For example, users who wanted to add a phrase containing two or more words had to either combine the words with no spaces (informationretrieval) or use an underscore to separate the words (information_retrieval). Which form to use also was not consistent across different social sites. Some sites are now allowing phrases to be entered using quotation marks ("information retrieval") as in Flickr's latest instructions to users when entering a phrase, but the tag still appears with no spaces in the tag cloud.

Strengths of tags and folksonomies, as reported by Quintarelli (2005), Kroski (2005), Peterson (2006), and Weinberger (2007), include that tags:

- reflect the user population's conceptual models and language,
- are current,
- are inclusive (present multiple viewpoints),
- reflect emerging concepts,
- accommodate diversity,
- are democratic and self-moderating,
- follow desire lines,
- offer insight into user behaviors,
- engender community, and
- offer a low-cost alternative to implementing and updating controlled vocabularies.

It is important for further research and also for practical applications, such as integrating tags and folksonomies into library OPACs or other retrieval systems, that the limitations and strengths be recognized. However, many of these limitations and strengths can be disputed and require further investigation, especially as social sites adapt to accommodate user tagging behaviors. For example, what evidence do we have that folksonomies will self-regulate or self-normalize or that tags will become more consistent over time without "external imposition of controls" (Trant, 2008: 8)? Udell (2005), Millen and Feinberg (2006), and Weinberger (2005) have begun to investigate this question in different contexts. For example, Udell illustrates how the tags in an individual's tag set in Delicious stabilize; and Millen and Feinberg saw a decline in unique or new tags within IBM's company system, dogear. Each of these studies includes a relatively small sample and examines tag evolution within only one social site, so, while their findings are an important first step in this research area, they are not very generalizable to other social sites and to the issue of folksonomy stabilization or normalization in general.

Comparing Tags and Folksonomies to Controlled Vocabularies

Research focused on vocabulary analysis within tags also includes the comparison of tags and/or folksonomies with existing controlled vocabularies (subject headings lists, thesauri, ontologies, and taxonomies). This research seeks to illustrate (1) the feasibility and usefulness of using tags and folksonomies as supplements to controlled vocabularies within information retrieval systems and (2) using the tags or folksonomies as a source of terms to add to existing controlled vocabularies. Research exploring these issues is reported briefly in the following section.

Spiteri's (2007) research examines whether or not tag structures follow the prescribed standards for developing controlled vocabularies. She compares the tags generated by users over a 30-day period in the bookmarking sites Delicious, Furl, and Technorati with the NISO standard for controlled vocabulary development. A total of 75 tags from Delicious, 208 for Furl, and 229 for Technorati were analyzed. Section 6 of the NISO standard (including guidance of term choice, scope, and form) was applied to the tags. Her findings indicate that tags from the three sites correspond closely to a number of the NISO guidelines, "namely in the types of concepts expressed, the predominance of single tags, the predominance of nouns, the use of recognized spelling, and the use of primarily alphabetic characters" (Spiteri, 2007: 21). Potential problem areas include "inconsistent use of the singular and plural form of count nouns, the difficulty with creating multi-term tags in Delicious, and the incidence of ambiguous tags in the form of homographs and unqualified abbreviations or acronyms" (Spiteri, 2007: 21). Again, while Spiteri's research presents very useful findings and also methods for future research, because of the small sample size one is cautioned about generalizing her findings to other social sites and to tag structures in general.

A few other researchers have reported comparing tags and folksonomies to controlled vocabularies. These include Lin and colleagues' (2006) study comparing tags from the Connotea social site with *Medical Subject Headings* (MeSH) used within the PubMed database. Their findings showed that only 11 percent of the 540 Connotea tags analyzed matched those used in PubMed's MeSH headings and that the tags in general were less formal, more personalized, and focused on specific subject matter covered in the article, rather than the overall subject.

Bruce (2008) compared tags from CiteULike articles to descriptors assigned by professional indexers to articles in the ERIC (Education Resources Information Center) database, which uses the ERIC Thesaurus as the controlled vocabulary. The total metadata analyzed included 2,899 unique ERIC descriptors, 3,176 unique CiteULike tags, and 1,083 unique CiteULike users. His findings show that only 7.6 percent or 240 descriptors matched the CiteULike tag, leading Bruce (2008) to conclude that "CiteULike users do not use the same terminology as subject specialists who maintain descriptors in the ERIC thesaurus."

Thomas, Caudle, and Schmitz (2009) conducted an extent of match study between LibraryThing tags assigned to ten books and records from six public and academic library OPACs that employ Web 2.0–enabled interfaces. They chose the specific library OPACs because of the Web 2.0 features they included, such as users being allowed to contribute tags or reviews, or that the interface included faceted or visual search. The goal of their study was to determine if the tags matched with *Library of Congress Subject Headings* (LCSH) assigned to the records for the ten books. Using an extent of match scale originally developed by Voorbji (1998) and later modified by Kipp (2006), as well as using Golder and Huberman's (2006) categories to filter out the subject-related tags, they compared tags from the ten LibraryThing records to the records and any tags from the library OPACs. After filtering, the subject-related tags harvested included 3,721 tags or 46 percent of the total tags (Thomas, Caudle, and Schmitz, 2009). Their findings indicate that only 14 percent of the subject-related tags match exactly with the LCSH and 62 percent of the subject-related tags match to some degree with the LCSH as broader term, narrower term, related term relationships, a natural language synonym (as determined by the researchers), or a valid LCSH subject heading that was *not* assigned to the books. While this research presents some useful findings, it is not clear whether or not they filtered out the LCSH assigned to the bibliographic record portion of the LibraryThing records or if they just used the tag sets of the LibraryThing records. In other words, do the 14 percent of exact matches with LCSH result from the bibliographic records harvested by LibraryThing users when creating their records, or are the Library of Congress headings used as part of the tag clouds for the books? The researchers also note that "the taggers seem to have a familiarity with the controlled vocabulary [LCSH]" (Thomas, Caudle, and Schmitz, 2009: 425). LibraryThing users include a large population of librarians, and it is possible that the tags analyzed may have been contributed by members of this population, but the research does not report if this is the case or not.

Rolla (2009) took a different tact on comparing LCSH to LibraryThing tags. Instead of conducting an extent of match study, he compared the LibraryThing tags for 45 books with OCLC's WorldCat records for each book. His analysis was focused more on whether or not the records from each system represented the subjects covered in each of the 45 books and to what level of granularity they did so. For example, did the tags/LCSH cover all subjects in the books or just general subjects? How specific were the terms in either the tags or the LCSH? His findings include the following: (1) user tags included at least one concept not covered by the LCSH in the WorldCat records; however, in 55.6 percent of the records, LCSH brought out concepts about the books' subjects that the LibraryThing tags did not; (2) in 35 of the books (75.6 percent), the LCSH and tags represented the same subject or concept but used different terms to express the subjects; (3) user tags generally included very general and broad subject terms; (4) LibraryThing tags generally did not include chronological or geographic-related tags; and (5) tags included issues with synonymy and grammar (Rolla, 2009: 179–180). Rolla also points out that many of the differences seen in the analysis may be a result of cataloger adherence to the Library of Congress rules for assignment of subject headings. Taggers in systems like LibraryThing are not under the same constraints and are given little to no guidance on how to form tags. In conclusion, Rolla (2009: 182) states, "while user tags can enhance subject access to library collections, they cannot replace the valuable functions of a controlled vocabulary like LCSH." He also points out that adding tags may be more useful in public libraries rather than academic libraries and that if tags are added libraries will need to figure out a way to deal with inherent problems of folksonomies, namely, personal tags, lack of synonym control, and grammatical issues (Rolla, 2009: 182).

As we review this research it is evident that the studies reported have contributed useful findings to our understanding about how users tag, why they tag, the nature and form of the tags, and the similarities of tags to existing controlled vocabularies or how closely they follow standards for developing controlled vocabularies. It should also be noted that many of these studies are small in scale, thereby limiting the generalizability of each to other social sites and to the issues they explored in general. Much research is stilled needed in order to build upon and to validate the studies reported.

Also evident from these studies is the lack of research or reported findings on the issue of the socially-constructed *structures* themselves that support the tagging activities and in effect serve as the framework for users to represent their collections within these social sites. For example, Ying and colleagues (2009) report on the different attributes used by Flickr users (date, location, colors, and seasons) in contrast to those used in Delicious (mainly related to subject or name). LibraryThing also addressed the issue of structure of its system for representing books with its Common Knowledge project. Launched in October 2007, the Common Knowledge project used a wiki format to allow users to suggest fields to add to a user-centered field structure. The resulting structure then could be used to populate LibraryThing records. Users gave suggestions on which fields to include and which to delete. The resulting structure now is appended to each LibraryThing record, and users can add data about the books, including, for example, series information, canonical title, people/characters mentioned in book, important events or places mentioned, dedications, and other information not included in a bibliographic record but that the LibraryThing user community thinks is important. It would be interesting to know more about the decisions made while building this structure and also to examine the fields added as potential means to augment library bibliographic (MARC) record structure further. Similar research could be conducted in other social sites to determine user preferences when representing objects in information retrieval systems, such as library OPACs. Figure 6.10 illustrates the gaps in the research that have become evident through this review.

Figure 6.10. Gaps in Socially-Constructed Structures Research

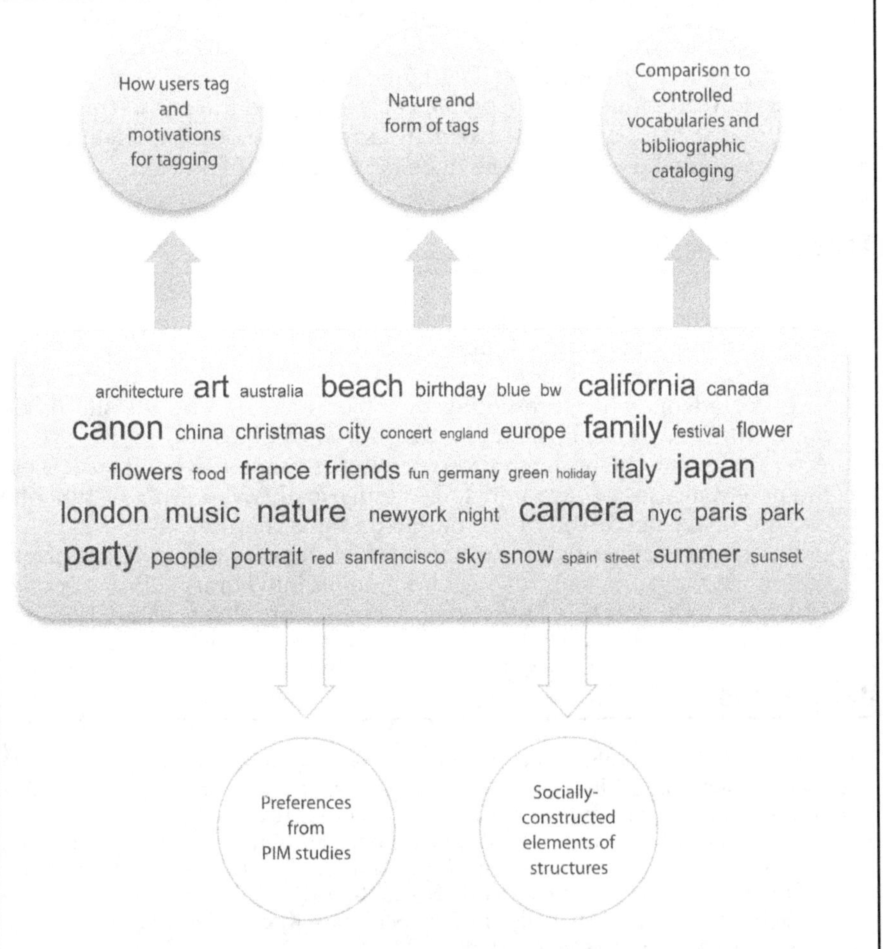

Conclusion

In this chapter we examined social organizing activities and the resulting socially-constructed structures for organizing knowledge that are being developed in Web 2.0 services, now commonly known as social bookmarking and social cataloging sites. These socially-constructed structures for organizing knowledge provide us with a window into how people naturally will organize objects in their personal knowledge spaces. The research is beginning to give us a better idea of social organizing activities and behaviors, but it does not address issues related to the structures people prefer for organizing objects within these socially-constructed knowledge spaces.

This chapter did not, however, address the practical applications suggested by the research findings—the integration of tags and folksonomies into library OPACs and other structures for organizing knowledge, such as adding tags to existing controlled vocabularies. These practical applications, as well as discussion on how to connect the disparate yet interrelated threads of traditional, personal, and socially-constructed structures for organizing knowledge into a coherent, or at least useful, whole will be the focus of Chapter 7.

Thought Exercises

1. Compare and contrast the different forms of social networking, social bookmarking, and/or social cataloging sites being used on the web. What do you see as their strengths and weaknesses? How useful are the structures for adequately representing the objects allowed by the site (bookmarks for Delicious, photos and videos for Flickr)?
2. After reviewing the research presented in the chapter, what do *you* see as the potential uses of tags and folksonomy(ies)? Make a list of potential uses that have not already been outlined in this chapter.
3. Brainstorm and create two separate lists of the benefits and problems of integrating tags, tagging features, or folksonomies into library OPACs or other structures for organizing knowledge, such as controlled vocabularies.

References

Abbas, June. 2001. "Smoothing the Information Seeking Path: Removing Representational Obstacles in a Middle School Digital Library Environment." Unpublished PhD dissertation. University of North Texas, Denton, Texas.

———. 2005. "Out of the Mouths of Middle School Children: I. Using Student Generated Keywords for Subject Access in a Digital Library." *Journal for the American Society of Information Science and Technology* 56, no. 14: 1512–1524.

———. 2007. "In the Margins: Reflections on Scribbles, Knowledge Organization and Access." *Knowledge Organization* 34, no. 2: 72–77.

———. 2010. "Social Software Use in Public Libraries." In *Handbook of Research on Social Interaction Technologies and Collaboration Software: Concepts and Trends* (pp. 451–461), edited by Tatyana Dumova and Richard Fiordo. Hershey, PA: IGI Global.

Bates, Mary Ellen. 2006. "Tag—You're It!" *Online* 30, no. 1: 64.

Bruce, Robert. 2008. "Descriptor and Folksonomy Concurrence in Education Related Scholarly Research." *Webology* 5, no. 3. Available: www.webology.ir/2008/v5n3/a59.html (accessed June 4, 2010).

Carlyle, Alyson. 1989. "Matching LCSH and User Vocabulary in the Library Catalog." *Cataloging and Classification Quarterly* 10, no. 1/2: 37–63.

Casey, M., and L. Savastinuk. 2006. "Library 2.0: Service for the Next Generation Library." *Library Journal* (September 1). Available: www.libraryjournal.com/article/CA6365200.html (accessed June 4, 2010).

Chan, Louis M. 1989. "Inter-indexer Consistency in Subject Cataloging." *Information Technology and Libraries* 8: 349–358.

Cooper, William S. 1969. "Is Interindexer Consistency a Hobgoblin?" *American Documentation* 20, no. 3: 268–278.

Delicious. "Help." Available: delicious.com/help/learn (accessed June 4, 2010).

Doyen, S., and D. Wheeler. 1989. "Use of a Controlled Vocabulary Index in Information Retrieval Tasks." In *Designing and Using Human–Computer Interfaces and Knowledge Based Systems* (pp. 226–231), edited by G. Salvendy and M. Smith. Amsterdam: Elsevier.

Drabenstott, Karen, and Diane Vizine-Goetz. 1990. "Search Trees for Subject Searching in Online Catalogs." *Library Hi Tech* 8, no. 3: 7–20.

Flickr. 2009. "About Flickr." Available: www.flickr.com/about (accessed June 4, 2010).

Giral, A., and Arlene G. Taylor. 1993. "Indexing Consistency and Overlap between the Avery Index to Architectural Periodicals and the Architectural Periodicals Index." *Library Resources & Technical Services* 37: 19–44.

Golder, Scott, and Bernardo Huberman. 2006. "Usage Patterns of Collaborative Tagging Systems." *Journal of Information Science* 32, no. 2: 198–208.

Gordon-Murnane, Laura. 2006. "Social Bookmarking, Folksonomies, and Web 2.0 Tools." *Searcher* 14, no. 6: 26–38.

Greenberg, Jane. 2001. "Automatic Query Expansion via Lexical–Semantic Relationships." *Journal of the American Association for Information Science* 52, no. 6: 487–498.

Guy, Marieke, and Emma Tonkin. 2006. "Folksonomies: Tidying Up Tags?" *D-Lib Magazine.* 12, no. 1. Available: www.dlib.org/dlib/january06/guy/01guy.html (accessed June 7, 2010).

Hadro, Josh. 2008. "Tagging Added to WorldCat.org." *Library Journal* 133, no. 17 (October 15): 21.

Hastings, Samantha. 1995. "An Exploratory Study of Intellectual Access to Digitized Art Images." *Proceedings of the Fifty-ninth Annual Meeting of the American Society for Information Science* 32: 3–8.

Kipp, Margaret. 2006. "Exploring the Context of User, Creator, and Intermediary Tagging." IA Summit 2006, Vancouver, BC. Available: www.iasummit.org/2006/files/109_Presentation_Desc.pdf (accessed June 7, 2010).

———. 2007. "@toread and Cool: Tagging for Time, Task, and Emotion." 8th Information Architecture Summit, Las Vegas, Nevada. Available: eprints.rclis.org/10445/ (accessed June 4, 2010).

Kroski, E. 2005. "The Hive Mind: Folksonomies and User-based Tagging." Info Tangle Blog. Available: infotangle.blogsome.com/2005/12/07/the-hive-mind-folksonomies-and-user-based-tagging (accessed June 4, 2010).

Leininger, K. 2000. "Inter-indexer Consistency in PsycINFO." *Journal of Librarianship and Information Science* 32: 4–8.

Lester, Marilyn Ann. 1989. "Coincidence of User Vocabulary and Library of Congress Subject Headings: Experiments to Improve Subject Access." Unpublished PhD dissertation, University of Illinois at Urbana-Champaign.

LibraryThing for Libraries. Available: www.librarything.com/wiki/index.php/LTFL:Libraries_using_LibraryThing_for_Libraries (accessed July 2, 2010).

Lin, X., J.E. Beaudoin, Y. Bui, and K. Desai. 2006. "Exploring Characteristics of Social Classification." *Advances in Classification Research* 17, Proceedings of the 17th ASIS&T Classification Research Workshop, Austin, Texas. Silver Spring, MD: American Society of Information Science and Technology.

MacGregor, George, and Emma McCulloch. 2006. "Collaborative Tagging as a Knowledge Organisation and Resource." *Library Review* 55, no. 5: 291–300.

Markey, Karen. 1984a. "Inter-indexer Consistency Tests: A Literature Review and Report of a Test in Consistency in Indexing Visual Materials." *Library and Information Science Research* 6: 155–177.

———. 1984b. *Subject Searching in Library Catalogs: Before and After the Introduction of Online Catalogs*. Dublin, OH: Online Computer Library Center.

Marlow, C., M. Naaman, d. boyd, and M. Davis. 2006. "HT06, Tagging, Paper, Taxonomy, Flickr, Academic Article, ToRead." *Proceedings of the 17th Conference on Hypertext and Hypermedia* (pp. 31–40). Available: doi.acm.org/10.1145/1149941.1149949 (accessed June 4, 2010).

Mathes, Adam. 2004. "Folksonomies—Cooperative Classification and Communication through Shared Metadata." Available: www.adammathes.com/academic/computer-mediated-communication/folksonomies.html (accessed June 4, 2010).

Merholz, P. 2004. "Metadata for the Masses." Available: www.adaptivepath.com/publications/essays/archives/000361.php (accessed June 4, 2010).

Millen, D.R., and J. Feinberg. 2006. "Using Social Tagging to Improve Social Navigation." Workshop on the Social Navigation and Community-Based Adaptation Technologies in Conjunction with Adaptive Hypermedia and Adaptive Web-Based Systems, Dublin, Ireland. Available: www.sis.pitt.edu/~paws/SNC_BAT06/crc/millen.pdf (accessed June 4, 2010).

Neal, Diane. 2006. "News Photography Image Retrieval Practices: Locus of Control in Two Contexts." Unpublished PhD dissertation. University of North Texas, Denton, Texas.

O'Connor, Brian C. 1996. *Explorations in Indexing and Abstracting: Pointing, Virtue and Power*. Englewood, CO: Libraries Unlimited.

O'Connor, Brian C., Jodi Kearns, and Richard Anderson. 2008. *Doing Things with Information*. Westport, CT: Libraries Unlimited.

O'Connor, Brian C., Mary K. O'Connor, and June Abbas. 1999. "User Reactions as Access Mechanism: An Exploration Based on Captions for Images." *Journal of the American Society for Information Science* 50, no. 8: 681–697.

Oder, Norman. 2008. "LC Seeks Community Tagging." *Library Journal* 133, no. 4 (March 1): 20.

Olson, Hope. 2002. *The Power to Name: Locating the Limits of Subject Representation in Libraries*. Dordrecht, the Netherlands: Kluwer Academic.

O'Reilly, T. 2005. "Web 2.0: Compact Definition?" *O'Reilly Radar* (October 1). Available: radar.oreilly.com/archives/2005/10/web_20_compact_definition.html (accessed June 4, 2010).

Ornager, S. 1997. "Image Retrieval: Theoretical Analysis and Empirical User Studies on Accessing Information in Images Digital Collections: Implication for Users, Funders, Developers, and Maintainers." *Proceedings of the 60th Annual Meeting of the American Society for Information Science* 34: 202–211.

Peterson, Elaine. 2006. "Beneath the Metadata: Some Philosophical Problems with Folksonomy." *D-Lib Magazine* 12, no. 11. Available: dlib.org/dlib/november06/peterson/11peterson.html (accessed June 4, 2010).

Quintarelli, E. 2005. "Folksonomies: Power to the People." ISKO, Italy—UniMIB Meeting, Milan. Available: www.iskoi.org/doc/folksonomies.htm (accessed June 4, 2010).

Reich, P., and E.J. Biever. 1991. "Indexing Consistency: The Input/Output Function of Thesauri." *College and Research Libraries* 52: 336–342.

Reuter, Kara, and Alison Druin. 2004. "Bringing Together Children and Books: An Initial Descriptive Study of Children's Book Searching and Selection Behavior in a Digital Library." *Proceedings of the 67th ASIST Annual Meeting* 41: 339–348. Medford, NJ: Information Today.

Rolla, Peter J. 2009. "User Tags versus Subject Headings: Can User-supplied Data Improve Subject Access to Library Collections?" *Library Resources and Technical Services* 53, no. 3: 174–184.

Sievert, M.C., and M.J. Andrews. 1991. "Indexing Consistency in Information Science Abstracts." *Journal of the American Society for Information Science* 46: 1–6.

Spiteri, Louise F. 2006. "The Use of Folksonomies in Public Library Catalogs." *Serials Librarian* 51, no. 2: 75–89.

———. 2007. "The Structure and Form of Folksonomy Tags: The Road to the Public Library Catalog." *Information Technology and Libraries* 26, no. 3: 13–25.

———. 2008. "Editorial: Folksonomies, the Web and Search Engines." *Webology* 5, no. 3, editorial 17. Available: www.webology.ir/2008/v5n3/editorial17.html (accessed June 4, 2010).

Taylor, Arlene. 1984. "Authority Files in Online Catalogs: An Investigation of Their Value." *Cataloging & Classification Quarterly* 4, no. 3: 1–17.

Thomas, Marliese, Dana M. Caudle, and Cecilia M. Schmitz. 2009. "To Tag or Not to Tag." *Library Hi Tech* 27, no. 3: 411–434.

Tonta, Y. 1991. "A Study of Indexing Consistency between Library of Congress and British Library Catalogers." *Library Resources & Technical Services* 35: 177–185.

Torunski, L. 2008. "Smart and Simple Web Crawler" (Version 1.1) [Computer software]. Santa Clara, CA: Sun Microsystems. Available: crawler.dev.java.net (accessed June 4, 2010).

Trant, Jennifer. 2008. "Studying Social Tagging and Folksonomy: A Review and Framework." *Journal of Digital Information* 10, no. 1. Available: journals.tdl.org/jodi/article/view/269/278 (accessed June 4, 2010).

Udell, J. 2005. "Jon Udell: Language Evolution in del.icio.us." Available: weblog.infoworld.com/udell.gems/delicious.html (accessed June 4, 2010).

Vander Wal, Thomas. 2006. "Folksonomy to Improve IA." Presented at the OZ IA, Sydney, Australia. Available: s3.amazonaws.com/2006presentations/OZIA/Folksonomy_for_IA.pdf (accessed June 4, 2010).

Voorbji, H.J. 1998. "Title Keywords and Subject Descriptors: A Comparison of Subject Search Entries of Books in the Humanities and Social Sciences." *Journal of Documentation* 54, no. 4: 466–476.

Weinberger, David. 2005. "Controlled and Suggested Vocabularies: Are Tags Making Us Dumb?" Jobo the Blog (blog). Available: www.hyperorg.com/blogger/2005/

03/26/controlled-and-suggested-vocabularies-are-tags-making-us-dumb/ (accessed June 4, 2010).
———. 2007. *Everything Is Miscellaneous: The Power of the New Digital Disorder*. New York: Times Books.
Wikipedia. 2009a. "List of Media Sharing Sites." Available: en.wikipedia.org/wiki/List_of_social_software (accessed June 4, 2010).
———. 2009b. "Social Bookmarking." Available: en.wikipedia.org/wiki/Social_bookmarking (accessed June 4, 2010).
———. 2009c. "Social Cataloging." Available: en.wikipedia.org/wiki/Social_cataloging_applications (accessed June 4, 2010).
Wolfram, Dietmar, Hope A. Olson, and Raina Bloom. 2009. "Measuring Consistency for Multiple Taggers Using Vector Space Modeling." *Journal of the American Society for Information Science and Technology* 60, no. 10: 1995–2003.
Ying, Ding, Elin K. Jacob, James Caverlee, and Zhixiong Zhang. 2009. "Profiling Social Networks: A Social Tagging Perspective." *D-Lib Magazine* 15, no. 3/4. Available: dlib.org/dlib/march09/ding/03ding.html (accessed June 4, 2010).
Zunde, P., and M.E. Dexter. 1969. "Indexing Consistency and Quality." *American Documentation* 20: 259–267.

Websites Noted in Text

CiteULike. Available: www.citeulike.org (accessed June 4, 2010).
Delicious. Available: delicious.com (accessed June 4, 2010).
Diigo. Available: www.diigo.com (accessed June 4, 2010).
Facebook. Available: www.facebook.com (accessed June 4, 2010).
Flickr. Available: www.flickr.com (accessed June 4, 2010).
GoodReads. Available: www.goodreads.com (accessed June 4, 2010).
LibraryCrunch blog. Available: www.librarycrunch.com/2007/10/we_know_what_library_20_is_and.html (accessed June 4, 2010).
LibraryThing. Available: www.librarything.com/ (accessed June 4, 2010).
MySpace. Available: www.myspace.com (accessed June 4, 2010).
Shelfari. Available: www.shelfari.com (accessed June 4, 2010).
Stashmatic. Available: stashmatic.com (accessed June 4, 2010).
Steve. The Museum Social Tagging Project. Available: www.steve.museum (accessed June 4, 2010).
Technorati. Available: technorati.com (accessed June 4, 2010).

7

Extending Our Thinking: Creating a Structure for Organizing Knowledge from Various Threads

Focus Points

- How can we "connect" the threads from the traditional approach, from personal organizing behaviors, and from socially-constructed structures into coherent and useful structures for organizing knowledge?
- What are the practical applications of this emerging structure, as well as the implications for library and information science and related professions and disciplines?
- How might these potentially new structures impact our everyday professional and work-related lives?

Introduction and Scope of the Chapter

In Chapter 6, socially-constructed structures for organizing knowledge, now commonly known as social bookmarking and social cataloging sites, were introduced and research into their use, tagging activities, and user studies were detailed, along with an overview of the research on issues related to structures for organizing knowledge. Tagging and the resulting folksonomies and structures for organizing knowledge are providing us with a window into the natural organizing behaviors of users as they freely upload and organize objects from their knowledge spaces. Social bookmarking and cataloging sites are, in effect, Petri dishes in which researchers in library and information science and related disciplines can learn more about the choices users make when organizing (describing) their objects (Abbas and Graham, 2006). Not only are we learning about the terms they choose by examining their tags but also the amount of terms they use, the level of granularity of their representations, and the attributes users *want* to use when representing objects. However, while research in this area is quite active and a picture is beginning to form, little is *really* known. What *is* clear is that tagging and use of social bookmarking and cataloging sites continues to be popular with users. What is also clear is that more research and application is needed to determine the feasibility of incorporating tagging and resulting folksonomies and other Web 2.0–related activities into existing structures for organizing knowledge. Furthermore, and perhaps of highest importance, is how do we begin to weave these seemingly disparate threads of traditional classification and structures for organizing knowledge, personal "natural" ways of organizing knowledge spaces, and socially-constructed structures for organizing knowledge into a coherent and useful structure for organizing knowledge? Or should we instead be considering a rich tapestry of possibilities and multiple structures?

In this chapter we will begin to address these issues by first reviewing briefly the "threads" we have to work with. We will then review examples of practical applications of tagging and other Web 2.0–related technologies into traditional library structures, such as library OPACs.

Review of Traditional, Personal, and Socially-Constructed Threads

The three "threads" discussed throughout this book (traditional, personal, and socially-constructed) contain many additional strands we need to address also, as illustrated in Figure 7.1. For example, those labeled as "traditional" include the formal structures developed by library and information science as well as the exemplars reviewed in Chapters 2 and 4 from other academic contexts, such as biology, zoology, and social science. The "personal" thread includes the more informal ways in which people naturally organize both their personal and work-related knowledge spaces. Last, "socially-constructed" refers to the emerging folksonomies and tagging practices and preferences that we are learning from, that take place in social bookmarking and cataloging sites. Some of the strands to consider include:

1. Traditional
    a. Controlled vocabularies such as subject headings lists or thesauri
    b. Classification schemes
    c. Domain-specific taxonomies
    d. Bibliographic structures for representing knowledge objects (e.g., MARC record structure)
    e. standards related to each of these (e.g., *Anglo-American Cataloguing Rules* and *Resource Description and Access*)
2. Personal
    a. Personal information management (PIM)

   b. Domain analysis
   c. Professional uses of traditional and socially-constructed structures for organizing knowledge
3. Socially-Constructed
   a. Emergent structures, such as social bookmarking and cataloging sites
   b. "Tag gardening" or the maintenance of personal or community-constructed ontologies/folksonomies
   c. Social cataloging—combining traditional with social
   d. Integration of folksonomies and tagging into OPACs
   e. Integration of folksonomies and tags into existing controlled vocabularies

Figure 7.1. Knowledge Threads: Additional Strands to Consider

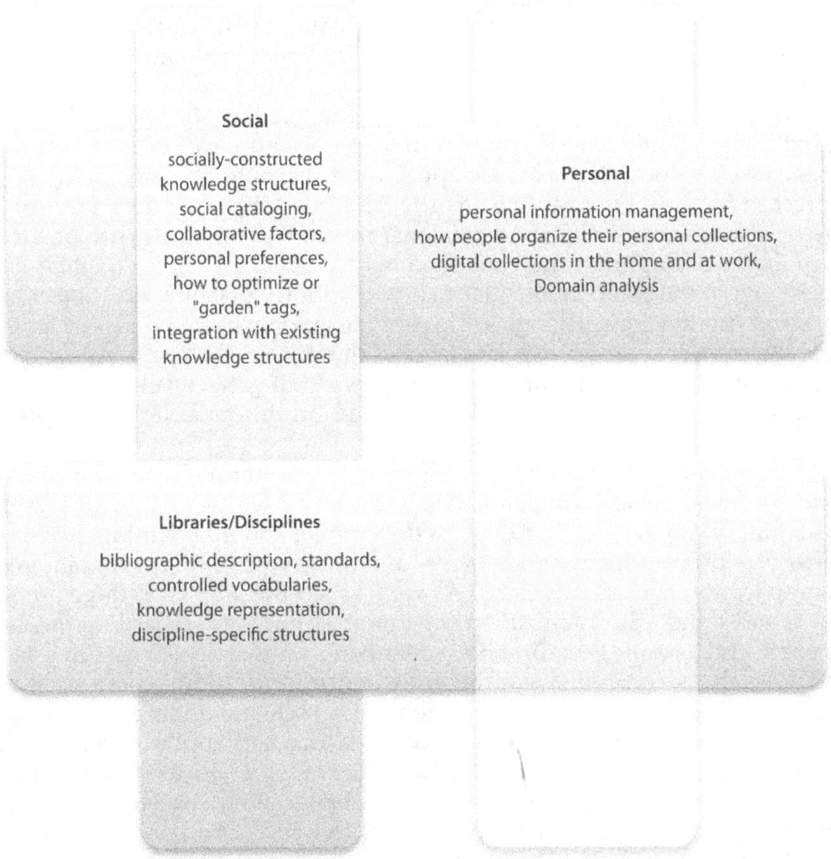

Traditional Structures for Organizing Knowledge

As learned throughout this book, there is a very rich and complex history related to the development and use of structures for organizing knowledge. Knowledge structures developed by library and information science include (1) library bibliographic catalogs (online public access catalogs—OPACs) and the metadata structure for representing data about objects in collections, the MARC structure; (2) related standards for encoding data, such as the *Anglo-American Cataloguing Rules*, and its continual revisions; (3) controlled vocabularies, including, for example, subject headings lists, discipline- and subject-specific thesauri, ontologies, and taxonomies; and (4) classification schemes. Those developed by natural sciences such as biology include (1) the Linnaeus taxonomy for scientific classification; (2) the international codes to implement the taxonomy, for example, the *International Code of Botanical Nomenclature*, the *International Code of Nomenclature of Bacteria*, the *International Code of Zoological Nomenclature*, and the *International Code of Nomenclature for Cultivated Plants*; and (3) the multiple metadata schemes and digital application and refinements of the Linnaeus taxonomy and the Codes, as outlined in Chapter 4.

The traditional structures for organizing knowledge tend to be rigidly structured and generally have extensive guidelines for application. Local best practices as well as local standards for application also might be used by catalogers or record creators. For example, in order to accurately apply the *Library of Congress Subject Headings* (LCSH) a cataloger must follow the rules established by the Library of Congress and contained in the *Subject Cataloging Manual*. These rules govern the choice and construction of Library of Congress subject headings and subdivisions. The rules also provide guidance related to how to represent the subject at an appropriate level of granularity or depth. As we saw in the biological code exemplars, the principles guiding the development and application of the formal standard are spelled out in detail and examples are given to assist the individual applying the code.

Each formal structure has been developed and refined over the course of many years by those individuals who will apply it within professional and/or disciplinary contexts. The process for developing and maintaining these structures also involves many stakeholders and those who have a vested interest in its application and effectiveness. As we learned in Chapter 3, there are standards and standards organizations that provide guidance regarding the development and use of structures for organizing knowledge. Structures in use today, such as controlled vocabularies and classification schemes, like the LCSH or Dewey Decimal Classification (DDC) scheme undergo continual review and revision at several levels: local practice and application (e.g., when catalogers suggest change or addition of terms in controlled vocabularies); professional review (e.g., when suggested changes to MARC record structure are reviewed or when structures such as the DDC are reviewed); and national/international standards review (e.g., when national or international standards organizations suggest changes to standards). These reviews and resulting revisions are predicated on the view that structures for organizing knowledge should not become static and should reflect the current and commonly used language and needs of those who will use them.

Critics, however, still point out the faults inherent in complex structures such as these, including that the structures are:

- out-of-date and do not contain new terms or logical divisions (classes) being used by users,
- biased toward Anglo-centric views and topics,
- not representative of cultural knowledges,
- not updated frequently enough,
- difficult to change, and
- not representative of how people would represent their own knowledge.

It is indeed interesting to note that folksonomies are viewed as a means to alleviate many of these weaknesses.

While review may be continual and from multiple levels, change to the structures and the standards is slow and can take many years. With new digital developments such as online subject headings lists and metadata schemes, additions and deletions to the structures can be made quickly rather than having to wait for the print edition. However, what is slow are the *decisions* that the controlled vocabulary, classification scheme, or metadata scheme should be changed, that new terms should be added, and that old terms or classes should be deleted or changed to reflect current usage. Furthermore, often these changes are effected at a local practice level first and then eventually at national/international levels. Change to a standard also can affect other related standards, which also might need to be revised as a result.

As noted in Chapter 6, little research has been conducted related to users' understanding of structures for organizing knowledge. Change to existing knowledge structures is often related to anecdotal experience rather than to research and may prove to be more of a temporary fix than a solution. For example, a significant development in the library and information science cataloging community is the development and implementation of the new standard for bibliographic representation, the *Resource Description and Access* (RDA), which is to replace the *Anglo-American Cataloguing Rules* (AACR2). The AACR2, often maligned for both its complex language and instructions and its ineffectiveness for addressing nonprint and digital objects, has continually been revised and refined since the first issue of the AACR in 1967. It was determined by the international cataloging community in 2005 to no longer revise the AACR2 and to instead develop a new standard for bibliographic description. The RDA was released in June 2010, five years after this decision. Many in the cataloging community, however, feel that, in light of developments in Web

2.0 environments, social bookmarking and social cataloging sites and resulting changes in user expectations, the RDA may be too little, too late.

The RDA has as its foundation the conceptual models developed from the findings of the *Functional Requirements for Bibliographic Records* (FRBR) studies designed to measure users' understanding and use of the structure of bibliographic records. FRBR used Charles Cutter's objects of a catalog as a basis for the functions the library catalog should provide to users. These include "(1) to enable a person to find a book on which either (a) author, (b) title, or (c) subject is known; (2) to show what a library has (a) by a given author, (b) on a given subject, (c) in a given kind of literature; and (3) to assist in the choice of a book (a) as to its edition and (b) as to its character" (Cutter, 1904, reprinted 1962: 12). Cutter's objects provided bibliographic code developers with the base set of elements that should be present in bibliographic records, (e.g., title, author, extent, publication information) in order to provide these functions. The functions provided are:

- Identification/Finding
- Collocation/Gathering
- Evaluation/Selecting

When library catalogs became automated, an additional objective was added: Location or Acquisition. The FRBR studies validated these functions (IFLA Study Group, 1998; Delsey, 2002, 2003) and extended our thinking of how to represent bibliographic objects for users.

The FRBR studies, however, represent a large conceptual leap for bibliographic and subject representation, as the findings indicate the need to restructure the traditional structure and usability of bibliographic records. The FRBR models provide a nonlinear, interconnected structure for representing knowledge within bibliographic records. The conceptual structure is more akin to the entity-relationship database model and hyperlinked connectivity seen in the web environment rather than to the flat file database model present at the time MARC record structure was developed. The entities and the relationships that have been defined in the FRBR model represent the key attributes of interest to users of bibliographic data. The entities have been divided into three groups. For example, the first group includes the products of intellectual or artistic endeavor that are named or described in bibliographic records: *work, expression, manifestation,* and *item* (although the user-friendly nature of these labels is suspect). The second group includes those entities responsible for the intellectual or artistic content, the physical production and dissemination, or the custodianship of such products: *person* and *corporate body*. The third group includes an additional set of entities that serve as the subjects of intellectual or artistic endeavor: *concept, object, event,* and *place* (IFLA Study Group, 1998: 12). Figure 7.2 shows a visual model of the first set of FRBR entities.

Figure 7.2. FRBR Model: First Group Entities

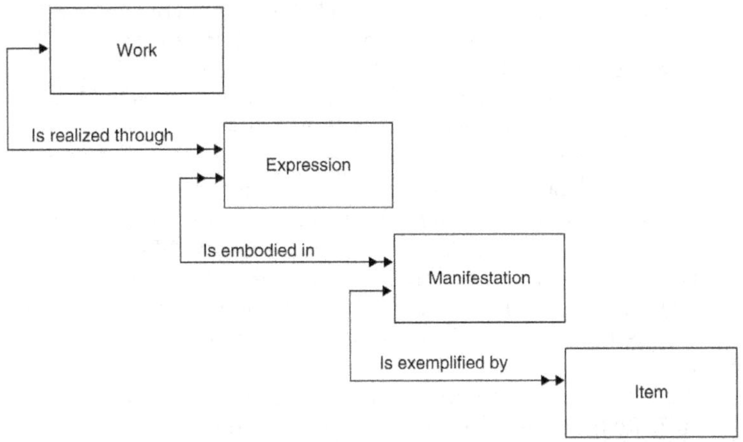

Source: *Functional Requirements for Bibliographic Records: Final Report* (IFLA Study Group, 1998: 13).

The RDA has the goals of supporting the new requirements for bibliographic description including rules for description of digital objects, as well as other nonprint objects, not adequately addressed in the AACR2.

Vendors, in response to Web 2.0 developments, the FRBR, and other related studies in classification, knowledge representation, and information retrieval, have developed what are now referred to as "Second Generation Catalogs" or next-generation OPACs. These new OPACs integrate faceted browsing and searching into more interactive interfaces. They also employ tag clouds as visual browsing/searching devices. However, to date, vendors have been hesitant to incorporate the FRBR conceptual model into OPAC design, waiting for the final development and implementation of the RDA. OPAC redesign in the future may include "FRBRizing" of MARC records to make connections between different manifestations of the same object, or related objects, more visible to users.

Implementation of the RDA and the FRBR models also requires that the MARC cataloging structure be revised as well. The MARBI (Machine-Readable Bibliographic Information) group is an interdivisional committee of the American Library Association (ALA): ALCTS (Association for Library Collections and Technical Services), LITA (Library and Information Technology Association), and RUSA (Reference and User Services Association). MARBI (accessed 2010) has begun to review and revise the MARC record structure to accommodate the changes made necessary by the RDA. See the MARBI website (www.ala.org/ala/mgrps/divs/alcts/mgrps/divgroups/marbi/marbi.cfm) for a summary of the changes made to the MARC structure.

Additional cataloging studies may also provide us with information on how to rework the MARC record structure. For example, William Moen (2009), with Shawne Miksa, conducted research to determine which fields in the MARC record structure are used most frequently by catalogers when developing bibliographic records in the OCLC WorldCat database. Using the entire database of WorldCat cataloging records as their data set (a total of 56,177,383 as of May 2005), they ran frequency analyses to determine which fields and related subfields were used most often in bibliographic records. Their findings indicate that a very small subset of the MARC fields and subfields available to catalogers are actually used to create bibliographic records. For example, in the Books, Pamphlets, and Printed Sheets format category, 14 fields (8.3 percent of the fields) occurred at least once in 80 percent of the records, and 21 fields (or 12.6 percent) occurred at least once in 80 percent of the records. Also, in Library of Congress–created records, 7 fields and 10 field/subfield combinations occurred commonly, and in non–Library of Congress–created records 10 fields and 18 field/subfield combinations occurred commonly (Moen, 2009). These findings indicate that the fields occurring commonly comprise the fields most often used by catalogers or what catalogers might view as the necessary or core fields to include in the bibliographic record.

However, while the Moen and Miksa study (Moen, 2009) is looking at the structure of bibliographic records from a *cataloger's* use perspective, their findings are indicative of catalogers' actual practices, which may indeed be very telling. However, because of the nature of their study, these findings do not indicate *why* catalogers used only a small subset of the MARC elements when developing bibliographic records. For example, did catalogers choose not to use specific fields because they thought they were unnecessary or that the description in the field would not be useful to users? Or were their choices simply for practical reasons related to time or to knowledge of the resource and/or the cataloging codes? There also is no evidence of how these commonly used fields support the user tasks identified in the FRBR study.

What do these developments and research findings suggest? Are efforts to revise cataloging standards (the RDA) and resulting changes to MARC record structures too little, too late? Have these efforts gone far enough to incorporate what we are learning about users' expectations and uses of Web 2.0 technologies?

Personal Structures for Organizing Knowledge

As noted in Chapter 5, there are few studies about personal structures that individuals use to organize the objects in their personal knowledge spaces, particularly in the home. Much of the research in this area is focused on work-related knowledge structures by researchers in personal information management (PIM). Studies such as Jones and colleagues' Keeping Found Things Found Project has explored many dimensions of PIM in work-related contexts. See the project website (kftf.ischool.washington.edu/index.htm) for more on this ongoing project and the findings. The Digital Lives project (Williams, John, and Rowland, 2009; Williams et al., 2008), as outlined in Chapter 5, will potentially provide even greater understanding of personal organization within home environments.

What we have learned about how people naturally organize knowledge spaces is summarized briefly:

- People vary greatly in their approaches to organizing information. Even within the same work environment or discipline, their approaches and organizing strategies may differ.
- People employ a variety of structures that are available through the technology they are using to store the information. They might use hierarchies or taxonomies in which folders containing various knowledge objects in various formats are structured.
- They may employ multiple hierarchical structures within one computer but also may/may not replicate these same structures on various computers or USB drives.
- People may keep information *without* a specific purpose in mind. There are many factors (cognitive, temporal, attentional) that affect both whether or not people keep information and their organizing strategies. Filing information away may be little more than an attempt to remove a distracting file or resource from one's desktop (physical or personal computer).
- As the amount of personal information stored increases, refinding a specific file may become more difficult. Alternative strategies of using tagging or labels may allow visual browsing, but, as the volume of loosely organized information increases, browsing also becomes problematic.
- Organizing and maintaining decisions can be based on various criteria, including (1) future use and (2) the value we place on the information (Jones, 2008: 160).
- The structure(s) we employ for organizing personal information in both work- and non-work-related environments may reflect how we conceptually think about and structure the routines, tasks, projects, etc., that we are engaged in on a daily basis and over a lifetime.

In contrast to formal, traditional structures for organizing knowledge, there may not be a standard or agreed upon way to organize the information objects in one's personal knowledge spaces. As outlined earlier, individuals use a variety of different structures for organizing their knowledge spaces, and these also vary within and between information devices. In the home environment, for example, multiple family members may use the same computer, and each may have his or her own way of organizing files. The family may have decided on a basic structure for organizing files, but there is no guarantee that this decision is followed or that it is maintained by family members. However, there is limited research exploring this area, so only assumptions and scenarios can be used to illustrate this point. In the office or work-related environment, both personal and group use of the files may be necessary.

In a personal office space, as outlined in Chapter 5, individuals use different strategies for organizing their office space. Whether a "filer" or a "piler," files for personal use may not reflect any community or group decisions on how to organize. Files organized and maintained on a corporate intranet, for example, may include agreed upon file structures or best practices that may have been developed within the work community or within different project groups so that all members of the community or group have access to and can find and refind the needed files. Jones (2008: 314) refers to the project file structure (the folders, files, and resulting hierarchies) as a visual representation of a project, its current stages, as well as its history. Project members can use project file structures to view the progress of a project and its gaps or needs, to find and refind project files, or to determine the next stage(s) of the project.

Some of the issues inherent in the personal approach include:

- no prior thought given to how to organize information objects, so there may exist multiple and poorly organized folder and file structures within one knowledge space;
- lack of consensus on how to organize files/folders within a specific project (or on a home computer) and also within multiple projects;
- lack of consistency in labeling of files/folders; and
- difficulty finding/refinding files within complex file structures.

More PIM research is needed. Little research has focused on the unique and creative home-related "artful" structures (Taylor and Swan, 2005) for organizing home/family knowledge, such as calendars, notebooks, and white boards, or organizing spaces, such as the kitchen table, and the role they play in family knowledge organization. While some research has focused on project file structure or disciplinary or professional work-related structures, there is definitely more work to be done in this area.

Socially-Constructed Knowledge Structures

Chapter 6 presented an overview of the various social bookmarking and cataloging sites on the web. We also looked at the research streams related to emerging structures for organizing knowledge within socially-constructed spaces, tagging and the resulting folksonomies, and the potential uses and issues with applying these emerging structures within different contexts such as library OPACs or into existing controlled vocabularies.

In contrast to formal, traditional structures, or those employed within personal work-related spaces, social bookmarking and cataloging sites provide very little guidance to users on how to organize their personal information objects within the space. In fact, many of the structures present in these sites are quite rudimentary and do not give the user many options for describing their objects. For example, Flickr allows users to tag photos with terms they feel represent the photo. No guidelines or standards are evident that instruct the user in term choice or form of word (plural, singular) or identify what aspects of the photo to represent (subject, color, date, size). Within formal, traditional structures, standards are essential for maintaining consistency of entries and word choices and forms. Effective retrieval within systems like databases and OPACs is dependent on standards and standardization of entries. In personal work-related structures, we see evidence of some attempts within work communities or projects to maintain some consistency in labeling and structures.

In socially-constructed spaces, lack of structure may be the draw for some users, while it may frustrate other users. It was also intriguing to note that while some of these social structures (e.g., Flickr) are designed for individual use and sharing of objects, communities are developing within them and communal standards may be emerging. For example, in LibraryThing's Common Knowledge project users contributed suggestions for fields to add to LibraryThing records. Using a wiki so that all users could see the process as decisions were made, consensus on fields to add emerged. The Common Knowledge fields are appended to the end of the LibraryThing records, and users can contribute their metadata to these fields as well. This project illustrates how even within the socially-constructed, communal environment, informal standards are being developed to serve the community of users. As the Common Knowledge project is continually updated by users of LibraryThing, the resulting structure will continue to be refined by the stakeholders of this community. It will be intriguing to revisit this development in future months to see how structures have changed and if standards continue to emerge.

Within socially-constructed knowledge spaces, users can tag and contribute comments to their own and others' collections of objects. However, as seen in Chapter 6 and as illustrated in this section, these contributions are within the limitations of the specific system and as predetermined by the system's designers or owners. Flickr gives users limited choices for organizing their photos and videos, which may, in fact, not accurately reflect how users *would* represent their objects if given the same flexibility and functionality present in their home computers or shoe boxes. Delicious allows users to organize their bookmarks by using tags but eschews the use of folders. In answer to user demand, Delicious now allows users to organize their tags into "bundles," but even these structures are limited and searching can only be conducted within individual bundles, not across sitewide bundles.

In reflection, even in a freer, non-standards-based social environment, with the possible exception of LibraryThing, users have little control over the elements (attributes) that are provided for their representations of their personal photos, bookmarks, or books. These spaces have provided limited sets of elements to use to represent objects: those chosen by the site's designers/owners, with little input from users or research supporting their choices. As a result, can we realistically compare these limited choices of structures for organizing knowledge to those used by individuals in personal home and work-related knowledge spaces? Are they, in essence, an accurate reflection of how individuals *want* to organize knowledge spaces?

Practical Applications of the Threads

In Chapter 6, a model of Adoption/Development/Use Cycles was presented as a framework for examining social bookmarking and cataloging sites and the activities of users. The tagging research to date reflects the first stage, or Early Exploration stage. The second and third stages, the Application and Refinement stages, respectively, are representative of both the practical applications of the research findings and the natural progression present in the use of any new technology. Under the Application stage, practical issues of how to integrate socially-constructed technologies (in this instance, tags and their resulting folksonomies) into existing structures for organizing knowledge, such as library OPACs or existing controlled vocabularies (e.g., subject headings lists, thesauri) are being explored. During the Refinement stage, which may occur concurrently with the Application phase, methods for refining or enhancing the technology are proposed and developed. In the case of socially-constructed knowledge structures, refinements to emerging tags and folksonomies are being explored, which include automatic and manual methods of "tag gardening" or reviewing and augmenting personal and/or community-based folksonomies. Research has also focused on the issues and potentials of incorporating facets into folksonomies in an effort to make the folksonomy more useful for both representation and searching.

Integration of Tags and Folksonomies within Library OPACs

Louise Spiteri (2006: 76) spells out the potential value of adding folksonomies to public library catalogs:

- They enable users to organize personal information spaces.
- They are more user-centered, intuitive supplements to existing controlled vocabularies.
- They provide a means to create online communities of interests.

Spiteri (2009a: 69–70) points out that users' expectations of library catalogs have changed as a result of their use of Web 2.0 environments. She suggests adding social features to library catalogs in an effort to make catalogs more interactive and dynamic. These features include:

- Hyperlinked names of authors, titles, and subject headings in library catalogs
- User reviews and/or ratings
- User-created discussion boards
- User-contributed tags
- User-contributed recommendations.

Features of second-generation library catalogs, which are incorporating more personalization functions into their interfaces, can support the development and use of personal information spaces and the creation of online communities of interests. What is, however, more problematic is the incorporation of tags and folksonomies within library OPACs. There are technical, logistical, ethical, and managerial issues that come into play and that most likely are resolved at a local level. As presented in Chapter 6, there is as yet little evidence to support the integration of tags and folksonomies within library catalogs as supplements to existing controlled vocabularies such as LCSH. Studies examining folksonomies' adherence to existing standards for developing controlled vocabularies (Spiteri, 2007) and extent of match studies of tags and controlled vocabulary term assignment conducted by Lin et al. (2006), Bruce (2008), Thomas, Caudle, and Schmitz (2009), and Rolla (2009) illustrate the *potential* for using tags as supplements to controlled vocabulary terms within catalog records. These studies, while contributing useful findings, are focused on the similarity between tags and controlled vocabulary terms and on illustrating the limitations of existing controlled vocabularies. The studies do not provide empirical evidence to support the assertion that incorporating tags within library catalog records can improve retrieval by representing library information objects using terms that are more intuitive and natural to users.

There have, however, been a number of libraries and museums experimenting with the feasibility of incorporating tags into library OPACs or museum information organization systems. As noted in Chapter 6, many efforts to explore this issue are currently underway, including, for example:

- The Steve.Museum Project, one of the first large-scale research efforts to learn more about the feasibility of using user-contributed tags to index images on museums' websites (Trant et al., 2006; Trant, 2009)
- The PennTags project at the University of Pennsylvania, which is inviting the university community and users to tag or comment on library resources within the library's OPAC
- Library integrated system vendors' integration of tagging, faceted, and visual search and classification into library OPACs
- Libraries' implementation of user-contribution features into their library OPACs by either developing their own homegrown systems (as is the case in the SOPAC system developed by Ann Arbor District Library) or by using LibraryThing for Libraries (LTFL), which currently boasts a total of 1,672 li-

braries and library consortia as users (LibraryThing for Libraries, accessed 2010)
- OCLC WorldCat's integrating of item tagging functionality into its catalog (Hadro, 2008)

At this point limited literature reports on the success or failure of integrating tagging features within library OPACs. Westcott, Chappell, and Lebel (2008) report on the first academic library to use LFTL, the Claremont University Consortium's Libraries at Claremont College. Although they briefly present the strengths (ease of use, ease of implementation, and tags and suggestions from multiple users) and weaknesses (limited tag searching and display within search interface, search of only one tag at a time, and an LTFL record set generated only for items that contain ISBNs) of implementing and using LTFL, their article does not include any details on whether or not a study of LTFL use was conducted. A few instances of how librarians used LTFL to assist academic users are briefly described, but no empirical data are presented to support their conclusions.

Gilmour and Stickland (2009) explain how their academic library used the Delicious widget and tag cloud to address specialized cataloging issues, such as adding more user-centered and discipline-specific subject headings to filmographies. Their article presents information on the mechanics of how to use Delicious and suggestions for other uses, such as creating new book lists and class resource lists, but it presents only an anecdotal account of the effectiveness of adding tags to library cataloging.

Mendes, Quinonez-Skinner, and Skaggs (2009) describe implementation of LTFL into the academic library catalog in the Oviatt Library of California State. Based on an analysis of 170 days of the OPAC's usage statistics, their study examined interface design issues, such as where to position the LTFL tag cloud on the OPAC search page and whether or not use of tags, recommendation links, and FRBR-like links improved resource discovery. Their findings indicate that use of LTFL data was low, at a level of about 1–2 percent. While both tags and recommendations were used equally, this use was lower than other OPAC search features. The researchers attribute the low level of use of LTFL features to the time period during which the data were captured (during spring break and summer months) and to the placement of the LTFL features at the bottom of the search page. Furthermore, they note that due to the quantitative nature of the study, user behavior and user perception of relevancy of tags could not be studied (Mendes, Quinonez-Skinner, and Skaggs, 2009: 38–39).

Integration of Tags and Folksonomies within Controlled Vocabularies

The next natural step for tags and folksonomies, as suggested by numerous authors (e.g., Mathes, 2004; Spiteri, 2006, 2007, 2009a; Abbas, 2005, 2007; Graham and Abbas, 2007; Rolla, 2009; Steele, 2009), is to either incorporate tags and/or folksonomies into existing controlled vocabularies or to use tags and folksonomies as a data set to learn more about users' choices and preferences for describing their objects. As noted, many authors have written about incorporating tags into knowledge structures such as LCSH, but limited application of this idea has been tried.

Yi and Chan (2009) present the first study to explore the feasibility of linking LCSH terms with a folksonomy, a select subset of the Delicious folksonomy. Using word mapping and converting LCSH into a tree structure, they examined (1) the characteristics of folksonomies, (2) the overlap of folksonomies and LCSH, and (3) the distribution of folksonomies over the LCSH tree. They found that (1) about 61 percent of user-assigned tags can be directly found in LCSH, with an additional 10 percent having potential matches; and (2) linking of the controlled, professionally-constructed controlled vocabulary with a folksonomy "holds great potential. . . . [T]he linking of two such resources is valuable in that it can integrate the views of both the users and systems in indexing and information organization" (Yi and Chan, 2009: 897). Furthermore, Yi and Chan (2009: 897) identified potential barriers to linking controlled vocabularies and folksonomies:

- occurrence of many specific technology-related tags [due to use of Delicious which has a user base of many technology and computer programmers],
- pervasiveness of many inconsistent forms and patterns of multiword tags that result in failure in matching headings,
- incompatibility issues between word forms used in tags such as abbreviations or acronyms used in tags and terms in LCSH.

Again, it should be noted that the barriers uncovered in their study overlap the weaknesses of folksonomies identified in studies related to the nature and structure of tags and in studies that compared controlled vocabularies and folksonomies. (See Chapter 6 for a summary of these studies.) The Yi and Chan study illustrates the variability of tags and tag forms and the impact of the weaknesses for searching and representation within systems. In the next section, solutions to "cleaning up" or "gardening" tags and adding facets to folksonomies will present potential solutions to these issues.

Refining Folksonomies

Chapter 6 outlined many of the limitations or weaknesses of tags and their resulting folksonomies, including that tags are:

- sloppy,
- imprecise,
- redundant,
- nonsensical,

- ambiguous,
- for single use,
- contain misspelling,
- often applied inaccurately,
- contain no synonym or homonym control,
- contain both plurals and singular forms, and
- are of informal or personal nature (me, my, naming specific individuals) (as reported in Mathes, 2004; Bates, 2006; Gordon-Murnane, 2006; Golder and Huberman, 2006; Guy and Tonkin, 2006; Peterson, 2006; MacGregor and McCulloch, 2006; and Spiteri, 2006).

Efforts to enrich or optimize tags and folksonomies are being developed to alleviate some of these issues and to lower barriers to incorporating tags and folksonomies into other retrieval systems and controlled vocabularies. For Peters and Weller (2008), "a gradual refinement of folksonomy tags and a stepwise application of additional structure to folksonomies is a promising approach." Social bookmarking and cataloging sites already include some features that allow users to edit and reuse their tags and personal folksonomies (referred to by Peters and Weller as "personomies"). For example, Delicious allows users to "bundle" their tags into logical/connected structures; Flickr presents users with various versions of tag clouds, including the alphabetical list, that allow users to view tags and identify form, spelling, and grammar issues in their tags and to edit them globally if desired.

Automatic methods of restructuring folksonomies have been proposed by Grahl, Hotho, and Stumme (2007), Begleman, Keller, and Smadja (2006), and Jaschke et al. (2007). Peters and Weller (2008) describe a manual process, called "tag gardening," of enriching or optimizing tags and folksonomies. The term "tag gardening" was introduced by James Governor in a blog post in 2006. Peters and Weller (2008) further develop this analogy of a folksonomy as a "garden," each tag as a "plant," and the process of vocabulary control through editing and enriching the folksonomy as "gardening." Some examples of the process include:

- synonym control using landscape design—combining similar "species" or topics into one garden;
- providing labels or sign posts and paths between them to show semantic interrelationships between terms;
- seeding the garden(s) with high-use terms that others might also use and emulate; and
- weeding out unuseful or poorly formed terms and replacing them if necessary.

While automatic and manual methods of optimizing tags and folksonomies are intriguing, adding facets to folksonomies has also been proposed by numerous researchers and within different social tagging environments (e.g., Beaudoin, 2007; Feldstein, n.d.; Lichtblau, Trice, and Wartik, 2006; Quintarelli, Resmini, and Rosati, 2007). Louise Spiteri (2009b) conducted an analysis of the methodologies used to incorporate facets within folksonomies as a way to facilitate more effective retrieval in social tagging applications. She concludes that while incorporating facets into social tagging environments has definite benefits of helping to clarify the meaning and context of tags and to create more efficient and structured browsing mechanisms (Spiteri, 2009b: 105–106), there are several issues that need to be addressed:

1. A methodological framework to create, evaluate, and monitor facets needs to be developed and applied.
2. A common definition of "facet" should be developed and adopted.
3. The optimal number of facets that are useful to users should be determined.
4. The appropriate level of facet granularity should be determined and consistently applied.

The Missing Part of This Conversation

The missing, or seldom discussed, part of this conversation remains the issue of how to develop structures for organizing knowledge that reflect the actual information practices and engagement needs of users. We hinted about developments in bibliographic record (MARC) restructuring due to the FRBR studies and development of the RDA, as well as the study conducted by Moen and Miksa (Moen, 2009) that seeks to uncover the most commonly used fields in bibliographic records. Moen and Miksa acknowledge, however, that their studies do not indicate if the fields used support the FRBR user tasks. Nor do their findings indicate why specific fields are commonly used to develop bibliographic records. What both the FRBR and Moen and Miksa studies do in fact indicate is our *need* to learn more about actual user expectations for using library catalogs in order to determine which fields will be most useful to users in bibliographic records. As noted earlier, even the socially-constructed knowledge spaces of social bookmarking and cataloging sites may not, in effect, be accurate reflections of how users want to organize their knowledge objects, as these sites' choices of representational elements are determined by the site owner/designers and not by users.

As described in Chapter 4, the metadata scheme development community (e.g., the Dublin Core, the Darwin Core, and the CDWA [Categories for the Description of Works of Art]), have been developing user-centered and discipline-specific structures for organizing knowledge of diverse communities, such as biologists or museums. These structures represent a more user-centered approach to knowledge structures than the structure present in library and/or museum catalogs. However, do these structures go far enough? For example, development of digital libraries and digital museums' metadata or museum online catalogs often represent the information museum professionals gathered and feel is necessary to include in their records. These records and the knowledge structures were developed for use by museum staff and researchers, not by the general public. Projects like Blobgects, an experimental interface to the museum catalog at the University of Cambridge's Museum of Archaeology and Anthropology (MAA), illustrate the inappropriateness to users of many of the metadata elements included in the museum's library catalog. Even when Blobgects incorporated tagging and commenting into the catalog, it still was not seen as useful to users (Srinivasan et al., 2009). The study's conclusions provide insights into how to better integrate Web 2.0 practices (tagging and commenting) into the museum or library catalog and also point out the "missing piece"—designing a structure that is representative of the "voices" of the users and that allows them to engage and to contribute meaningfully to the system (Srinivasan et al., 2009: 674). Most telling is Srinivasan and colleagues' conclusion that even

> in the rich, diverse, dynamic nature of cultural knowledge production, we continue to create static systems that mediate our interactions and preserve our practices, still focused on retrieval questions that are displaced from practice and active engagement. Even though the presence of social Web software (Web 2.0) has opened up our categories from meta ontologies, within the domain of multicultural systems and publics, these systems fall short of actually sharing knowledges according to the contexts in which they were produced. (Srinivasan et al., 2009: 676)

While Srinivasan and colleagues' statement is focused on museum catalog records, the issues presented extend to other structures for organizing knowledge, namely, bibliographic records, controlled vocabularies, and classification systems. Figure 7.3 illustrates the rich tapestry of possibility that might be possible if we weave these four threads together into an integrated, user-centered structure.

As this chapter has explored, there is work underway to merge or to incorporate aspects of the three threads of traditional, personal, and socially-constructed structures for organizing knowledge. Because these developments are very recent, only time will tell the outcome of the efforts and how this tapestry will potentially be woven together.

Thought Exercises

1. Although the traditional, personal, and socially-constructed structures for organizing knowledge appear quite different, can you see overlap between the three? Think specifically about how they are structured, the types of information that is included in each, and their underlying guiding principles.

Figure 7.3. Knowledge Threads: Tapestry of Possibilities

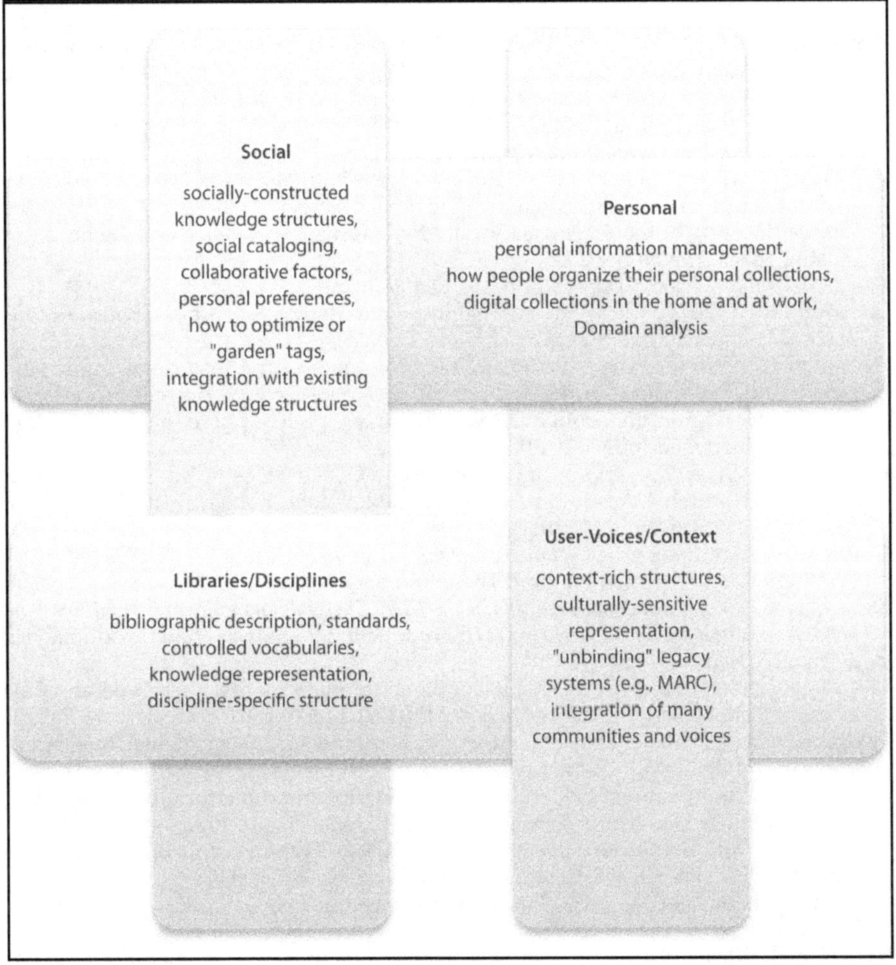

2. Brainstorm potential ideas for weaving the three threads together. Draw a picture of how the three might be merged together. Describe what your picture looks like. Do you envision one coherent structure or several interconnected ones?
3. Does the tapestry metaphor hold? If not, what metaphor would be more useful?

References

Abbas, June. 2005. "Out of the Mouths of Middle School Children: I. Using Student Generated Keywords for Subject Access in a Digital Library." *Journal for the American Society of Information Science and Technology* 56, no. 14: 1512–1524.

———. 2007. "In the Margins: Reflections on Scribbles, Knowledge Organization and Access." *Knowledge Organization* 34, no. 2: 72–77.

Abbas, June, and Jenn Graham. 2006. "So, Let's Talk about Tagging, User-defined/Supplied Descriptors . . . A Research and Curricular Agenda." Poster presented at the Annual Meeting of the American Society for Information Science and Technology, Austin, Texas, November 2006.

Bates, Mary Ellen. 2006. "Tag—You're It!" *Online* 30, no. 1: 64.

Beaudoin, Joan. 2007. "Flickr Image Tagging: Patterns Made Visible." *Bulletin of the American Society for Information Science and Technology* 34, no. 1: 26–29.

Begleman, G., P. Keller, and F. Smadja. 2006. "Automatic Tag Clustering—Improving Search and Exploration in the Tag Space." *Collaborative Web Tagging Workshop* at *WWW2006*, Edinburgh, Scotland. Available: www.pui.ch/phred/automated_tag_clustering (accessed June 5, 2010).

Bruce, Robert. 2008. "Descriptor and Folksonomy Concurrence in Education Related Scholarly Research." *Webology* 5, no. 3. Available: www.webology/ir/2008/v5n3/a59.html (accessed June 4, 2010).

Cutter, C.A. 1904. *Rules for a Dictionary Catalog*, 4th ed. Washington, DC: Government Printing Office; reprinted London: The Library Association, 1962.

Delsey, Tom. 2002. *Functional Analysis of the MARC 21 Bibliographic and Holdings Formats*. Available: www.loc.gov/marc/marc-functional-analysis/functional-analysis.html (accessed June 4, 2010).

———. 2003. "Functional Requirements for Bibliographic Records: User Tasks and Cataloguing Data: Part 1." *Catalogue & Index* 150 (Winter): 1–4.

Feldstein, Michael. n.d. "The Obligatory Folksonomy Post." Available: mfeldstein.com/the_obligatory_folksonomy_post/ (accessed June 4, 2010).

Gilmour, Ron, and Jennifer Stickland. 2009. "Social Bookmarking for Library Services: Bibliographic Access through Delicious." *C&RL News* 70, no. 4 (April): 234–237.

Golder, Scott, and Bernardo Huberman. 2006. "Usage Patterns of Collaborative Tagging Systems." *Journal of Information Science* 32, no. 2: 198–208.

Gordon-Murnane, Laura. 2006. "Social Bookmarking, Folksonomies, and Web 2.0 Tools." *Searcher* 14, no. 6: 26–38.

Governor, J. 2006. "On the Emergence of Professional Tag Gardeners." Comment posted October 1, 2006. Available: www.redmonk.com/jgovernor/2006/01/10/on-the-emergence-of-professional-tag-gardeners/ (accessed June 4, 2010).

Graham, Jenn, and June Abbas. 2007. "Tagging the Tags . . . Process, Observations and Analysis of Conversations in Metatagging at an ASIST Interactive Poster Session." Poster presented at the Annual Meeting of the American Society for Information Science and Technology, Milwaukee, Wisconsin, November 2007.

Grahl, M., A. Hotho, and G. Stumme. 2007. "Conceptual Clustering of Social Bookmarking Sites." In *Proceedings of I-KNOW '07* (pp. 356–364). Graz, Austria: Know Center.

Guy, Marieke, and Emma Tonkin. 2006. "Folksonomies: Tidying Up Tags?" *D-Lib Magazine*. 12, 1. Available: www.dlib.org/dlib/january06/guy/01guy.html (accessed June 4, 2010).

Hadro, Josh. 2008. "Tagging Added to WorldCat.org." *Library Journal* 133, no. 17 (October 15): 21.

IFLA Study Group. 1998. *Functional Requirements for Bibliographic Records: Final Report.* Munchen: K.G. Saur. Available: www.ifla.org/publications/functional-requirements-for-bibliographic-records (accessed June 4, 2010).

Jaschke, R., L. Marinho, A. Hotho, L. Schmidt-Thieme, and G. Stumme. 2007. "Tag Recommendations in Folksonomies." *Lecture Notes in Artificial Intelligence* 4702: 506–514.

Jones, William. 2008. *Keeping Found Things Found: The Study and Practice of Personal Information Management*. New York: Morgan Kaufmann Publishers.

Keeping Found Things Found. Available: kftf.ischool.washington.edu/index.htm (accessed June 4, 2010).

LibraryThing for Libraries. Available: www.librarything.com/wiki/index.php/LTFL:Libraries_using_LibraryThing_for_Libraries (accessed June 4, 2010).

Lichtblau, Dale E., Andrew W. Trice, and Steven P. Wartik. 2006. "Taxonomic and Faceted Classification for Intelligent Tagging and Discovery in Net-Centric Command and Control." Paper presented at the 2006 Command and Control Research and Technology Symposium, June 20–22, 2006, San Diego, California. Available: stinet.dtic.mil/cgi-bin/GetTRDoc?=AD=ADA463288&Location=U2&doc=GetTRDcoc.pdf (accessed June 4, 2010).

Lin, X., J.E. Beaudoin, Y. Bui, and K. Desai. 2006. "Exploring Characteristics of Social Classification." *Advances in Classification Research* 17, Proceedings of the 17th ASIS&T Classification Research Workshop, Austin, Texas. Silver Spring, MD: American Society of Information Science and Technology.

MacGregor, George, and Emma McCulloch. 2006. "Collaborative Tagging as a Knowledge Organisation and Resource." *Library Review* 55, no. 5: 291–300.

MARBI. Available: www.ala.org/ala/mgrps/divs/lita/litamembership/litacommittees/marbicomm/machinereadable.cfm (accessed June 4, 2010).

Mathes, Adam. 2004. "Folksonomies—Cooperative Classification and Communication through Shared Metadata." Available: www.adammathes.com/academic/computer-mediated-communication/folksonomies.html (accessed June 4, 2010).

Mendes, Luiz H., Jennie Quinonez-Skinner, and Danielle Skaggs. 2009. "Subjecting the Catalog to Tagging." *Library Hi Tech* 27, no. 1: 30–41.

Moen, William. 2009. NISO Webinar: Bibliographic Control Alphabet Soup, October 14. Draft of Report. Available: www.mcdu.unt.edu (accessed June 4, 2010).

Peters, Isabella, and Katrin Weller. 2008. "Tag Gardening for Folksonomy Enrichment and Maintenance." *Webology* 5, no. 3, Article 58. Available: www.webology.ir/2008/v5n3/a58.html (accessed June 4, 2010).

Peterson, Elaine. 2006. "Beneath the Metadata." *D-Lib Magazine* 12, no. 11. Available: dlib.org/dlib/november06/peterson/11peterson.html (accessed June 4, 2010).

Quintarelli, Emanuele, Andrea Resmini, and Luca Rosati. 2007. "FaceTag: Integrating Bottom-Up and Top-Down Classification in a Social Tagging System." Paper presented at the IA Summit 2007: Enriching Information Architecture, Las Vegas, Nevada, March 22–26, 2007. Available: www.facetag.org/download/facetag-20070325.pdf (accessed June 4, 2010).

Rolla, Peter J. 2009. "User Tags versus Subject Headings: Can User-supplied Data Improve Subject Access to Library Collections?" *Library Resources and Technical Services* 53, no. 3: 174–184.

Spiteri, Louise F. 2006. "The Use of Folksonomies in Public Library Catalogs." *Serials Librarian* 51, no. 2: 75–89.

———. 2007. "The Structure and Form of Folksonomy Tags: The Road to the Public Library Catalog." *Information Technology and Libraries* 26, no. 3: 13–25.

__________. 2009a. "The Impact of Social Cataloging Sites on the Construction of Bibliographic Records in the Public Library Catalog." *Cataloging & Classification Quarterly* 47, no. 1: 52–73.

———. 2009b. "Incorporating Facets into Social Tagging Applications: An Analysis of Current Trends." *Cataloging & Classification Quarterly* 48, no. 1: 94–109.

Srinivasan, Ramesh, Robin Boast, Katherine M. Becvar, and Jonathan Furner. 2009. "Blobgects: Digital Museum Catalogs and Diverse User Communities." *Journal of the American Society for Information Science and Technology* 60, no. 4: 666–678.

Steele, Tom. 2009. "The New Cooperative Cataloging." *Library Hi Tech* 27, no. 1: 68–77.

Taylor, Alex, and Laurel Swan. 2005. "Artful Systems in the Home." In *Proceedings of the 2005 SIGCHI Conference on Human Factors in Computing Systems* (pp. 641–650). New York: ACM Press.

Thomas, Marliese, Dana M. Caudle, and Cecilia M. Schmitz. 2009. "To Tag or Not to Tag." *Library Hi Tech* 27, no. 3: 411–434.

Trant, Jennifer. 2009. "Tagging, Folksonomy and Art Museums: Early Experiments and Ongoing Research." *Journal of Digital Information* 10, no. 1. Available: journals.tdl .org/jodi/article/view/270/277 (accessed June 4, 2010).

Trant, J. and the Participants in the Steve.Museum Project. 2006. "Exploring the Potential for Social Tagging and Folksonomy in Art Museums: Proof of Concept." *New Review of Hypermedia and Multimedia* 12, no. 1:83–105.

Westcott, Jezmynne, Alexandra Chappell, and Candace Lebel. 2008. "LibraryThing for Libraries at Claremont." *Library Hi Tech* 27, no. 1: 78–81.

Williams, Pete, Katrina Dean, Ian Rowlands, and Jeremy Leighton John. 2008. "Digital Lives: Reports on Interviews with the Creators of Personal Digital Collections." *Ariadne* no. 55 (April). Available: www.ariadne.ac.uk/issue55/williams-et-al (accessed June 4, 2010).

Williams, Peter, Jeremy Leighton John, and Ian Rowland. 2009. "The Personal Curation of Digital Objects: A Lifecycle Approach." *Aslib Proceedings: New Information Perspectives* 61, no. 4: 340–363.

Yi, Kwan, and Lois Mai Chan. 2009. "Linking Folksonomy to Library of Congress Subject Headings: An Exploratory Study." *Journal of Documentation* 63, no. 6: 872–900.

Websites Noted in Text

Keeping Found Things Found Project. Available: kftf.ischool.washington.edu/index .htm (accessed June 4, 2010).

MARBI. Library of Congress. Available: www.ala.org/ala/mgrps/divs/lita/ litamembership/litacommittees/marbicomm/machinereadable.cfm (accessed June 4, 2010).

8

Thinking Ahead: Are We at a Crossroads?

Focus Points

- If you painted a picture of today's user of knowledge structures, what would you include? Are there similarities between users of knowledge structures developed in the MARC era and users of the Web 2.0 world?
- What would a merged knowledge structure need to include? How do we move from a MARC-based world to one that re-creates not just the structures but also our thinking about how to represent knowledge?
- What lessons have we re-learned, and which should we revisit?

Envisioning Exercise #1

In this chapter let's conduct two thought exercises to frame our discussion. In the first one, let's envision a picture of today's users. Our first exercise is this: Develop a picture of today's users and the information needs they bring to organization systems. For example, it could be a 20-something professional who is seated at an outdoor restaurant conducting a business interview via the speaker of her cell phone, while simultaneously searching the web for information to complete a project prospectus and also blogging on her laptop, or the grandmother who engages in playful activities with her grandchildren within a virtual world environment. If we take to heart the views from popular media, then the picture might portray today's users as wired, multitasking individuals who use multiple information devices and multiple media forms to conduct information searches and to obtain information resources. Personal observation and conversations with others observing this phenomenon support this view for some users but not necessarily for all. For example, what is known about users in remote locations or who live in underdeveloped countries?

What devices and structures are they using to locate information? Are their characteristics similar to or different from the users outlined in the popular media's scenario? Have they developed novel approaches or routines that should be included in our picture?

We might also include in this exploration the heavy Flickr users, who not only tag and comment on their own images and videos but also those of other participants; or who develop or contribute to emerging professional and personal groups forming in the social site; or the LibraryThing users who are passionate enough about organizing their collections and the structure of LibraryThing that they contributed to the Common Knowledge project to enhance the structure of LibraryThing for all users. What are the daily information-gathering routines of these users, and what do they suggest about the intentionality of their use of information systems? What features of structures for organizing knowledge are intuitive to them? Most useful to them? Or not useful/used?

The picture we paint might actually need to be multidimensional, multifaceted, and very complex. It should also include information about how users have incorporated the three threads explored within this book into their daily personal and work-related routines and information-gathering activities. In addition, we might also ask, are these routines guided/driven by factors related to convenience, time-saving, and/or a desire to use the latest technologies?

These are but a few scenarios and questions that could inform our exploration, but there are many others to pose. Researchers from library and information studies, human–computer interaction, and personal information management (PIM) have been investigating the information-seeking and -gathering activities of users for decades, and a large body of literature has been developed from their findings. With the emergence of the web and related technologies, information behavior and PIM research has also explored users and their use of the web and new technologies for seeking, finding, and refinding information. In Chapter 5 we reviewed the findings of PIM research and what this area contributes to our portrayal of today's user. Again, what seems to be missing from the picture we are painting of users is their *preference* or the natural manner in which they wish to organize information and knowledge. While examining socially-constructed knowledge structures is indeed very useful in helping us to better understand users, these structures are unfortunately imposing a predetermined view of how information should be organized on the user group rather than allowing them to "artfully" design their own structures for organizing knowledge.

Envisioning Exercise #2

For our second thought exercise, let's envision what a merged knowledge structure might include. Our second exercise is this: If we were charged with developing a structure for organizing knowledge that takes into account the traditional, personal, and socially-constructed structures as discussed in earlier chapters, what do we envision that structure to include? Would we use existing structures as a foundation and build from there, or would we start from "scratch"? Incorporate into your model your own experiences using existing structures and how you would like to see systems changed (elements to add or delete, labels to change, etc.). For example, in libraries, we depend on the MARC metadata scheme as the foundation of bibliographic library records. We based this structure on Cutter's objects of a catalog, as well as early cataloging principles, as are outlined in Chapters 2 and 3. The structures used to accomplish these purposes include the MARC record structure or metadata scheme, classification schemes, and controlled vocabularies.

The representations we create to serve as surrogates for the objects in collections provide information the community of catalogers has chosen to highlight about each object in order to enable users to find or indentify an object, to collocate or gather like items together, and to evaluate or select an object. The format of both the printed book catalog and later the card catalog imposed an artificial, though practical, limitation on what we could include in bibliographic records. When this print format was automated in the form of the MARC record structure, little was changed. Although the basic core of the records was expanded to accommodate various media present in collections, the MARC structure is often criticized as (1) inadequately addressing the unique needs of multimedia in collections or (2) not including elements that users find necessary. Would it be possible to remove the "boundaries" from MARC records and make this rich store of bibliographic data shareable with the data and data structures of the web? What would need to be changed about the existing MARC structure to explore this potential further?

Scenario One

One possible structure we could envision might use the MARC record structure as the core elements to include in the knowledge structure. For example, we might include the MARC fields:

1XX	Main Entry Fields (authorized name of creator)
20X–24X	Title and Title-Related Fields (title of work and also names of those responsible for the work)
25X–28X	Edition, Imprint, Etc. Fields (version information)
3XX	Physical Description, Etc. Fields (details about the physical nature of the work, including, for example, pagination, whether or not illustrated, dimensions, format, etc.)
4XX	Series Statement Fields (association with other works)
5XX	Notes Fields (multiple uses that could be developed further)

6XX	Subject Access Fields (controlled vocabulary terms that describe various aspects of subjects, including topical, genre, chronological, and geographic relationships)
70X–75X	Added Entry Fields (entries that show relationships to other creators)
76X–78X	Linking Entry Fields (additional relationships to main series, e.g., subseries entries, language, translations, etc.)
80X–83X	Series Added Entry Fields (entries that show relationships to other series creators)
84X–88X	Holdings, Location, Alternate Graphics, Etc. Fields (local or institutional holdings information and links to electronic access to the work)

We could add to this frame some of the socially-constructed fields from LibraryThing, including:

- Titles of works in the series, including order of publication of each
- People/characters present in the work/series
- Important places/events in the work
- Related items (movies, music, etc.)
- Other works by the creator
- Websites associated with the work
- Awards and honors for the work

Taking a closer look at this proposed model shows both the complexity of the MARC structure and also the overlaps and additions needed. For example, the MARC 4XX and 80X–83X fields provide series information, but they do not provide the information that LibraryThing users have built into the Common Knowledge Structure (e.g., other works in the series and the order in which they were published or where they fall within the series; people or characters in the series; other works or links to related works). Also, if we examine closely the elements that *can* be included in the 5XX or Notes fields in the MARC structure, there are many elements that might provide some of the desired relationships if used and displayed in a manner users find useful. For example, the MARC Notes fields include possible entries shown in Figure 8.1.

The MARC structure, especially the 5XX fields, includes elements that could be used to provide some of the additional information that users of LibraryThing feel were needed. However, existing research does not provide information about the extent the 5XX fields are used by catalogers, which fields are actually used, and how and why they are used. More in-depth research in this area might provide further insights focused on how existing structures could provide more user-centered information about objects of the collection.

Figure 8.1. MARC 5XX Notes Fields

500 - General Note
501 - With Note
502 - Dissertation Note
504 - Bibliography, etc. Note
505 - Formatted Contents Note
506 - Restrictions on Access Note
507 - Scale Note for Graphic Material
508 - Creation/Production Credits Note
510 - Citation/Refere
511 - Participant or P
513 - Type of Report
514 - Data Quality No
515 - Numbering Pec
516 - Type of Computer ... or Data Note
518 - Date/Time and Place of an Event Note
520 - Summary, etc.
521 - Target Audience Note
522 - Geographic Coverage Note
524 - Preferred Citation of Described Materials Note
525 - Supplement Note
526 - Study Program Information Note
530 - Additional Physical Form available Note
533 - Reproduction Note
534 - Original Version Note
535 - Location of Originals/Duplicates Note
536 - Funding Information Note
538 - System Details Note
540 - Terms Governing Use and Reproduction Note
541 - Immediate Source of Acquisition Note
542 - Information Relating to Copyright Status
544 - Location of Other Archival Materials Note
545 - Biographical or Historical Data
546 - Language Note
547 - Former Title Complexity Note
550 - Issuing Body Note
552 - Entity and Attribute Information Note
555 - Cumulative Index/Finding Aids Note
556 - Information About Documentation Note
561 - Ownership and Custodial History
562 - Copy and Version Identification Note
563 - Binding Information
565 - Case File Characteristics Note
567 - Methodology Note
580 - Linking Entry Complexity Note
581 - Publications About Describ
583 - Action Note
584 - Accumulation and Frequen
585 - Exhibitions Note
586 - Awards Note
588 - Source of Description Note
59X - Local Notes

Research might also support restructuring of the 5XX fields or breaking them out into more usable elements of the MARC ten-tag structure.

We would also need to address technical issues related to reworking the MARC structure so that the data in library records could be more easily shared and integrated into other data generated by the many web communities, such as publishers, services such as Google Scholar and Google Book Search, Open Library, and others. Karen Coyle (2010a) explains some of the technical issues related to "unbinding" MARC records, as well as some developments to do so.

For example, the MARC record structure is not the same as any other community's structure, which means sharing data outside of the library community is not easily accomplished. Coyle (2010a: 18) notes that the development of XML for MARC, using Unicode, "is a step toward the transformation of library-specific data into something that could be used by anyone, anywhere in an information system."

Developments related to *Functional Requirements for Bibliographic Records* (FRBR) modeling within Integrated Library Systems (ILSs) may also provide some of the functions for linking together different versions of a work, related works (such as movies, music, other related books or websites, etc.) indicated as important to LibraryThing's Common Knowledge participants. However, as few vendors have incorporated FRBR into their ILSs at this time, little is known about the changes FRBR might afford. Implementation of the *Resource Description and Access* (RDA) bibliographic standard also supports additional or restructured metadata and additional connections or relationships that users feel are necessary in bibliographic records.

Additionally, from the socially-constructed thread, the research focused on socially-constructed sites and the collaborative and individual features for organizing objects provided within these sites suggests that adding features such as author- and user-supplied tagging (subject and descriptive terms) is important to users. Being able to provide feedback on the object or write reviews might also be a useful feature. Chapter 7 outlined the efforts to incorporate Web 2.0 features, such as tagging, folksonomies, and reviews, into library ILSs, as well as initiatives to use folksonomies as additions to controlled vocabularies, such as the *Library of Congress Subject Headings* (LCSH).

PIM research in both the home and workplace indicates the need for customization or incorporating "artful" capabilities into the structure. Unfortunately, PIM research cannot at this point provide many specifics about common ways or structures people use to organize their knowledge in either home or work contexts other than that there is a high degree of personal variability in their structures and that novel, ad hoc structures and tools have been used (e.g., notebooks, white/black boards, paper and electronic calendars). PIM research might then suggest the need for multiple, customizable interfaces of ILSs and other information systems, but at this point PIM findings may be difficult to include in this thought exercise.

Scenario Two

A second scenario we could envision might be to start from scratch and, taking a top-down approach, develop an entirely new structure for bibliographic records. We are indeed at a crossroads if we take this route, and cautions should also be recognized before we proceed. For example, we should ask the following questions:

- Would records created with this "new" structure be easily integrated into existing library systems (ILSs) or other information systems? How would existing systems have to be altered or adapted to enable interoperability with this "new structure"?
- What resources would be needed to develop and implement a "new" structure (e.g., financial resources, time, training, intellectual capital of record creators, etc.)?
- What other standards and systems will be affected?
- Are there unforeseen issues that might also impact this change?

It might sound like, on first reading, Scenario Two should not be attempted because of the potential issues outlined, but this is not the intention of the author. Many bold initiatives to re-create the MARC wheel have been successfully implemented. Take, for example, XML-MARC efforts that use the flexibility of the XLM data encoding scheme to create relationships and links within MARC records; the innovative approach taken by the Joint Steering Committee to re-engineer the *Anglo-American Cataloguing Rules* (AACR2) standard, thereby extending the potential functionalities of bibliographic records using the FRBR model rather than to continue to revise a standard that many have felt inadequate and confusing; or the many metadata schemes and taxonomies and ontologies (as outlined in Chapters 4 and 5) that have been developed or are being developed by the Semantic Web and other specialized communities. Karen Coyle (2010b: 7) views initiatives such as these as a

> time of opportunity . . . because the cataloging community has stepped back to rethink its work. The Functional Requirements for Bibliographic Records (FRBR) and *Resource Description and Access* (RDA) provide new models and new rules, and they have come at a time when the way data is stored and managed has resulted in an entirely new technology with which we can distribute our catalog entries and make them available to users. That technology is the World Wide Web, and more specifically the burgeoning use of the linked data standard to facilitate interconnections between information resources.

What might also be relevant to this conversation are the questions, "Which direction would the 'new' structure take? Would a more simplified structure be warranted, or is a more complex structure needed?" While a more simplified structure might be useful for display to users, would it include all of the elements needed in the records so that systems could search and display results from the varying information needs of users and diverse user groups (e.g., children, researchers, public library users)? Or would users prefer the simplicity they are becoming accustomed to through their use of search engines such as Google or the collaborative and/or contributory features afforded by Web 2.0 sites? There is also no guarantee that users will continue to collaborate or contribute to structures developed that incorporate Web 2.0 features. How successful can a folksonomy-enabled OPAC be if users are not contributing tags? This scenario is envisioned in Figure 8.2.

Figure 8.2. Factors in Developing New Structure

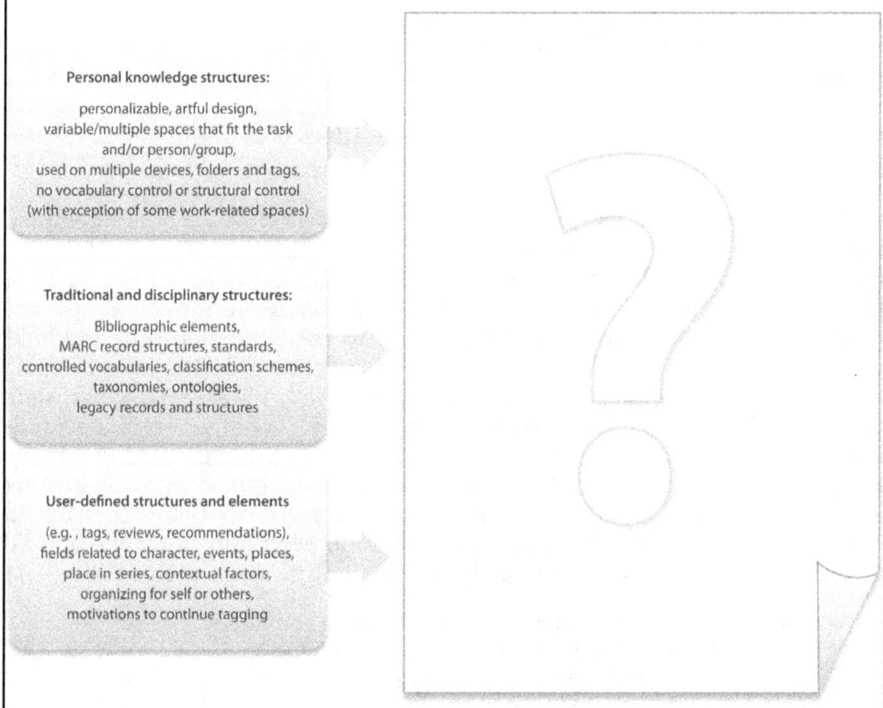

This chapter will not attempt to answer these questions, nor will it propose a structure for Scenario Two. That is for the reader to envision. However, it should be emphasized that there is a real need for more in-depth understanding about how users interact and perhaps, more important, *how they want to interact with or design* information systems. As illustrated in Chapters 6 and 7, little is known about the elements or features that users find useful or desirable in structures for organizing knowledge.

So Where Does This Leave Us?

We are indeed at a crossroads, and only time and exploration will provide the road to take. This is an exciting opportunity for the knowledge organization community! This book provided potential approaches to consider as choices are made. It outlined ideas to review and expand upon or to disregard altogether. Also illustrated is the apparent need for more research and further exploration of the issues proposed throughout the book—those specific to learning more about user needs and uses of structures for organizing knowledge and those related to how people naturally organize their personal knowledge spaces. Perhaps it is also time for library and information science educators and professionals to revisit lessons we have learned in the past (or should have learned) about melding the traditional, present, and future practices so that we take this opportunity to fashion structures for organizing knowledge into integrated, multidimensional, but enriched tapestries.

References

Coyle, Karen. 2010a. "Changing the Nature of Library Data." *Library Technology Reports* 46, no. 1: 14–29.

———. 2010b. "Library Data in the Web World." *Library Technology Reports* 46, no. 2: 5–11.

Index

Special conventions used in the index: Page references for figures are followed by an italicized "f" and tables are followed by an italicized "t." Common abbreviations are used instead of full names when appropriate, with cross-references directing the reader to the preferred entry.

D

M

N

About the Author

Dr. June Abbas, PhD, is an Associate Professor in the School of Library and Information Studies (SLIS) at the University of Oklahoma, Norman Campus, in Norman, Oklahoma. She obtained her PhD in Information Science from the University of North Texas in 2001 and taught in the Department of Library and Information Studies at the State University of New York in Buffalo from 2001 to 2008 before joining the SLIS in August 2008. Her research focuses on the intersections of users, technology, and structures for organizing knowledge. The outcomes of her research are applied to the development of user-centered, culturally sensitive digital libraries, institutional repositories, and other knowledge organization structures; the potential uses and applications of Web 2.0 technologies within libraries and knowledge structures; and the development of age- and cognitive-appropriate knowledge organization structures for children and young adults. The courses she teaches include those related to the organization of information and knowledge resources, cataloging and classification, indexing and surrogation, digital libraries, and digital information retrieval. She has also served as project manager on seven digital libraries projects and as a consultant to numerous projects related to the development of university institutional repositories, digitization and oral history projects in cultural heritage organizations, and content and knowledge management in private enterprise. Currently she is serving as Chair of the ALA Resource Description and Access (RDA) Programming Taskforce.

CPSIA information can be obtained
at www.ICGtesting.com
Printed in the USA
LVHW080746200120
644143LV00013B/488

9 781555 706999